_____

A GIFT FOR

_____

FROM

_____

DATE

*May this exploration bring you into deeper
knowledge, appreciation, and love of God's Word.*

Published in Nashville, Tennessee, by Thomas Nelson. Thomas Nelson is a registered trademark of HarperCollins Christian Publishing, Inc.

Thomas Nelson titles may be purchased in bulk for educational, business, fund-raising, or sales promotional use. For information, please e-mail SpecialMarkets@ThomasNelson.com.

Unless otherwise indicated, all Scriptures are taken from the New International Version®, NIV®. Copyright © 1973, 1978, 1984 by Biblica, Inc®. Used by permission of Zondervan. All rights reserved worldwide. www.zondervan.com. The "NIV" and "New International Version" are trademarks registered in the United States Patent and Trademark Office by Biblica, Inc®. Scripture quotations marked NASB are taken from the New American Standard Bible®. Copyright © 1960, 1962, 1963, 1968, 1971, 1972, 1973, 1975, 1977, 1995 by The Lockman Foundation. Used by permission. (www.Lockman.org) Scripture quotations marked NKJV are taken from the New King James Version®. © 1982 by Thomas Nelson. Used by permission. All rights reserved. Scripture quotations marked KJV are taken from the King James Version. Public domain.

Italics in Scripture indicate the author's emphasis.

ISBN: 978-0-7180-3249-4

Printed in China

16 17 18 19 20 DSC 5 4 3 2 1

THE
COMPLETE
BIBLE
ANSWER
BOOK

COLLECTOR'S EDITION
REVISED AND UPDATED

HANK HANEGRAAFF

Thomas Nelson
Since 1798

CONTENTS

HANK HANEGRAAFF

Foreword

The Complete Bible Answer Book Collector's Edition—revised and updated—was born out of almost three decades of hosting the internationally syndicated *Bible Answer Man* radio broadcast. In this book I've taken my on-air answers to hundreds of questions and chiseled them until only the gems emerge—questions involving biblical interpretation, cults, religions, science, ethics, afterlife, apparent contradictions, and much, much more.

The successes of my previous *Bible Answer Books* are quite simply astounding: half a million copies are now in print. And now the revised, updated edition contains over fifty new entries, including twenty-six new "Hankronyms." My goal in using such acronyms is to take the complex and make it simple and memorable so that readers will not only *remember* but also *recall*.

Questions you'll encounter in this volume run the gamut from the common to the complex. In the category of common, I answer such questions as *"What are the ABCs of redefining marriage?"* and *"What is a near-death experience?"* In the category of complex, I tackle questions such as *"What is replacement theology?"* and *"What is the Euthyphro dilemma?"* (Euthyphro what??? While you may never have even conceived of such a question, it's one every student will eventually encounter!)

Perhaps the question I have been asked more than any other is *"Why does God allow bad things to happen to good people?"* At first blush it may seem as though there are as many responses to this question as there are religions. In reality, however, you will discover that there are only three basic answers—and only Christian theism answers the question satisfactorily!

Along with questions I answered in previous *Bible Answer Books*, I have added answers to questions such as *"Is America going to P-O-T?" "What are the characteristics of C-U-L-T-S?"* and *"Is soul sleep biblical?"*

In a category called "Apparent Contradictions," I address such questions as *"How many asses did Jesus ride into Jerusalem?"* and *"Did the cock crow once or twice after Peter denied Christ?"* I even tackle the tired old canard *"Does the Bible begin with two contradictory creation accounts?"*

Also part of this revised and updated version is a *Legacy Reading Plan* (see pages 616–617) that will equip you to read the Bible in books rather than bits. You'll even discover recommended resources for further study as well as Scripture passages specifically related to the subject matter at hand.

Finally, a concluding note on how this book came to be. Three words: *Jack! Jack! Jack!* Without ol' Countryman, this book would as yet remain an unfinished monument. After years of his urging, I finally took the ancient sage's advice and began to write. As they say, the rest is history. I am, of course, also deeply grateful to my personal assistant of twenty-five years, Stephen Ross, and to the entire Thomas Nelson gift book team, particularly Laura and Lisa. (How do you spell *dynamite*?)

Hank Hanegraaff
Charlotte, North Carolina

BASIC CHRISTIAN THOUGHT
AND SPIRITUAL GROWTH

What must I do to be saved?

No one gets out of this world alive, so this is beyond a doubt the most important question you can ever ask yourself! In fact, the Bible was written "so that you may know that you have eternal life" (1 John 5:13).

First, according to Scripture, you need to realize that you are a sinner. If you do not realize you are a sinner, you will not recognize your need for a savior. The Bible teaches we "all have sinned and fall short of the glory of God" (Romans 3:23).

Furthermore, you must repent of your sins. *Repentance* is an old English word that describes a willingness to turn from our sin toward Jesus Christ. It literally means a complete U-turn on the road of life—a change of heart and a change of mind. It means that you are willing to follow Jesus and to receive Him as your Savior and Lord. Jesus said, "Repent and believe the good news!" (Mark 1:15).

Finally, to demonstrate true belief means to be willing to receive. To truly receive is to trust in and depend on Jesus Christ alone to be the Lord of our lives here and now and our Savior for all eternity. It takes more than knowledge (the devil knows about Jesus and trembles). It takes more than agreement that the knowledge we have is accurate (the devil agrees that Jesus is Lord). What it takes is to trust in Jesus Christ alone for eternal life. The requirements for eternal life are based not on what you can do but on what Jesus Christ has done. He stands ready to exchange His perfection for your imperfection.

According to Jesus Christ, those who realize they are sinners, repent of their sins, and receive Him as Savior and Lord are "born again" (John 3:3)—not physically, but spiritually. The reality of our salvation is not dependent on our feelings but rather on the promise of the Savior who says: "I tell you the truth, whoever hears my word and believes him who sent me has eternal life and will not be condemned; he has crossed over from death to life" (John 5:24).

> *"For God so loved the world that He gave His only begotten Son, that whoever believes in Him shall not perish but have everlasting life."*
> JOHN 3:16 NKJV

For further study, see Hank Hanegraaff, *The Prayer of Jesus: Secrets to Intimacy with God* (Nashville: W Publishing Group, 2001).

What are the secrets to spiritual growth?

ccording to Jesus Christ, those who repent of their sins and receive Him as Savior and Lord are "born again" (John 3:3)—not physically, but spiritually. And with this spiritual birth must come spiritual growth. It is crucial, therefore, to be intimately acquainted with the ABCs of spiritual growth.

First, no relationship can flourish without constant, heartfelt communication. This is true not only in human relationships but also in our relationship with God. If we are to nurture a strong relationship with our Savior, we must be in constant communication with Him. The way to do that is through *prayer*.

Furthermore, it is crucial that we spend time reading God's written revelation of Himself—*the Bible*. The Bible not only forms the foundation of an effective prayer life but also is foundational to every other aspect of Christian living. While prayer is our primary way of communicating with God, the Bible is God's primary way of communicating with us. Nothing should take precedence over getting into the Word and getting the Word into us. If we fail to eat well-balanced meals on a regular basis, we will eventually suffer the physical consequences. What is true of the outer man is also true of the inner man. If we do not regularly feed on the Word of God, we will starve spiritually.

Finally, it is crucial for new believers to become active participants in a healthy, well-balanced church. In Scripture, the church is referred to as *the body of Christ.* Just as our physical body is one yet has many parts, so, too, the body of Christ is one but is composed of many members (1 Corinthians 12). Those who receive Christ as the Savior and Lord of their lives are already a part of the church universal. It is crucial, however, that all Christians become vital, reproducing members of a local body of believers as well. Christian growth doesn't happen in isolation.

Adapted from *The Face That Demonstrates the Farce of Evolution*

For everyone who partakes only of milk is unskilled
in the word of righteousness, for he is a babe. But
solid food belongs to those who are of full age, that
is, those who by reason of use have their senses
exercised to discern both good and evil.
HEBREWS 5:13–14 NKJV

For further study, see Hank Hanegraaff, *The Covering: God's Plan to Protect You from Evil* (Nashville: W Publishing Group, 2002).

What is essential Christian
D-O-C-T-R-I-N-E?

The importance of essential Christian doctrine can hardly be overstated. First, these are the very doctrines that form the line of demarcation between the kingdom of Christ and the kingdom of the cults. While we may debate nonessentials without dividing over them, when it comes to essential Christian doctrine there must be unity. Hence, the maxim: *In essentials, unity; in nonessentials, liberty; and in all things, charity.*

Furthermore, essential Christian doctrine is the North Star by which the course of Christianity is set. Just as the North Star is an unchanging reference point by which sailors safely guided their ships, so essential Christian doctrine has safely guided the church through doctrinal storms that have sought to sink it. Shooting stars may light the sky for a moment; following them, however, leads to shipwreck.

Finally, essential Christian doctrine is the foundation on which the gospel of Jesus Christ rests. Covering topics ranging from His deity to the eschatological certainty that He will appear a second time to judge the living and the dead, essential Christian doctrine is foundational to the gospel. All other religions compromise, confuse, or contradict these essentials. Muslims, for example, dogmatically denounce the doctrine of Christ's unique deity as the unforgivable sin of *shirk*, of putting something created on the same level as the Creator. They readily affirm the sinlessness of Christ, but they adamantly deny His sacrifice upon the cross and His subsequent resurrection as the only hope of salvation.

I am so passionate about inscribing the essentials on the tablet of your heart that I've organized them around the acronym D-O-C-T-R-I-N-E. It is my prayer that you will become so familiar with essential Christian doctrine that when a counterfeit looms on the horizon you will know it instantaneously.

DEITY OF CHRIST. The biblical witness is clear and convincing that Jesus Christ is the eternal Creator God (John 1; Colossians 1; Hebrews 1; Revelation 1). Throughout His earthly ministry Jesus claimed to be God in word and deed (Mark 14:61–62; John 5:18, 20; 8:58; 10:30–33). He vindicated His claim to deity by living a sinless life (John 8:46; 2 Corinthians 5:21; Hebrews 4:15; 1 John 3:5; 1 Peter 2:22); by manifesting His power over nature (Mark 4:39), over fallen angels (Luke 4:35), over sickness (Matthew 4:23), and even over death itself (John 4:50; 11:43–44; 1 Corinthians 15); and by accurately prophesying God's judgment on Jerusalem through the destruction of the temple that occurred in AD 70 (Matthew 24:1–2, 32–35).

ORIGINAL SIN. Sin is not just murder, rape, or robbery. *Sin* refers to any thought, word, deed, or state of being that fails to meet God's standard of holiness and perfection. The Bible unambiguously proclaims that "all have sinned and fall short of the glory of God" (Romans 3:23). While the notion of generational curses and spirits is foreign to the text of Scripture, there is a sense in which all people are cursed as a result of an ancestor's sin: Adam's rebellion brought death to us all and tainted every aspect of our being (Genesis 3; 1 Corinthians 15:21–22; cf. Ephesians 2:3). God, however, has provided redemption through the atoning work of the Second Adam, Jesus Christ (Romans 5:12–21).

CANON. The Hebrew Scriptures along with the Greek New Testament constitute the Christian canon (meaning "standard of measurement"). While inspiration provides the divine authority for the Scriptures (2 Timothy 3:16), canonization provides human acknowledgment of that authority. As such, the canon was *determined* by God and *discovered* by church fathers who accepted books as part of the canon on the basis that they were widely used within the churches and ultimately traceable to the authority of the apostles and prophets.

TRINITY. Although the word *Trinity* is found nowhere in the Bible, it aptly codifies the essential biblical truths that (1) there is only one God (Deuteronomy 6:4; Isaiah 43:10); (2) the Father is God, the Son is God, and the Holy Spirit is God (1 Corinthians 8:6; Hebrews 1:8; Acts 5:3–4); and (3) Father, Son, and Holy Spirit are eternally distinct (Matthew 28:19; John 15:26; 17:1–26). It is important to note that when Trinitarians speak of one God, they are referring to the nature or essence of God. Moreover, when they speak of Persons, they are referring to personal self-distinctions within the Godhead. Put another way, Trinitarians believe in one *What* and three *Whos*.

RESURRECTION. All four canonical Gospels record the bodily resurrection of Jesus Christ from the dead. The immutable fact of Jesus' resurrection is the cornerstone of Christian faith, because it not only vindicates Jesus' claims to deity but also ensures the future bodily resurrection unto eternal life of all who believe in Jesus Christ as their Savior and proclaim Him as Lord (1 Corinthians 15; 1 Thessalonians 4:13–18). The historical reality of the resurrection can be demonstrated by eyewitness accounts of the fatal torment Jesus suffered on the cross; the empty tomb (early Christianity could not have survived an identifiable tomb containing the corpse of Christ); the post-resurrection appearances of Jesus; and the transformation of believers throughout the ages whose lives have been radically altered upon experiencing the resurrected Lord.

INCARNATION. The doctrine of the incarnation is aptly summed up in the words of the apostle John: "In the beginning was the Word, and the Word was with God, and the Word was God. . . . And the Word became flesh and dwelt among us, and we beheld His glory, the glory as of the only begotten of the Father, full of grace and truth" (John 1:1, 14 NKJV). The clear testimony of Scripture is that, in the incarnation, Jesus Christ was, and will forever remain, fully God *and* fully man; that is, the eternal Son of God, the second Person of the Triune Godhead, added to Himself an additional nature such that He exists as the perfect unity of a divine nature and a human nature in one Person (John 1; Colossians 1). As *Theanthropos* ("God-man"), the spotless Lamb of God (John 1:29) lived a perfectly sinless human life and died a sinner's death to sufficiently atone—once, for all—for the sins of humanity (Romans 5:1–21; Hebrews 10:11–18).

NEW CREATION. The essential doctrine of New Creation is aptly codified in the words of the apostle Paul: "If anyone is in Christ, he is a new creation; old things have passed away; behold, all things have become new" (2 Corinthians 5:17 NKJV). All who believe in the resurrection of Jesus Christ and confess Him as Lord are reconciled to God and inherit eternal life in His glorious presence (John 3:16; Romans 10:9–10). Jesus' resurrection from the dead inaugurated the renewal of all things. The new creation of faithful believers and the new creation of the natural world will be consummated in the resurrection when Jesus returns bodily to earth as the conquering King (Romans 8:18–25).

ESCHATOLOGY. The word *eschatology* is an intimidating word with a simple meaning: the study of end times. While the meaning of eschatology is simple to grasp, its importance is difficult to overemphasize. Far from being a mere branch in the theological tree, eschatology is the root that provides life and luster to every fiber of its being. Put another way, eschatology is the thread that weaves the tapestry of Scripture into a harmonious pattern. It is the study of everything we long and hope for. Early in Genesis, Adam and Eve fell into a life of constant sin terminated by death. The rest of Scripture chronicles God's unfolding plan of redemption. Although Christians debate secondary aspects of eschatology, such as the timing of the Tribulation or the meaning of the Millennium, we are united in the truth that just as Christ came to earth once to bear the sins of the world, so, too, He will return again to gather the elect and to usher in the resurrection of all things (1 Thessalonians 4:13–18; Hebrews 9:27–28). On that day, the just will be resurrected to eternal life and the unjust to eternal conscious torment and separation from the love and grace of God (John 5:28–29). Paradise lost will become paradise restored, and the problem of sin and Satan will be fully and finally resolved (Revelation 20–22).

> *Watch your life and doctrine closely.*
> *Persevere in them, because if you do, you*
> *will save both yourself and your hearers.*
> 1 TIMOTHY 4:16

The essential tenets of the Christian faith are:

DEITY OF CHRIST

ORIGINAL SIN

CANON

TRINITY

RESURRECTION

INCARNATION

NEW CREATION

ESCHATOLOGY

For further study, see the plethora of articles at www.equip.org.

What is the biblical definition of faith?

he shield of faith described by the apostle Paul in his letter to the Ephesian Christians is of paramount importance to believers because it is the grace "with which you can extinguish all the flaming arrows of the evil one" (Ephesians 6:16). This is not an uncertain promise. Rather, it is divine assurance that faith equips us to escape the very extremities of evil. But what is faith?

First, the Bible defines *faith* as "being sure of what we hope for and certain of what we do not see" (Hebrews 11:1). Thus, biblical faith is a *channel of living trust—an assurance*—that stretches from man to God. Moreover, it is the *object* of faith that renders faith faithful.

Furthermore, faith is the assurance that God's promises will never fail, even if sometimes we do not experience their fulfillment during our mortal existence. Hebrews 11 underscores the fact that we trust God to fulfill His promises for the future (the unseen) based on what He has already fulfilled in the past. Thus, our faith is not blind, but based squarely on God's proven faithfulness.

Finally, the faith that serves to protect us in spiritual warfare is not to be confused with mere knowledge. Millions worldwide believe in the trustworthiness of Billy Graham. They have heard him proclaim the good news on television and yet do not believe that his message corresponds to reality. Thus, they have the knowledge that it takes to be saved but do not have saving faith. Others hear the message, agree that it corresponds to reality, but, due to the hardness of their hearts, do not bow. Rather, like the demons, they continue to live in fearful anticipation of the judgment to come (James 2:19). Some, however, have what Scripture describes as genuine justifying faith—a faith that not only knows about the gospel and agrees that its content corresponds to reality, but a faith by which they are transformed.

In part adapted from *The Covering*

Though He slay me, yet will I trust Him.
JOB 13:15 NKJV

For further study, see Hank Hanegraaff, *The Covering: God's Plan to Protect You from Evil* (Nashville: W Publishing Group, 2002), chapter 7; and Hank Hanegraaff, *Christianity in Crisis: 21st Century* (Nashville: Thomas Nelson, 2009), Part Two.

What is sin?

While it has become politically incorrect to talk about sin, the Scriptures make it crystal clear that "all have sinned and fall short of the glory of God" (Romans 3:23). But what is sin from a biblical perspective?

First, sin is not just murder, rape, or robbery. Sin is failing to do the things we should and doing those things that we should not. In short, *sin* is a word that describes anything that fails to meet God's standard of perfection. Thus, sin is the barrier between you and a satisfying relationship with God. Just as light and dark cannot exist together, neither can God and sin.

Furthermore, sin is a barrier between us and other people. You need only read the newspaper or listen to a news report to see how true this statement really is. We live in a time when terrorism abounds and when the world as we know it can be instantly obliterated by nuclear aggression.

Finally, sin is the deprivation of good. As such, sin is characterized by a lack of something rather than being something in itself. As noted above, sin is a break in relationship with God and with others rather than being an ontological substance.

Adapted from *The Face That Demonstrates the Farce of Evolution*

But God demonstrates His own love toward us, in that while we were still sinners, Christ died for us. Much more then, having now been justified by His blood, we shall be saved from wrath through Him.

ROMANS 5:8–9 NKJV

For further study, see Carl F. H. Henry, *Basic Christian Doctrines* (Grand Rapids: Baker Book House, 1962).

Sin is failing to do the things we should . . .

Sins of Omission

Failing to believe in Jesus (John 3:16–18; 6:29; 1 John 5:12)

Failing to love God (Deuteronomy 6:4; Mark 12:30)

Failing to love your neighbor as yourself (Mark 12:31)

Failing to trust God (Proverbs 3:5; Isaiah 26:4)

Failing to worship God (Deuteronomy 6:13)

Failing to honor God (Proverbs 3:9; John 5:23)

Failing to honor the Son (John 5:23)

Failing to honor one's parents (Exodus 20:12)

Failing to give thanks to God in everything (Psalm 105:1; Romans 1:21; 1 Thessalonians 5:18)

Failing to glorify God (Psalm 34:3; Romans 1:21)

Failing to fear the Lord (Deuteronomy 6:13; Proverbs 3:7)

Failing to do the good one knows one ought to do (James 4:17)

Failing to test new teaching by Scripture (1 Thessalonians 5:21; Acts 17:11)

Failing to discern and guard against false teachers and prophets (Matthew 7:15–20; Acts 20:28–31)

Failing to learn and believe Scripture (Deuteronomy 6:6; 2 Timothy 2:15)

Failing to guard life and doctrine (1 Timothy 4:16)

Failing to repay debts (Romans 13:7)

Failing to care for orphans and widows in distress (James 1:20)

Failing to defend the faith (1 Peter 3:15: Jude v. 3)

Failing to share the gospel (Matthew 28:19)

Failing to honor others (Romans 12:9)

Failing to keep your fervor (Romans 12:9)

Failing to serve or give (Romans 12:9)

Failing to live at peace (Romans 12:18)

Failing to be clear-minded and alert (1 Peter 5:8)

Failing to rejoice (1 Thessalonians 5:16)

Failing to pray without ceasing (Luke 18:1; Ephesians 6:18; 1 Thessalonians 5:17)

Failing to pray for fellow believers (James 5:16)

Failing to forgive (Matthew 6:15)

and doing those things that we should not.

SINS OF COMMISSION

Idolatry (Exodus 20:3–6; Romans 1:21–25; 1 John 5:21)

Blasphemy (Mark 3:29)

Misusing the Lord's name (Exodus 20:7)

Covetousness (Exodus 20:17; Romans 1:29; 7:7; 13:9)

Wrong teaching (Matthew 23:15; Galatians 1:8; James 3:1)

Insincere love (Romans 12:9)

Causing someone else to sin (Mark 9:42)

Sexual impurity (Matthew 5:28; Romans 1:24)

Adultery (Exodus 20:14; Hebrews 13:4)

Homosexuality (Leviticus 18:22; Romans 1:26–27; 1 Corinthians 6:9)

Selfish ambition (Galatians 5:20)

Fits of rage (Galatians 5:20)

Slave trading (1 Timothy 1:10)

Lying (Exodus 23:1; Romans 13:9; Revelation 21:8)

Hypocrisy (1 Peter 2:1)

Drunkenness (1 Corinthians 6:10)

Stealing (Exodus 20:15; 1 Corinthians 6:10)

Sorcery (Deuteronomy 18:10)

Witchcraft (Deuteronomy 18:10)

Divination (Deuteronomy 18:10)

Interpreting Omens (Deuteronomy 18:10)

Consulting the dead (Deuteronomy 18:11)

Astrology (Deuteronomy 18:9–13; Isaiah 47:13–14)

Depravity (Romans 1:29)

Envy (Romans 1:29; 1 Peter 2:1)

Deceit (Romans 1:29; 1 Peter 2:1)

Murder (Romans 1:29)

Strife (Romans 1:29)

Malice (Romans 1:29; 1 Peter 2:1)

Gossip (Romans 1:29)

Slander (Romans 1:30; 1 Peter 2:1)

Hating God (Romans 1:30)

Insolence (Romans 1:30)

Arrogance (Romans 1:30)

Boastfulness (Romans 1:30)

Inventing evil (Romans 1:30)

Disobeying parents (Romans 1:30)

Disobeying the governing authorities (Romans 13:1–7)

Worrying (Luke 12:22–32)

How can I be certain I haven't committed the unforgivable sin?

T his is one of the most frequently asked questions on the *Bible Answer Man* broadcast, and it stems from the following words spoken by Christ: "I say to you, any sin and blasphemy shall be forgiven people, but blasphemy against the Spirit shall not be forgiven. Whoever speaks a word against the Son of Man, it shall be forgiven him; but whoever speaks against the Holy Spirit, it shall not be forgiven him, either in this age or in the age to come" (Matthew 12:31–32 NASB). As a result of these words, Christians are often paralyzed by fear.

In response, let me first point out that from a historic perspective, the Pharisees mentioned by Matthew militantly hated Christ and attributed His miracles to Beelzebub, the prince of demons. Unlike people who are afraid they have committed the unforgivable sin, the Pharisees were totally unconcerned about receiving Christ's forgiveness. Instead, with premeditation and persistence, they willfully blasphemed the Holy Spirit's testimony that Christ was the Son of the living God. It is crucial to recognize that the unforgivable sin is not a single act but a continuous, ongoing rejection of Jesus.

Furthermore, those who have committed the unpardonable sin have no godly regrets. As Paul emphasized in the book of Romans, they not only continue in their evil ways but approve of others who do so as well (1:32). Conversely, "godly sorrow brings repentance that leads to salvation" (2 Corinthians 7:10). Sorrow for sin and the desire for Christ's forgiveness are proof positive that you have not rejected the Savior of your soul. Never forget that three times Peter denied his Lord with vile oaths. Yet not only did Christ forgive him, but his confession, "You are the Christ, the Son of the living God" (Matthew 16:16 NASB) became the cornerstone of the Christian church.

Finally, the Bible consistently teaches that those who spend eternity separated from God do so because they willingly, knowingly, and continuously reject the gospel. John referred to this as the "sin that leads to death" (1 John 5:16) in the sense that those who refuse forgiveness through Christ will spend eternity separated from His grace and love. Be assured that those who sincerely desire God's forgiveness can be absolutely certain that He will never turn them away.

These things I have written to you who believe in the name of the Son of God, that you may know that you have eternal life, and that you may continue to believe in the name of the Son of God.

1 JOHN 5:13 NKJV

For further study, see Hank Hanegraaff, "The Unforgivable Sin," available from the Christian Research Institute at http://www.equip.org.

To grow in your understanding of and relationship with God, see J. I. Packer, *Knowing God* (Downers Grove, IL: InterVarsity Press, 1993).

Must Christians attend church?

From first to last, the Scriptures teach us that the Christian life is to be lived in the context of the family of faith (Ephesians 3:4–15; Acts 2). Indeed, the Bible knows nothing of Lone Ranger Christians! Far from being born again as rugged individuals, we are born into a body of believers of which Christ is the head. Thus, as Hebrews commands, "Let us not give up meeting together, as some are in the habit of doing" (10:25).

Furthermore, spiritual growth is impossible apart from membership in a healthy, well-balanced church. It is in the church that we receive the Word and sacraments as means of God's grace. Thus, it is crucial that we emulate the early Christians who "devoted themselves to the apostles' teaching and to the fellowship, to the breaking of bread and to prayer" (Acts 2:42).

Finally, although it is in the church that we enter into worship, experience fellowship, and are equipped to witness, church membership itself does not save us. As has been well said, walking into a church does not make you a Christian any more than walking into a garage makes you a car. We are rescued from God's wrath, forgiven of all our sins, and declared righteous before God solely by grace, through faith, on account of Jesus Christ (Romans 1:17; 3:21–4:8; Ephesians 2:8–9).

Let us consider one another in order to stir up love and good works, not forsaking the assembling of ourselves together, as is the manner of some, but exhorting one another, and so much the more as you see the Day approaching.

Hebrews 10:24–25 NKJV

For further study, see "How do I find a good church? (G-O-D)" (pp. 23–26).

How do I find a good church? (G-O-D)

This question has taken on added significance as pop culture beckons and post-modern Christians take the bait. Far too many modern churches partake of an unhealthy diet of fast-food Christianity—long on looks, dreadfully short on substance. A healthy church is one in which *God* is revered, *oneness* is realized, and *discipleship* is an experiential reality.

GOD. The first sign of a healthy, well-balanced church is the commitment to worship God through prayer, praise, and proclamation. Prayer is so inextricably woven into the fabric of worship that it would be unthinkable to have a Lord's Day without it. From the inception of the early Christian church, prayer has been a primary means of worshipping God. Jesus Himself set the pattern for prayer when He taught His disciples to pray, "Our Father who art in heaven" (Matthew 6:9 NASB).

Praise is likewise a key ingredient of worshipping God: "praise God in his sanctuary" (Psalm 150:1). Paul urged the church at Ephesus to "speak to one another with psalms, hymns and spiritual songs" (Ephesians 5:19). In the Psalms—the hymnbook of the early church—we see a stunning portrayal of God who is indeed worthy of praise and adoration.

In addition to prayer and praise, the *proclamation* of the Word is vital to the worship of God. Paul exhorted Timothy, "Devote yourself to the public reading of Scripture, to preaching and to teaching" (1 Timothy 4:13). Through the proclamation of God's Word, God is honored and believers are edified, educated, and equipped. It is through prayer, praise, and proclamation that we as believers are "being built into a spiritual house to be a holy priesthood, offering spiritual sacrifices acceptable to God through Jesus Christ" (1 Peter 2:5).

ONENESS. A second sign of a church's health is *oneness*. Jesus Christ has broken through the barriers of sex, race, and background that can divide, and He makes us into one body under the banner of love. Communism claimed to turn men into comrades, but Christ turns us into a body. The oneness we share as the body of Christ is tangibly manifested through *communion*, *creed*, and *contribution*.

Communion (the Eucharist) is the chief expression of our oneness with Christ and with one another. As we all partake of the same elements, we also partake of that which the elements signify: Christ, who binds us together as one. Our fellowship on earth, celebrated through the centrality of communion, is a foretaste of the heavenly communion we will share when the elements give way to eternity.

Commonality in creedal confession unites us around essential Christian doctrine. These doctrines—codified in the creeds and confessions of the Christian church—form the basis of our unity as the body of Christ. They mark the line of demarcation between the kingdom of Christ and the kingdom of the cults. We can disagree agreeably on nonessential or secondary doctrines, but when it comes to essential Christian doctrine, codified in the creeds, there must be oneness: "In essentials, unity; in nonessentials, liberty; and in all things, charity."

Contribution of time, talent, and treasure also demonstrates oneness in Christ. A healthy, well-balanced church is commissioned to "prepare

God's people for works of service, so that the body of Christ may be built up" (Ephesians 4:12). God has given the individual members of the body special gifts to be used "for the common good" (1 Corinthians 12:7). No human being is an island! Many logs together burn brightly, but when a log falls to the side, its embers quickly die out.

DISCIPLESHIP. In the Great Commission, Christ calls us to make not only *converts* but *disciples* (Matthew 28:19). A disciple is a learner or follower of the Lord Jesus Christ. Discipleship is demonstrated through the testimony of our *love*, *lips*, and *lives*. One secret of the early church's growth was the testimony of its *love*. The love of Christ was so contagious that it swept through the Roman Empire like wildfire. Jesus said, "All men will know that you are my disciples, if you love one another" (John 13:35).

New Testament Christianity was likewise characterized by the testimony of its *lips*. The book of Acts tells us that on the day Stephen was martyred, a great persecution arose against the church in Jerusalem, and all except the apostles were scattered through Judea and Samaria (Acts 8:1). Those who were scattered preached the word wherever they went. While it is true that not everyone is called to be an *evangelist*, everyone is called to *evangelize*.

Closely related to the testimony of our lips is the testimony of our *lives*. The aroma of the indwelling Christ should so characterize our life that people are attracted to our lives as are bees to honey. If our lives contradict the testimony of our lips, we conversely drag Christ's name through the mud. The testimony of our lives and lips must be in sync.

My prayer for you and for myself is that we are daily reminded of the privilege of being vitally connected to a healthy, well-balanced body of believers: a body in which *God* is worshipped, in which *oneness* is experienced, and in which *discipleship* is an experienced reality. Indeed, you and I are "a chosen people, a royal priesthood, a holy nation, a people belonging to God, that you may declare the praises of him who called you out of darkness into his wonderful light" (1 Peter 2:9).

> *They [followers of Christ] continued steadfastly*
> *in the apostles' doctrine and fellowship, in*
> *the breaking of bread, and in prayers.*
> ACTS 2:42 NKJV

For further study, see Hank Hanegraaff, "How to Find a Healthy Church," available from the Christian Research Institute at www.equip.org.

Why pray if God already
knows what we need?

As the father of twelve, I sometimes know what my children need before they ask. However, what I as an earthly father only sometimes know, our eternal heavenly Father always knows. That fact inevitably leads to the question "If God knows what we need before we even ask, why bother asking at all?"

First, it is crucial to recognize that supplication should not be seen as the sole sum and substance of our prayers. Far from merely being a means of presenting our daily requests to God, prayer is a means of pursuing a dynamic relationship with Him.

Furthermore, God ordains not only the ends but also the means. Thus, to ask, "Why pray if God already knows what we need?" is akin to asking, "Why get dressed in the morning and go to work?" For that matter, if God is going to do what He is going to do anyway, why bother doing anything? God has ordained that both the work we do and the prayers we utter produce results. The fact that God knows the future does not imply that our futures are fatalistically determined any more than our knowledge that the sun will rise causes the sun to rise.

Finally, while our heavenly Father knows what we need

before we even ask, our supplications are in and of themselves an acknowledgment of our dependence on Him. And that alone is reason enough to "pray without ceasing" (1 Thessalonians 5:17 NKJV).

Adapted from *The Prayer of Jesus*

"When you pray, do not use vain repetitions as
the heathen do. For they think that they will
be heard for their many words. Therefore do
not be like them. For your Father knows the
things you have need of before you ask Him."
MATTHEW 6:7–8 NKJV

For further study, see Hank Hanegraaff, *The Prayer of Jesus: Secrets to Real Intimacy with God* (Nashville: W Publishing Group, 2001).

What are some secrets to
effective prayer?

Everyone wants to know the secret to something. Golfers want to know the secret to playing golf like Jack Nicklaus or Rory McIlroy. Investors want to know the secret to making a fortune on Wall Street. Parents want to know the secret to raising healthy, happy kids. And Christians desperately want to know the secrets to effective prayer. So what are the secrets to real intimacy through prayer with God?

The first secret to effective prayer is *secret prayer*, and Jesus provided the ultimate example. As Dr. Luke put it, Jesus "often withdrew to lonely places and prayed" (Luke 5:16). Unlike the religious leaders of His day, Jesus did not pray to be seen by men. He prayed because He treasured fellowship with His Father. Hypocrites gain their reward through public prayer. They may be perceived as spiritual giants, but by the time they are finished, they have received everything they will ever get— their prayer's worth and nothing more.

A further secret is to recognize the connection between prayer and *meditation*. Our prayers are only as inspired as our intake of Scripture. Scripture feeds meditation, and meditation gives food to our prayers. Meditating on Scripture allows us to more naturally transition into a marvelous time of meaningful prayer. Author Donald Whitney, who rightly refers to meditation as the missing link between the intake of Scripture and prayer, notes that if there was a secret to the prayer life of evangelist George Müller, it was his discovery of the connection between meditation and prayer.

A final secret is to discover your secret place, a place where you can drown out the noise of the world and hear the voice of your heavenly Father. The issue, of course, is not location but motivation. We are all unique creations of God. Thus, your secret place will no doubt be different from mine. The point is that we all desperately need a place away from the invasive sounds of this world so that we can hear the sounds of another place and another Voice.

Adapted from *The Prayer of Jesus* and *The Covering*

"When you pray, go into your room, and when
you have shut your door, pray to your Father
who is in the secret place; and your Father
who sees in secret will reward you openly."

MATTHEW 6:6 NKJV

For further study, see Hank Hanegraaff, *The Prayer of Jesus: Secrets to Intimacy with God* (Nashville: W Publishing Group, 2001).

A few prayers in the Bible

Abraham's servant prayed for success in finding a wife for
Isaac (Genesis 24:12–14).

Jacob prayed for protection (Genesis 32:9–12).

Job prayed for conviction of sin (Job 13:23).

Moses prayed for mercy (Exodus 32:11–13, 31–32;
Deuteronomy 9:26–29).

Moses prayed to know God and to see His glory (Exodus
33:12–18).

Manoah prayed for guidance in raising his son, Samson
(Judges 13:8).

Hannah prayed to exalt God with thanksgiving and praise
(1 Samuel 2:1–10).

Elijah prayed for vindication and proof of God's power
(1 Kings 18:36–37).

Hezekiah prayed for deliverance from enemies (2 Kings
19:15–19).

Solomon prayed for forgiveness of sins for Israel
(2 Chronicles 6:21).

David, throughout Psalms, prayed with thanksgiving and praise for mercy and grace, conviction of sin, forgiveness, instruction, and deliverance from enemies.

Jeremiah prayed to complain (Jeremiah 20:7–18).

Ezra prayed to confess his people's sin (Ezra 9:6–15).

Daniel prayed for help with thanksgiving (Daniel 6:10–11).

Daniel prayed to confess his people's sin (Daniel 9:9–19).

Jonah prayed for restoration (Jonah 2:1–9).

Jesus prayed for God's will (Matthew 26:36–46).

Jesus prayed for Himself, for the disciples, and for all believers (John 17:1–26).

Jesus prayed for forgiveness for His enemies (Luke 23:34).

The apostles prayed for selection of Judas's replacement (Acts 1:24–25).

The apostles prayed for the bold proclamation of the gospel with miracles (Acts 4:29–30).

Stephen prayed for the Lord to receive his spirit and to forgive his killers (Acts 7:59–60).

What is the
F-A-C-T-S prayer guide?

T he word F-A-C-T-S serves as a memorable outline providing a wonderful structure to my daily prayer time. In place of merely snorkeling in the surface waters of prayer, F-A-C-T-S provides me a means by which I can dive deep beneath the tumult and turbulence of the ocean surface to a place that is silent and serene, a place where my harried requests may give way to the quietness of union with the Lover of my soul.

FAITH. Think of faith as *a channel of living trust—an assurance—* that stretches from a human being to God. It is the object of faith, however, that renders faith faithful. Faith is more than mere *knowledge* and *agreement*; it involves living *trust*. Jesus summed up the prayer of faith with these words: "If you remain in me and my words remain in you, ask whatever you wish, and it will be given you" (John 15:7).

ADORATION. Faith in God naturally leads to adoration. The beauty of adoration is that it unshackles us from preoccupation with self and places our focus directly on the Sovereign of our souls. Through adoration we express our genuine heartfelt love and longing for God. Adoration inevitably leads to praise and worship as we focus our thoughts on God's surpassing greatness. We can pray the psalms in particular as passionate prayers of adoration.

CONFESSION. It is quite natural for your prayers to transition from adoration of God to confession of guilt. Indeed, one inevitably leads toward the other. When we touch the transcendence of God, we are inevitably reminded of our own unworthiness. We can develop intimacy with the Lord through prayer only when we confess our need for forgiveness and contritely seek His pardon. The apostle John summed it up beautifully when he wrote, "If we confess our sins, He is faithful and just to forgive us our sins and to cleanse us from all unrighteousness" (1 John 1:9 NKJV).

THANKSGIVING. Scripture exhorts us to "enter [God's] gates with thanksgiving" (Psalm 100:4). Failure to do so makes prayer the stuff of pagan babblings and carnal Christianity. Pagans, said Paul, knew about God, but "they neither glorified him as God *nor gave thanks to him*" (Romans 1:21). Each new day we ought to approach God "overflowing with thankfulness" (Colossians 2:7) as we devote ourselves "to prayer, being watchful and thankful" (4:2). Such thankfulness is an action that flows from the sure knowledge that our heavenly Father knows exactly what we need and will supply it.

SUPPLICATION. It is proper and right that our supplications tend toward the end rather than the beginning of our prayers, for it is in the context of a relationship with God that our requests make any sense at all. As John wrote, "Now this is the confidence that we have in Him, that if we ask anything *according to His will*, He hears us. And if we know that He hears us, whatever we ask, we *know* that we have the petitions that we have asked of Him" (1 John 5:14–15 NKJV).

While our Father knows what we need before we even ask, our supplications in and of themselves are an acknowledgment of our dependence on Him. And that alone is reason enough to "pray without ceasing."

Rejoice always, pray without ceasing,
in everything give thanks; for this is the
will of God in Christ Jesus for you.

1 THESSALONIANS 5:16–18 NKJV

FAITH

ADORATION

CONFESSION

THANKSGIVING

SUPPLICATION

For further study, see Hank Hanegraaff, *The Prayer of Jesus: Secrets to Real Intimacy with God* (Nashville: W Publishing Group, 2001).

Why is it so crucial to pray
"Your will be done"?

J esus not only taught His disciples to pray, "Your will be done" (Matthew 6:10), but He modeled those very words in His own life and ministry. And Jesus' example raises the question, "Why is it so crucial to pray in this way?"

First, to pray "Your will be done" is to recognize the sovereignty of God over every aspect of our daily lives. In effect, it is a way of saying, "Thank God this world is under His control, not mine!" We would be in deep trouble if God gave us everything for which we asked. The fact is, we don't know what's best for us! We only see a snapshot of our lives while God sees the entire panoply. Thus, His perspective is far superior to ours.

Furthermore, to pray "Your will be done" is daily recognition that our wills must be submitted to His will. One of the most comforting thoughts that can penetrate a human mind yielded to the will of God is that He who has created us also knows what is best for us. Thus, if we walk according to His will, rather than trying to command Him according to our own wills, we will indeed have, as He promised, not a panacea, but peace in the midst of the storm. In the yielded life we find great peace in knowing that the One who taught us to pray "Your will be done" has every detail of our lives under control. Not only is God the Object of our faith, He is also the Originator of our faith. Indeed, He is the Originator of our salvation and, yes, even the Originator of our prayers. Thus, whatever we pray for, whether it's healing or a house, when our will is in harmony with His will, we will receive what we request 100 percent of the time. However, when we pray as Christ prayed, "Nevertheless, not my will but yours be done" (Luke 22:42), we can rest assured that even in sickness and tragedy "all things work together for good to those who love God, to those who are the called according to His purpose" (Romans 8:28 NKJV).

Finally, to pray "your will be done" is daily recognition that God will not spare us from trial and tribulation, but rather He will use the fiery furnace to purge impurities from our lives. Ultimately, this is the message of the book of Job. Job endured more tragedy in a single day than most people experience in a lifetime. Yet in his darkest hour Job uttered the ultimate words of faith, "Though he slay me, yet will I trust in him" (Job 13:15 KJV). For the child of God, the hope is not perfect health and happiness in this lifetime, but a resurrected body and a heavenly dwelling in the life to come.

Adapted from *The Prayer of Jesus*

Why do people end their prayers with *amen*?

E veryone is familiar with the word *amen*. But have you ever taken the time to consider what it really means? Is ending our prayers with *amen* a mere ritual? Or is there a majestic richness to the word that we often miss?

First, *amen* is a universally recognized word that is far more significant than simply signing off or saying, "That's all." With the word *amen* we are in effect saying, "May it be so in accordance with the will of God." It is a marvelous reminder that prayer is a means of bringing us into conformity with God's will, not a magic mantra that ensures God's conformity to ours.

Furthermore, the word *amen* is a direct reference to Jesus, who taught us to pray "your will be done" (Matthew 6:10). In Revelation, Jesus is referred to as the "Amen, the faithful and true witness, the ruler of God's creation" (3:14). Also, Jesus not only taught us to pray, "Your will be done," but He modeled those words in His life. In His passionate prayer in the Garden of Gethsemane, He prayed, "My Father, if it is possible, may this cup be taken from me. Yet *not as I will, but as you will*" (Matthew 26:39).

Finally, although Jesus is our greatest example, He is certainly not our only example of submitting to God's will. His brother

James warned those who are prone to "boast and brag" that they ought to pray instead, "If it is the Lord's will, we will live and do this or that" (James 4:15). Christ's closest friend during His earthly ministry, the apostle John, echoed the words of the Master when he wrote, "This is the confidence we have in approaching God: that if we ask anything *according to his will*, he hears us" (1 John 5:14).

Next time you end your prayer with the word *amen*, it is my prayer that you will remember that far from being a formality, this way of closing a prayer is fraught with meaning. Not only is *amen* a direct reference to the Savior, but it is a reminder that even the seemingly insignificant details of our lives are under the Savior's sovereign control.

Adapted from *The Prayer of Jesus*

Now this is the confidence that we have in Him,
that if we ask anything according to His will,
He hears us. And if we know that He hears
us, whatever we ask, we know that we have
the petitions that we have asked of Him.

1 JOHN 5:14–15 NKJV

For further study, see Hank Hanegraaff, *The Prayer of Jesus: Secrets to Real Intimacy with God* (Nashville: W Publishing Group, 2001).

Must I forgive those who refuse forgiveness?

Jesus taught His disciples to pray, "Forgive us our debts, as we also have forgiven our debtors" (Matthew 6:12). Does that mean we have to forgive someone even when they refuse to reconcile?

First, the debts we owe one another are small change compared to the infinite debt we owe our heavenly Father. Because we have been forgiven an infinite debt, it is a horrendous evil to even consider withholding our forgiveness from those who seek it. Thus, we must always manifest the kind of love that is *willing* to forgive those who wrong us.

Furthermore, forgiveness is by definition a two-way street leading to the restoration of fellowship. It requires someone who is *willing* to forgive and someone who is *wanting* to be forgiven. If you are to forgive me, I must be repentant; otherwise, there can be no restoration of fellowship (i.e., forgiveness).

Finally, we must never suppose that our standard of forgiveness is higher than God's standard. He *objectively* offers us forgiveness and the restoration of fellowship with Him. We do not *subjectively* realize His forgiveness, however, until we repent (Luke 6:37–38).

In part adapted from *The Prayer of Jesus*

HANK HANEGRAAFF

SPIRITUAL GIFTS

What does it mean to say that
the Holy Spirit is *in* you?

Over the past several decades, I have been asked the "in" question in a variety of different ways: "What does it mean to say God is in my life, Jesus is in my heart, or the Holy Spirit is in me? Does it mean that everyone simultaneously has a little piece of God in them?" Or is the Bible communicating something far more precious?

First, to say that the Holy Spirit is *in* you is not to point out *where* the Holy Spirit is physically located, but rather to acknowledge that you have come into an intimate, personal relationship with Him through faith and repentance. As such, the preposition *in* is not a *locational* but a *relational* term. Similarly, when Jesus said, "The Father is in me, and I in the Father" (John 10:38), He was speaking not of physical location but of intimacy of relationship.

Furthermore, to deny that the Holy Spirit is *spatially* locatable within us is not to deny that He is *actively* locatable within us, working redemptively to conform us to the image of Christ. Far from detracting from our nearness to the Holy Spirit, the classic Christian view intensifies the intimacy of our relationship to the Creator as well as the benefits of our redemption.

The glorious reality is that you and I can experience union with God—the interpenetration of His uncreated energy with our humanity. While we cannot experience God in His essence, we can experience His energies (Colossians 1:29). As Peter put it, we may as yet participate in the divine nature (2 Peter 1:4; cf. John 17:11; 2 Corinthians 3:18).

Finally, according to the Scriptures, the Holy Spirit is not a physical being; thus, to ask *where* the Holy Spirit is, is to confuse categories. Asking spatial questions about a Being who does not have extension in space makes about as much sense as asking what the color blue tastes like. King Solomon revealed the utter futility of believing that the infinite Holy Spirit can be physically contained in any finite space, let alone the human body, when he exclaimed, "Will God really dwell on earth? The heavens, even the highest heaven, cannot contain you. How much less this temple I have built!" (1 Kings 8:27).

> *Do you not know that your body is the temple*
> *of the Holy Spirit who is in you, whom you*
> *have from God, and you are not your own?*
> 1 CORINTHIANS 6:19 NKJV

For further study, see "Is there a difference between *indwelling* and *infilling*?" (pp. 44–45).

Is there a difference between *indwelling* and *infilling*?

First, all members of true Israel are *indwelt* by the Holy Spirit (Romans 8:1–17; 1 Corinthians 12:13; Ephesians 1:13; 1 John 4:13). As such, the Spirit dwelt in Moses (Isaiah 63:11) as well as Matthew (John 14:17), and both Joshua (Numbers 27:18) and James (Acts 15). In every epoch of time, believers are regenerated and restored (John 3:3–6) as well as sanctified and sealed (Romans 15:16; Ephesians 1:13; 4:30) by the indwelling Holy Spirit.

Furthermore, those who are in Christ are not only indwelt by but also *infilled* with the Holy Spirit. When Jesus said to His disciples, "I will ask the Father, and he will give you another Counselor to be with you forever" (John 14:16), He was not suggesting that the Holy Spirit was not already working redemptively within His followers. Jesus was saying that the Spirit would manifest in the special empowerment of each believer to proclaim the gospel (Acts 1:8; 13:52).

Finally, while the indwelling of the Spirit happens at conversion, the infilling of the Spirit happens continually (Ephesians 5:18). As such, we daily seek the Holy Spirit to empower us for our prayers to God and our proclamations of the gospel.

Indeed, whenever the gospel penetrates the human heart it is "'not by might nor by power, but by my Spirit,' says the LORD Almighty" (Zechariah 4:6).

> Create in me a clean heart, O God,
> And renew a steadfast spirit within me.
> Do not cast me away from Your presence,
> And do not take Your Holy Spirit from me.
> Restore to me the joy of Your salvation,
> And uphold me by Your generous Spirit.
> Then I will teach transgressors Your ways,
> And sinners shall be converted to You.
>
> PSALM 51:10–13 NKJV

For further study, see "Is speaking in tongues *the* evidence of the baptism of the Holy Spirit?" (p. 46).

Is speaking in tongues *the* evidence of the baptism of the Holy Spirit?

I t has become increasingly common for Christians to suppose that the full gospel includes the baptism of the Holy Spirit with the evidence of speaking in tongues. Thus the question: "Is speaking in tongues *the* evidence of being baptized by the Holy Spirit?"

First, as the apostle Paul made plain, believers are "all baptized by one Spirit into one body" (1 Corinthians 12:13), yet not all who believe speak in tongues (vv. 10, 30). Thus, tongues may be a manifestation of the baptism of the Holy Spirit, but tongues cannot be *the* manifestation.

Furthermore, even if individuals do speak in tongues, it is not a guarantee that they have been baptized in the Holy Spirit. For as Paul put it, "If I speak in the tongues of men and angels, but have not love, I am only a resounding gong or a clanging cymbal" (1 Corinthians 13:1). Indeed, said Paul, without love, "I am nothing" (v. 2). Moreover, sociopsychological manipulation tactics such as peer pressure or the subtle power of suggestion can induce ecstatic utterances wholly apart from the Spirit.

Finally, as Scripture makes clear, the normative sign of the baptism of the Holy Spirit is not speaking in tongues but the confession of Jesus Christ as Lord, repentance from sin, and obedience to God (Romans 8:1–17; 1 John 4:12–16; cf. Ephesians 1:13–15). "Those who live in accordance with the Spirit have their minds set on what the Spirit desires. The mind of sinful man is death, but the mind controlled by the Spirit is life and peace" (Romans 8:5–6). As such, the fruit of the Spirit is not merely speaking in tongues, but "love, joy, peace, patience, kindness, goodness, faithfulness, gentleness and self-control" (Galatians 5:22–23). In sum, righteousness, not tongues, is the core of Christianity compressed in a single word.

Do not be drunk with wine, in which is dissipation;
but be filled with the Spirit, speaking to one
another in psalms and hymns and spiritual songs,
singing and making melody in your heart to
the Lord, giving thanks always for all things to
God the Father in the name of our Lord Jesus
Christ, submitting to one another in the fear of God.

EPHESIANS 5:18–21 NKJV

For further study, see "What does it mean to say that the Holy Spirit is *in* you?" (pp. 42–43).

THE NATURE AND
CHARACTER OF GOD

Is the Trinity biblical?

hile it is popular to suggest that the doctrine of the Trinity is derived from pagan sources, in reality this Christian essential is thoroughly biblical. The word *Trinity*—like *incarnation*—is not found in Scripture; however, it aptly expresses what God has condescended to reveal to us about His nature and being. In short, the Trinitarian platform contains three planks: (1) there is but one God; (2) the Father is God, the Son is God, and the Holy Spirit is God; (3) Father, Son, and Holy Spirit are eternally distinct.

The first plank underscores that there is only one God. Christianity is not polytheistic but fiercely monotheistic. "'You are my witnesses,' declares the LORD, 'and my servant whom I have chosen, so that you may know and believe me and understand that I am he. *Before me no god was formed, nor will there be one after me*'" (Isaiah 43:10).

The second plank emphasizes that, in hundreds of Scripture passages, the Father, the Son, and the Holy Spirit are each declared to be fully and completely God. As a case in point, the apostle Paul said that "there is but one God, the Father" (1 Corinthians 8:6). The Father, speaking of the Son, said, "Your throne, O God, will last for ever and ever" (Hebrews 1:8). And when Ananias "lied to the Holy Spirit," Peter pointed out that he had "not lied to men but to God" (Acts 5:3–4; cf. Matthew 28:19).

The third plank of the Trinitarian platform asserts that the Father, Son, and Holy Spirit are eternally distinct. Scripture clearly portrays subject/object relationships between Father, Son, and Holy Spirit. For example, the Father loves the Son (John 3:35); the Son prays to the Father (John 17); and the Father sends the Holy Spirit (John 15:26). Additionally, Jesus proclaimed that He and the Father are two distinct witnesses and two distinct judges (John 8:14–18). If Jesus were Himself the Father, His argument would have been not only irrelevant but also fatally flawed; and if such were the case, He could not have been fully God.

It is important to note that when Trinitarians speak of one God, they are referring to the nature or essence of God. Moreover, when they speak of Persons, they are referring to personal self-distinctions within the Godhead. Put another way, we believe in one *What* and three *Whos*.

Hear, O Israel: The LORD our God, the LORD is one!
DEUTERONOMY 6:4 NKJV

For further study, see Donald Fairbairn, *Life in the Trinity: An Introduction to Theology with the Help of the Church Fathers* (Downers Grove, IL: IVP Academic, 2009).

If God is one, why does the Bible refer to Him in plural?

ow could the Israelites be fiercely monotheistic and yet refer to their God using the plural *Elohim* (Genesis 1:1; Deuteronomy 6:4)?

First, this usage cannot be explained away as a royal plural or plural of majesty. Nowhere in the Hebrew language of the Old Testament does a first-person plural refer solely to the speaker.

Furthermore, while the Bible from Genesis to Revelation reveals that God is one in nature or essence (Deuteronomy 6:4; Isaiah 43:10; Ephesians 4:6), it also reveals that this one God eternally exists in three distinct Persons: the Father, the Son, and the Holy Spirit (1 Corinthians 8:6; Hebrews 1:8; Acts 5:3–4). Thus, the plural ending of *Elohim* points to a plurality of Persons, not to a plurality of gods.

Finally, although *Elohim* is *suggestive* of the Trinity, this word alone is not sufficient to prove the Trinity. Thus, instead of relying on a singular grammatical construction, Christians must be equipped to demonstrate that the one God revealed in Scripture exists in three Persons who are eternally distinct.

What does it mean to say that God is omnipresent?

The Bible clearly portrays God's omnipresence. But what exactly does that term mean? Is God dispersed throughout the universe? Or does *omnipresence* refer to God's nearness to all of creation all of the time?

First, when Scripture speaks of God as omnipresent or present everywhere (Psalm 139), it is not communicating that He is physically distributed throughout the universe. *Omnipresence* means that God is simultaneously present—in all His fullness—to every part of creation. Thus Scripture communicates God's creative and sustaining relationship to the cosmos rather than any physical location in the cosmos.

Furthermore, to speak of God's omnipresence in terms of a physical location in the world rather than His relationship to the world has more in common with the panentheism of heretical process theology (currently popular in liberal circles) than with classical Christian theism. Panentheism holds that God is intrinsically *in* the world like a hand in a glove, while classical theism holds that God properly exists outside of time and space (Isaiah 57:15).

Finally, the danger of speaking about God in locational

terms is that it logically implies that He is by nature a material being. The apostle John clearly communicated that "God is Spirit, and those who worship Him must worship in spirit and truth" (John 4:24 NKJV).

> *Where can I go from Your Spirit?*
> *Or where can I flee from Your presence?*
> *If I ascend into heaven, You are there;*
> *If I make my bed in hell, behold, You are there.*
> *If I take the wings of the morning,*
> *And dwell in the uttermost parts of the sea,*
> *Even there Your hand shall lead me,*
> *And Your right hand shall hold me.*
> PSALM 139:7–10 NKJV

For further study, see Gordon R. Lewis, "Attributes of God," in Walter A. Elwell, ed., *Evangelical Dictionary of Theology*, 2nd ed. (Grand Rapids: Baker Academic, 2001), 492–99.

Does God know the future?

A contingency in Christianity—namely, open theists—are currently communicating that God does not have perfect knowledge of the future. How do we respond to this crisis within Christianity?

First, from beginning to end, the Bible teaches the omniscience of God. In the words of Isaiah, God knows "the end from the beginning" (Isaiah 46:10). As such, God's knowledge is exhaustive, including even those things in the future (cf. Job 37:16; Psalm 139:1–6; 147:5; Hebrews 4:12–13).

Furthermore, if God's knowledge of the future is fallible, biblical predictions that depend on human agency might well have turned out wrong. Then even Jesus' predictions in the Olivet Discourse could have failed, thus undermining His claim to deity. God Himself could have failed the biblical test for a prophet (Deuteronomy 18:22). Indeed, if God's knowledge of the future is incomplete, we would be foolish to trust Him to answer our prayers, thus negating the "confidence we have in approaching God: that if we ask anything according to his will, he hears us. And if we know that he hears us—whatever we ask—we know that we have what we asked of him" (1 John 5:14–15).

Finally, open theists suggest that God cannot know the future exhaustively because He changes His plans as a result of what people do. In reality, however, it is not God who changes, but people who change in relationship to God. By way of analogy, if you walk into a headwind, you struggle against the wind; if you make a U–turn on the road, the wind is at your back. It is not the wind that has changed, but you have changed in relationship to the wind. As such, God's plan to destroy Nineveh was not aborted because He did not know the future. Instead, God did not destroy the Ninevites because they, who had walked in opposition to God, turned from walking in their wicked ways. Indeed, all of God's promises to bless or to judge must be understood in light of the condition that God withholds blessing when we disobey and withholds judgment when we repent (Ezekiel 18; Jeremiah 18:7–10).

> *Remember the former things of old,*
> *For I am God, and there is no other;*
> *I am God, and there is none like Me,*
> *Declaring the end from the beginning,*
> *And from ancient times things that are not yet done,*
> *Saying, "My counsel shall stand,*
> *And I will do all My pleasure."*
>
> Isaiah 46:9–10 NKJV

For further study, see "Does God repent?" (p. 57).

HANK HANEGRAAFF

Does God repent?

he classic King James Version of the Bible says, "It repented the LORD that he had made man on the earth, and it grieved him at his heart" (Genesis 6:6). Elsewhere, God says, "It repenteth me that I have set up Saul to be king: for he is turned back from following me, and hath not performed my commandments" (1 Samuel 15:11 KJV). If God is perfect, how could He repent?

First, the Bible unequivocally teaches that God is perfectly good and thus incapable of doing evil (Psalm 5:4–5; James 1:13; 3 John v. 11). As such, God's repentance must not be understood as entailing moral guilt. Indeed, the moral perfection of the Creator sets Him apart from His sin-tainted creation (Leviticus 11:44–45; 19:2; 20:7; 1 Peter 1:15–16).

Furthermore, although God does not change, the meaning of the word *repent* has changed over time. Thus, in place of the word *repent*, most modern English translations substitute the word *regret* or *grieve*. Indeed, as a human father grieves over rebellion on the part of his children, so our heavenly Father grieves over rebellion on the part of His creation.

Finally, God's repentance must be understood as an anthropomorphism (talking about God in terms we would use to talk about a human being) that communicates the full measure of

God's grief over the horror of sin rather than a change of heart or a change of mind. With respect to the faithlessness of Saul, God said, "It repenteth me that I have set up Saul to be king" (1 Samuel 15:11 KJV). Yet the very same chapter says that "the Strength of Israel will *not* lie *nor repent*: for he is not a man, that he should *repent*" (v. 29 KJV). Apart from an anthropomorphic understanding, such passages would be self-refuting.

> *"The Glory of Israel will not lie or change His mind;*
> *for He is not a man that He should change His mind."*
>
> 1 SAMUEL 15:29 NASB

For further study, see Millard J. Erickson, *What Does God Know and When Does He Know It?* (Grand Rapids: Zondervan, 2003).

If jealousy is sin, how can God be jealous?

Scripture describes God as jealous and jealousy, as sin. The second commandment explicitly says that God is a jealous God (Exodus 20:4–5; cf. 34:14); yet in Galatians Paul condemned jealousy in the same breath as idolatry (Galatians 5:19–20). How can this be?

First, there is such a thing as sanctified jealousy. As such, jealousy is the proper response of a husband or wife whose trust has been violated through infidelity. Indeed, when an exclusive covenant relationship is dishonored, sanctified jealousy is the passionate zeal that fights to restore that holy union. The jealousy of God for His holy name and for the exclusive worship of His people as such is sanctified.

Furthermore, as there is sanctified jealousy, so, too, there is sinful jealousy. In this sense, jealousy is painfully coveting another's advantages. Accordingly, the apostle Paul listed jealousy as an act of the sinful nature: "The acts of the sinful nature are obvious: sexual immorality, impurity and debauchery; idolatry and witchcraft; hatred, discord, *jealousy*, fits of rage, selfish ambition, dissentions, factions and envy; drunkenness, orgies, and the like" (Galatians 5:19–21).

Finally, as God personifies sanctified jealousy, so those who reflect His character must be zealous for the things of God. The Bible is replete with heroes such as Elijah (1 Kings 19:10, 14), David (Psalm 69:9), and Paul (2 Corinthians 11:2), whose jealousy for God's glory motivated self-sacrifice and radical reform. The quintessential example, however, is found in the incarnate Christ who exercised the epitome of sanctified jealousy by overturning the tables of the moneychangers in the temple—a symbolic gesture condemning the Jewish leaders of His day for dishonoring God through their contemptible religiosity (Matthew 21:12–13; John 2:17; cf. Jeremiah 7:9–15).

I am jealous for you with godly jealousy. For I have betrothed you to one husband, that I may present you as a chaste virgin to Christ.

2 CORINTHIANS 11:2 NKJV

For further study, see J. I. Packer, *Knowing God* (Downers Grove, IL: InterVarsity Press, 1982), 151–58.

Does God have a gender?

I t has become increasingly popular in Christian circles to apply politically correct sentiments to language for God. Some have even supplemented the Trinitarian language of Father, Son, and Holy Spirit with feminine forms such as Mother, Child, and Womb. This raises an important question: "Does God have a gender?"

First, the Bible tells us that "God created man in His own image; in the image of God He created him; male and female He created them" (Genesis 1:27 NKJV). As God created both male and female in His image, He does not participate in one or the other gender, but rather transcends gender.

Furthermore, while the Bible uses masculine titles for God, such as Father and Son, it also employs feminine images for God, such as mother (Isaiah 49:14–15; 66:13) and midwife (Isaiah 66:9). Likewise, God's judgment of Israel is likened to that of a mother bear robbed of her cubs (Hosea 13:8). Whether masculine or feminine, all such images are anthropomorphisms or personifications that reveal God to us in ways we can understand.

Finally, the language we use for God must *clarify* rather than *confuse*. In the absence of biblical warrant, we ought to refrain from tampering with the traditional titles for God. Indeed, it would be a grave mistake to sacrifice theological clarity concerning the nature of God and the nature of the relationships between the divine Persons of the Godhead on the altar of political correctness.

> *There is neither Jew nor Greek, there is neither slave nor free, there is neither male nor female; for you are all one in Christ Jesus. And if you are Christ's, then you are Abraham's seed, and heirs according to the promise.*
> GALATIANS 3:28–29 NKJV

For further study, see Leslie Zeigler, "Christianity or Feminism?" in William A. Dembeski and Jay Wesley Richards, eds., *Unapologetic Apologetics* (Downers Grove, IL: InterVarsity Press, 2001), 179–86.

Can God create a rock so heavy that He cannot move it?

This question is a classic straw man that can have many Christians looking like the proverbial deer in the headlights. At best, it challenges God's omnipotence. At worst, it undermines His existence.

First, there is a problem with the premise of the question. While it is true that God can do anything that is consistent with His nature, it is absurd to suggest that He can do everything. God cannot lie (Hebrews 6:18), He cannot be tempted (James 1:13), and He cannot cease to exist (Psalm 102:25–27).

Furthermore, just as it is impossible to make a one-sided triangle, so it is impossible to make a rock too heavy to be moved: what an all-powerful God can create, He can obviously move. Put another way, God can do everything that is logically possible.

Finally, we should note that a wide variety of similar questions are raised in an attempt to undermine the Christian view of God. Thus, it is crucial that we learn to question the question rather than assuming the question is valid.

What is apologetics?

Living as we do in what has been described as post-Christian America, Christians absolutely must know *what* they believe as well as *why* they believe it. The apostle Peter put it this way: *"Always* be prepared to give an answer [*apologia*] to everyone who asks you to give the reason for the hope that you have. But do this with gentleness and with respect" (1 Peter 3:15).

First, apologetics is the defense of the faith "once for all entrusted to the saints" (Jude v. 3). The word *apologetics* is derived from the Greek *apologia*, which means "a reasoned defense." As such, apologetics involves providing an *answer*, not an *apology* in the contemporary sense of the word. Just as good attorneys defend their clients in courts of law by presenting solid evidence and sound reasoning, so, too, apologists defend the truth of Christianity with well-reasoned answers to the questions of skeptics and seekers alike.

Furthermore, apologetics is *pre-evangelism*. As such, apologetics is the handmaiden to evangelism. It is using our logical answers as springboards or opportunities to share the good news of the gospel. The Christian faith is not a blind faith but rather a faith firmly rooted in history and evidence.

Finally, apologetics is *post-evangelism*. In the swirling waves of doubt and despair that can threaten to submerge our faith, it is crucial to be familiar with the pillars or posts on which our faith is founded—namely, God created the universe; Jesus Christ demonstrated He is God through the immutable fact of His resurrection; and the Bible is demonstrably divine rather than merely human in origin.

This, in a nutshell, is what apologetics is all about. And remember—if you are looking for a truly rewarding experience, try becoming an apologist. Not only will you experience the power and presence of the Holy Spirit working through you, but you may just find yourself in the middle of an angelic praise gathering when you've helped a lost son or daughter of Adam find his or her way into the kingdom of God.

> *Walk in wisdom toward those who are outside,*
> *redeeming the time. Let your speech always be with*
> *grace, seasoned with salt, that you may know*
> *how you ought to answer each one.*
> Colossians 4:5–6 NKJV

For further study, see William Lane Craig, *On Guard: Defending Your Faith with Reason and Precision* (Colorado Springs, CO: David C. Cook, 2010).

Is apologetics really necessary?

Too often people suppose the task of apologetics to be the exclusive domain of scholars and theologians. Not so! The defense of the faith is not optional. It is basic training for *every Christian*. And that means *you*!

First, the Bible informs us that apologetics is not just a nicety; it is a necessity for every believer. Writing in a world steeped in mystery cults, the apostle Peter admonished believers to "always be prepared to give an answer [*apologia*] to everyone who asks you to give the reason for the hope that you have" (1 Peter 3:15). As such, Paul vigorously defended the gospel (Acts 17:15–34; 18:4) and charged Timothy and Titus to do the same (2 Timothy 2:23–26; 4:2–5; Titus 1:9–14).

Furthermore, apologetics is necessary for the preservation of the faith. Not only must the church defend herself against objections from without, but she must also guard against false teachings from within. Thus, Paul admonished Timothy to "preach the Word, be prepared in season and out of season; correct, rebuke and encourage—with great patience and careful instruction. For the time will come when men will not put up with sound doctrine. . . . They will turn their ears away from the truth and turn aside to myths" (2 Timothy 4:2–4). Defending essential Christian doctrine against perversions by pseudo-Christian cults is a crucial task of the Christian apologist.

Finally, apologetics is necessary for the cultural relevance of the church. In a post-Christian society in which theism is no longer in vogue and belief in the possibility of miracles is viewed as simpleminded superstition, apologetics creates intellectual room for the acceptance of the gospel. In place of merely pontificating dogmatic assertions, Christian apologists are commanded to provide defensible arguments "with gentleness and respect" (1 Peter 3:15).

Beloved, while I was very diligent to write to you concerning our common salvation, I found it necessary to write to you exhorting you to contend earnestly for the faith which was once for all delivered to the saints.

JUDE V. 3 NKJV

For further study, see J. P. Moreland, *Love Your God with All Your Mind: The Role of Reason in the Life of the Soul* (Colorado Springs: NavPress, 2007); see also Hank Hanegraaff and Tom Fortson, *7 Questions of a Promise Keeper* (Nashville: J. Countryman, 2006).

Can a person be argued into
the kingdom of God?

common mistake Christians make derives from the notion that someone can be talked into the kingdom of God. While the motivation may be sincere, the consequences are often devastating.

First, no matter how eloquent you may or may not be, you cannot change anyone else's heart—only the Holy Spirit can do that. Thus, while it is your responsibility to "always be prepared to give an answer to everyone who asks you to give the reason for the hope that you have" (1 Peter 3:15), it is God who changes the heart.

Furthermore, the problem is not that people *cannot* believe; it is that they *will not* believe. In other words, it is often not a matter of the mind but a matter of the will. To wit, the maxim: "A man convinced against his will is of the same opinion still." As Jesus Christ declared, "This is the verdict: Light has come into the world, but men loved darkness instead of light because their deeds were evil. Everyone who does evil hates the light, and will not come into the light for fear that his deeds will be exposed" (John 3:19–20). The Christian faith is reasonable, but reason alone will not compel a person to embrace Christ.

Finally, I am utterly convinced that if we are "prepared to give an answer," God will bring into our paths those whose hearts He has prepared. Thus, it is our responsibility to prepare ourselves to be the most effective tools in the hands of almighty God.

> *No one knows the things of God except the*
> *Spirit of God. Now we have received, not*
> *the spirit of the world, but the Spirit who is*
> *from God, that we might know the things*
> *that have been freely given to us by God.*
>
> *These things we also speak, not in words which man's*
> *wisdom teaches but which the Holy Spirit teaches,*
> *comparing spiritual things with spiritual. But the*
> *natural man does not receive the things of the Spirit*
> *of God, for they are foolishness to him; nor can he*
> *know them, because they are spiritually discerned.*
>
> 1 CORINTHIANS 2:11–14 NKJV

For further study, see William Lane Craig, *Reasonable Faith: Christian Truth and Apologetics*, 3rd ed. (Wheaton, IL: Crossway Books, 2008), chapter 1.

What are the most significant apologetics issues?

hankfully, learning to defend our faith is not nearly as difficult as one might think. In fact, it all boils down to being able to deal with three major apologetics issues.

First and foremost is the issue of *origins*. How people view their origins will determine how they live their lives. If you suppose you are merely a function of random processes, you will live your life by a different standard than if you know you are created in the image of God and accountable to Him. In the final analysis, more consequences for society hinge on this issue than on any other.

Furthermore, because of its centrality to Christianity, those who take the sacred name of Christ upon their lips must be prepared to defend the historical reality of His *resurrection*. The resurrection is not merely important to the historic Christian faith; without it, there would be no Christianity. The apostle Paul put it plainly, "If Christ has not been raised, our preaching is useless and so is your faith" (1 Corinthians 15:14). The resurrection of Jesus is the singular doctrine that elevates Christianity above all other world religions. Through the resurrection, Christ demonstrated that He does not stand in a line of peers with Abraham, Buddha, or Confucius. He is utterly unique. He has the power not only to lay down His life but to take it up again.

Finally, we must be equipped to demonstrate that the *Bible* is divine rather than merely human in origin. If we can successfully accomplish this, we can answer a host of other objections by simply appealing to the authority of Scripture. If the Bible is merely human in origin, then it stands in a long line of peers with other holy books. If, however, we can demonstrate the Old and New Testaments to be divine in origin, they are *the* authority by which to govern our lives.

Because of the transcendent importance of these apologetic issues, I have organized a memorable acronym for each of them. First is the F-A-R-C-E of evolution (Fossil record, Ape-men fictions, Recapitulation, Chance, Empirical science). Furthermore, the resurrection is the greatest F-E-A-T in the annals of recorded history (Fatal torment, Empty tomb, Appearances of Christ, Transformation). Finally, Bibles contain M-A-P-S demonstrating that its details and descriptions are rooted in history and evidence (Manuscripts, Archaeology, Prophecy, Scriptural Synergy).

Sanctify the Lord God in your hearts, and always be ready to give a defense to everyone who asks you a reason for the hope that is in you, with meekness and fear; having a good conscience, that when they defame you as evildoers, those who revile your good conduct in Christ may be ashamed.

1 PETER 3:15–16 NKJV

For further study, see "What is the F-A-R-C-E of evolution?" (pp. 104–107); "Resurrection: What are memorable keys to the greatest F-E-A-T in history?" (pp. 251–254); and "Is the Bible a reliable authority for faith and practice? (M-A-P-S)" (pp. 142–145).

Is there evidence for life after death?

A theists believe that death is the cessation of being. In their view, humans are merely bodies and brains. They reject metaphysical realities such as the soul, *a priori* (prior to examination), but there are convincing reasons to believe that humans have an immaterial aspect to their being that transcends the material and thus can continue to exist after death. Christian philosopher J. P. Moreland advances several sound arguments for the existence of the immaterial soul.

First, using logic, we can demonstrate that *the mind is not identical to the brain* by proving that the mind and brain have different properties. As Moreland explains: "The subjective texture of our conscious mental experiences—the feeling of pain, the experience of sound, the awareness of color—is different from anything that is simply physical. If the world were only made of matter, these subjective aspects of consciousness would not exist. But they *do* exist! So there must be more to the world than matter." An obvious example is color. A moment's reflection is enough to convince thinking people everywhere that the experience of color involves more than a mere wavelength of light.

Furthermore, from a legal perspective, if human beings were merely material, they could not be held accountable this year for a crime committed last year, because identity would change over time. Every day we lose multiplied millions of microscopic particles. In fact, every seven years or so, virtually every part of our material anatomy changes, apart from aspects of our neurological system. Therefore, from a purely material perspective, the person who previously committed a crime is presently not the same person. But, of course, a criminal who attempts to use this line of reasoning as a defense would not get very far. Legally and intuitively, we recognize *a sameness of soul* that establishes personal identity over time.

Finally, libertarian freedom (freedom of the will) presupposes that we are more than mere material robots. If I am merely material, my choices are simply a function of such factors as genetic makeup and brain chemistry, and my decisions are not free; they are fatalistically determined. The implications of such a notion are profound. In a worldview that embraces fatalistic determinism, I cannot be held morally accountable for my actions, because reward and punishment make sense only if we have freedom of the will.

While the logical, legal, and libertarian freedom arguments are convincing in and of themselves, an even more powerful and persuasive argument demonstrates the reality of life beyond the grave. That argument flows from the resurrection of Jesus Christ. The best minds of ancient and modern times have demonstrated beyond a shadow of doubt that Christ's physical trauma was fatal; that the empty tomb is one of the best-attested facts of ancient history; that Christ's followers experienced on several occasions tangible post-resurrection appearances of Christ; and that within weeks of the resurrection, not just one, but an entire community of at least ten thousand Jews experienced such an incredible transformation that they willingly gave up sociological and theological traditions that had given them their national identity.

Through the resurrection, Christ not only demonstrated that He does not stand in a line of peers with Abraham, Buddha, or Confucius but also provided compelling evidence for life after death.

Adapted from *Resurrection*

"Do not fear those who kill the body but cannot kill the soul. But rather fear Him who is able to destroy both soul and body in hell."

MATTHEW 10:28 NKJV

For further study, see Gary R. Habermas and J. P. Moreland, *Beyond Death: Exploring the Evidence for Immortality* (Wheaton, IL: Crossway Books, 1998).

Can chance account for the universe?

stronaut Guy Gardner, who has seen the earth from the perspective of the moon, points out that "the more we learn and see about the universe, the more we come to realize that the most ideally suited place for life within the entire solar system is the planet we call home." In other words, life on earth was designed by a benevolent Creator rather than directed by blind chance.

First, consider the ideal temperatures on planet Earth—not duplicated on any other known planet in the universe. If we were closer to the sun, we would fry. If we were farther away, we would freeze.

Furthermore, ocean tides—caused by the gravitational pull of the moon—play a crucial role in our survival. If the moon were significantly larger, thereby having a stronger gravitational pull, devastating tidal waves would submerge large areas of land. If the moon were smaller, tidal motion would cease, and the oceans would stagnate and die.

Finally, consider plain old tap water. The solid state of most substances is denser than their liquid state, but the opposite is true for water, which explains why ice floats rather than sinks. If water were like virtually any other liquid, it would freeze from the bottom up rather than from the top down, killing aquatic life, destroying the oxygen supply, and making earth uninhabitable.

From the temperatures to the tides and the tap water—and myriad other characteristics of this planet that we so easily take for granted—the earth is an unparalleled masterpiece. Like Handel's *Messiah* or da Vinci's *Last Supper*, it should never be carelessly pawned off as the result of blind evolutionary processes.

Adapted from *Fatal Flaws*

> *In the beginning God created the*
> *heavens and the earth.*
> Genesis 1:1 NKJV

For further study, see R. C. Sproul, *Not a Chance: The Myth of Chance in Modern Science and Cosmology* (Grand Rapids: Baker Book House, 1994).

How many explanations are there for the existence of our universe?

hilosophical naturalism—the worldview undergirding evolutionism—can provide only three explanations for the existence of our universe.

First, the universe is merely an illusion. This notion carries little weight in an age of scientific enlightenment.

Second, the universe sprang from nothing. This proposition not only flies in the face of the laws of cause and effect and of energy conservation, but it is self-evidently absurd. As has been well said, "Nothing comes from nothing, nothing ever could." Or, to put it another way, there simply are no free lunches.

Third, the universe eternally existed. The law of entropy, which predicts that a universe that has eternally existed would have died an "eternity ago" of heat loss, devastates this hypothesis.

There is, however, one other possibility. It is found in the first chapter of the first book of the Bible: "In the beginning God created the heavens and the earth" (Genesis 1:1 NKJV). In an age of empirical science, nothing could be more certain, clear, or correct (Romans 1:20).

Adapted from *Fatal Flaws*

Who made God?

Noneof the arguments forwarded by philosophical naturalism—(1) the universe is merely an illusion; (2) the universe sprang from nothing; (3) the universe eternally existed—satisfactorily account for the existence of the universe. Logically, we can turn only to the possibility that "God created the heavens and the earth" (Genesis 1:1). If that's the case, however, it immediately brings up the question "Who made God?"

First, unlike the universe—which, according to modern science, had a beginning—God is infinite and eternal. Thus, as an infinite eternal being, God logically can be demonstrated to be the uncaused First Cause.

Furthermore, to suppose that because the universe had a cause, the cause of the universe must have had a cause simply leads to a logical dead end. An infinite regression of finite causes does not answer the question of *source*; it merely makes the *effects* more numerous.

Finally, simple logic dictates that the universe is not merely an illusion; it did not spring out of nothing ("nothing comes from nothing; nothing ever could"); and it has not eternally existed (the law of entropy predicts that a universe that has eternally existed would have died an "eternity ago" of heat loss). Thus, the only philosophically plausible possibility that remains is that the universe was made by an unmade Cause greater than itself.

Adapted from *Fatal Flaws*

Before the mountains were brought forth,
Or ever You had formed the earth and the world,
Even from everlasting to everlasting, You are God.

PSALM 90:2 NKJV

For further study, see Paul Copan, *That's Just Your Interpretation: Responding to Skeptics Who Challenge Your Faith* (Grand Rapids: Baker Books, 2001), 69–73.

If we can't see God, how can we know He exists?

It is not uncommon for skeptics to suppose that Christians are irrational for believing in a God they cannot see. In reality, it is irrational for such skeptics to suppose that what cannot be seen does not exist.

First, the fact that something cannot be seen does not presuppose that it doesn't exist. We know that black holes, electrons, the laws of logic, and the law of gravity exist despite the fact that we cannot see them. Indeed, even a full-blown empiricist holds fast to the law of gravity while standing atop the Eiffel Tower.

Furthermore, as King David proclaimed, "The heavens declare the glory of God; the skies proclaim the work of his hands" (Psalm 19:1). Or, in the words of the apostle Paul, "God's invisible qualities—his eternal power and divine nature—have been clearly seen, being understood from what has been made, so that men are without excuse" (Romans 1:20). Put another way, the order and complexity of the visible, physical universe eloquently testify to the existence of an uncaused First Cause.

Finally, God can be seen through the Person and work of Jesus Christ. As Paul explained, "In Christ all the fullness of the Deity lives in bodily form" (Colossians 2:9). Indeed, the incarnation of Jesus Christ is the supreme act of God's self-revelation. Through the ministry of the Holy Spirit, we experience the power and presence of God in a way that is more fundamentally real than even our perceptions of the physical world in which we live.

> *Now we see in a mirror, dimly, but then*
> *face to face. Now I know in part, but then*
> *I shall know just as I also am known.*
> 1 CORINTHIANS 13:12 NKJV

For further study, see J. P. Moreland and William Lane Craig, *Philosophical Foundations for a Christian Worldview* (Downers Grove, IL: InterVarsity Press, 2003); see also Lee Strobel, *The Case for a Creator* (Grand Rapids: Zondervan, 2004).

What is truth?

This is the very question Pontius Pilate asked Jesus (John 18:38). In the irony of the ages, he stood toe-to-toe with the personification of truth and yet missed its reality. Postmodern people are in much the same position. They stare at truth but fail to recognize its identity.

First, truth is an aspect of the nature of God Himself. Thus, to put on truth is to put on Christ. For Christ is "truth" (John 14:6), and Christians are to be the bearers of truth. As Christian author and social critic Os Guinness explained, Christianity is not true because it works (pragmatism); it is not true because it feels right (subjectivism); it is not true because it is "my truth" (relativism). It is true because it is anchored in the Person of Christ.

Furthermore, truth is anything that corresponds to reality. As such, truth does not yield to the size and strength of the latest lobby group. Nor is truth merely a matter of preference or opinion. Rather, truth is true even if everyone denies it, and a lie is a lie even if everyone affirms it.

Finally, truth is essential to a realistic worldview. When sophistry, sensationalism, and superstition sabotage truth, our view of reality is seriously skewed. The death of truth spells the death of civilization. However, as Aleksandr Solzhenitsyn discovered, "One word of truth outweighs the entire world."

Adapted from *The Covering*

Pilate therefore said to Him, "Are You a king then?"

Jesus answered, "You say rightly that I am a king. For this cause I was born, and for this cause I have come into the world, that I should bear witness to the truth. Everyone who is of the truth hears My voice."

Pilate said to Him, "What is truth?"

JOHN 18:37–38 NKJV

For further study, see Os Guinness, *Time for Truth* (Grand Rapids: Baker Books, 2000).

What is the Euthyphro Dilemma?

The Euthyphro Dilemma is named after one of Plato's famed dialogues. The dialogue purportedly puts Greek gods on the horns of a dilemma: *Is something good because the gods will it, or do the gods will it because it is good?* This pseudo-dilemma is worthy of a response only because professors gone wild raise this question *ad nauseum ad infinitum* as a way of undermining the Christian worldview.

First, if we say that *something is good because the gods will it*, we immediately perceive a problem. Goodness—or the lack thereof—is left in the hands of capricious gods. Put another way, right or wrong and good or bad become arbitrary. For example, the gods might well have dictated pedophilia a moral imperative despite our intuitive revulsions.

Furthermore, if we say that *the gods will something because it is good*, we are gored by the opposite horn of the dilemma. Good and evil and right and wrong have now become autonomous. And if this is so, the gods are subordinate, not sovereign.

Finally, if we say that *something is good because it reflects the nature of God,* then good and evil, right and wrong, are neither arbitrary nor autonomous. *God* (not gods) *wills what He wills because* He is good*, and what He wills is right because it is reflective of and consistent with His nature.*

What we glean from this is that what is posited as a dilemma in reality is no dilemma at all. There *is* a third option, and it alone corresponds to reality. If Plato's Euthyphro serves a purpose, it is to teach us to question the question rather than assuming that the question is valid.

> *For the LORD is good;*
> *His mercy is everlasting,*
> *And His truth endures to all generations.*
>
> PSALM 100:5 NKJV

For further study, see Matthew Flannagan, "The Euthyphro Dilemma," *Christian Research Journal* 36, 1 (2013), available online from CRI at www.equip.org; William Lane Craig, *On Guard: Defending Your Faith with Reason and Precision* (Colorado Springs: David C. Cook, 2010), chapter 6.

Why does God allow bad things
to happen to good people?

his is perhaps the most common question Christian celebrities are asked to answer on secular television shows. At first blush, it may seem as though there are as many responses as there are religions. In reality, however, there are only three basic answers, namely, pantheism, philosophical naturalism, and theism. *Pantheism* denies the existence of good and evil because in this view god is all and all is god. *Philosophical naturalism* (the worldview undergirding evolutionism) supposes that everything is a function of random processes, thus there is no such thing as good and evil. *Theism* alone has a relevant response to the question of why bad things happen to good people—and only *Christian* theism can answer the question satisfactorily.

First, Christian theism acknowledges that God created the *potential* for evil because God created humans with freedom of choice. We choose to love or hate, to do good or evil. The record of history bears eloquent testimony to the fact that humans of their own free will have actualized the reality of evil through such choices.

Furthermore, without choice, love is meaningless. God is neither a cosmic rapist who forces His love on people, nor a cosmic puppeteer who forces people to love Him. Instead, God, the personification of love, grants us the freedom of choice. Without such freedom, we would be little more than preprogrammed robots.

Finally, the fact that God created the potential for evil by granting us freedom of choice will ultimately lead to the best of all possible worlds—a world in which "there will be no more death or mourning or crying or pain" (Revelation 21:4). How can that be? Those who choose Christ will be redeemed from evil by God's goodness and will forever be able *not* to sin.

Adapted from *Resurrection*

> *We know that all things work together for*
> *good to those who love God, to those who*
> *are the called according to His purpose.*
> ROMANS 8:28 NKJV

For further study, see Joni Eareckson Tada and Steven Estes, *When God Weeps* (Grand Rapids: Zondervan, 1997); Lee Strobel, *The Case for Faith* (Grand Rapids: Zondervan, 2000), chapter 1.

Is religion the root of evil?

A common refrain in the twenty-first century is that religion is the root cause of the great atrocities of human history. In reality, more people died as a result of secularist ideologies in the last century alone than have died in all the religiously motivated conflicts of Western history.

First, the Nazi philosophy that Jews were subhuman and that Aryans were supermen led to the extermination of six million Jews. In the words of Sir Arthur Keith, a militant anti-Christian physical anthropologist, "The German Führer, as I have consistently maintained, is an evolutionist; he has consciously sought to make the practice of Germany conform to the theory of evolution." Far from religiously motivated, Hitler's "Final Solution to the Jewish problem" was grounded in the naturalistic philosophy of survival of the fittest. In fact, Hitler overtly distanced himself from the historic Christian faith, proclaiming, "Christianity is a rebellion against natural law, a protest against nature. Taken to its logical extreme, Christianity would mean the systematic cultivation of the human failure."

Furthermore, the inherently atheistic utopian philosophy of communism eclipsed even the carnage of Hitler's Germany. Karl Marx saw in philosophical naturalism the scientific and sociological support for an economic experiment that led to the mass murder of multiplied millions worldwide. Mao Tse-tung's communist dictatorship of China accounted for the deaths of an estimated sixty-five million people, while the USSR under Stalin saw between twenty and thirty million murdered as a result of agrarian collectivization and the Great Purge. Add to that two million Cambodians—nearly a quarter of that nation's population—massacred by Pol Pot's Khmer Rouge regime, and the death toll resulting from the secular ideology of communism becomes a horror beyond comprehension.

Finally, a third ideology of modern secularism has led to even more ghastly consequences. Though not formally organized under a deranged dictator, this invisible holocaust continues to claim the lives of untold millions around the globe. Almost three thousand helpless victims—nearly the total casualties of 9/11—die each day in the United States alone. The secularist ideology to which I refer is, of course, abortionism. Indeed, the modern bioethical holocaust has eclipsed the carnage of Nazism and communism combined.

Even apart from the ongoing genocide of the unborn, over 100 million people died at the hands of secularist regimes during the twentieth century. Coupled with recognition of the innumerable humanitarian aid efforts motivated by religious commitments, these statistics should motivate secularists toward humble introspection rather than the haughty inculpation of religion.

It is a joy for the just to do justice,
But destruction will come to the workers of iniquity.

Proverbs 21:15 nkjv

For further study, see Os Guinness, *Unspeakable: Facing up to Evil in an Age of Genocide and Terror* (San Francisco: Harper San Francisco, 2005); see also "If Christianity is true, why are so many atrocities committed in the name of Christ?" (pp. 94–95).

If Christianity is true, why are so many atrocities committed in the name of Christ?

T his is a classic smoke-screen question often asked to avoid having to grapple with the evidence for authentic Christianity. At best, it involves a hasty generalization. At worst, it's a way of "poisoning the well."

To begin with, this question was anticipated by Christ, who long ago proclaimed that His followers would be recognized by the way they lived their lives (John 15:8). Thus, to classify as Christian those who are responsible for instigating atrocities is to beg the question of who Christ's disciples are to begin with. As Jesus pointed out, not everyone who calls Him "Lord" is the real deal (Matthew 7:21–23).

Furthermore, this question implies that Christianity must be false on the basis that atrocities have been committed in Christ's name. There is no reason, however, why we can't turn the argument around and claim that Christianity must be true because so much good has been done in the name of Christ. Think of the countless hospitals, schools, universities, and relief programs that have been instituted as a direct result of people who have the sacred name of Christ upon their lips.

Finally, those who use this argument fail to realize that the validity of Christianity does not rest on sinful men but rather on the perfection of Jesus Christ alone (Hebrews 7:26; 1 Peter 2:22). Moreover, the fact that professing Christians commit sins only serves to prove the premise of Christianity—namely, "all have sinned and fall short of the glory of God" (Romans 3:23); thus, all are in need of a Savior (1 John 3:4–5).

> *"Not everyone who says to Me, 'Lord, Lord,' shall enter the kingdom of heaven, but he who does the will of My Father in heaven. Many will say to Me in that day, 'Lord, Lord, have we not prophesied in Your name, cast out demons in Your name, and done many wonders in Your name?' And then I will declare to them, 'I never knew you; depart from Me, you who practice lawlessness!'"*
>
> MATTHEW 7:21–23 NKJV

For further study, see R. C. Sproul, *Reason to Believe* (Grand Rapids: Zondervan, 1982); Lee Strobel, *The Case for Faith* (Grand Rapids: Zondervan, 2000), chapters 4 and 7.

CHRISTIANITY
AND SCIENCE

Is the Big Bang biblical?

T he Big Bang postulates that billions of years ago the universe began as an infinitely dense point called a singularity and has been expanding ever since. Though the Big Bang is not taught in the Bible, the theory does lend scientific support to the scriptural teaching that God created the universe *ex nihilo* (out of nothing).

First, like the Bible, the Big Bang postulates that the universe had a beginning. As such, the Big Bang stands in stark opposition to the scientifically silly suggestion that the universe has eternally existed, not to the biblical account of origins.

Furthermore, if the universe had a beginning, it had to have a cause. Indeed, according to empirical science, whatever begins to exist must have a cause equal to or greater than itself. Thus, the Big Bang flies in the face of the philosophically preposterous proposition that the universe sprang from nothing apart from an uncaused First Cause.

Finally, though evolutionists hold to Big Bang cosmology, the Big Bang itself does not entail biological evolution. In other words, the Big Bang theory answers questions concerning the origin of the space-time universe as opposed to questions concerning the origin of biological life on earth.

While we must not stake our faith on Big Bang cosmology,

we can be absolutely confident that as human understanding of the universe progresses, it will ultimately point to the One who spoke and caused the universe to leap into existence.

> *The heavens declare the glory of God;*
> *And the firmament shows His handiwork.*
>
> PSALM 19:1 NKJV

For further study, see Paul Copan and William Lane Craig, *Creation Out of Nothing: A Biblical, Philosophical, and Scientific Exploration* (Grand Rapids: Baker Academic, 2004), 17–19; see also J. P. Moreland, *Scaling the Secular City: A Defense of Christianity* (Grand Rapids: Baker Book House, 1987), 33–34; and Lee Strobel, *The Case for a Creator* (Grand Rapids: Zondervan, 2004), especially chapter 5.

Did God create things with an appearance of age?

I t is frequently argued that God created the universe with the appearance of age. Does this notion correspond to the reality of Scripture and science?

First, some creationists suggest that Adam was created with the appearance of age. In truth, however, we simply do not know. Did he have a belly button? Baby teeth? Calluses on his feet? The Bible doesn't tell us.

Furthermore, the notion that God created His handiwork with the appearance of age is logically unfalsifiable: you can neither prove it nor disprove it. Just as you cannot prove you were not created five seconds ago and that your recollection of the previous paragraph is just an implanted memory, so, too, you can neither prove nor disprove that Adam was created with the appearance of age. To believe that you were created five seconds ago is to live in massive deception. Far better to trust that all such notions are inconsistent with our knowledge of God.

Finally, consider an observable astronomical event such as Supernova 1987A—an event with an identifiable *before* and *after*. Prior to 1987, this supernova was a star in a distant galaxy 168,000 light-years away (a light-year is not a measure of time but distance—specifically, the distance light travels in a year). On February 23, 1987, the star exploded in spectacular brilliance. In other words, 168,000 years ago the star exploded, and in 1987, the light of that event finally reached earth— unless, of course, God created the universe only six thousand years ago. Then the supernova might well be likened to a documentary film of an event that never really happened.

In sum, the notion that the universe is not authentically old but merely appears to be old creates more conundrums than it solves. Indeed, what good teacher would ask a student to put faith in a textbook intentionally filled with lies? Moreover, we should bear in mind that whatever our notions of age, the universe is finite.

In part adapted from *The Creation Answer Book*

It is impossible for God to lie.
HEBREWS 6:18 NKJV

For further study, see Hank Hanegraaff, *The Creation Answer Book* (Nashville: Thomas Nelson, 2012).

What is the danger of smuggling scientific paradigms into scriptural passages?

Smuggling scientific paradigms into scriptural passages has given Christianity one black eye after another. Misunderstanding hermeneutics (interpretation) is often at the root of the problem.

First, churchmen once swallowed the dangerous contention that the earth was stationary on the basis of Psalm 93:1—"The world is firmly established; it cannot be moved." This interpretation, however, is obviously misguided. A quick look at context along with some common sense readily unveils the meaning: the kingdom of the Lord who is "robed in majesty" (hardly a comment on His clothing, v. 1) cannot be shaken by the pseudo-powers of earth.

Furthermore, in an attempt to find concord between science and Scripture, Isaiah has been robbed of meaning and magnificence. Some creationists contend that Isaiah teaches sphericity ("circle of the earth," 40:22); others, that he communicates Big Bang cosmology ("stretches out the heavens," v. 22). On the other side of the fence, anti-creationists believe that Isaiah was either a flat-earther ("spreads [the heavens] out like a tent,"

v. 22) or an evolutionist contending that people evolved from pests ("people are like grasshoppers," v. 22). The very thought must surely cause Isaiah to turn over in his grave (literalist alert!).

Finally, with astronomy texts in one hand and the Bible in the other, some conclude that, like Isaiah, Job was hip to Big Bang cosmology: "[God] alone stretches out the heavens and treads on the waves of the sea" (Job 9:8). Conversely, anti-supernaturalists contend that an unevolved Job thought that earth was set on pillars: "He shakes the earth from its place and makes its pillars tremble" (v. 6).

While the earth is spherical and Big Bang cosmology does accord well with the first few words of Genesis, the dangers of smuggling scientific paradigms into biblical passages should be evident. Far better that we recommit ourselves to mastering the art and science of biblical interpretation—or, for that matter, of literature in general.

In part adapted from *The Creation Answer Book*

What is the
F-A-R-C-E of evolution?

Macro-evolution has been rightly called "a fairy tale for grownups," but it is more rightly rendered a *farce*. It is not only patently improbable; it is plainly impossible. And as the acronym F-A-R-C-E makes plain, the arguments used to buttress the theory are astonishingly weak.

FOSSILS. While Darwin predicted hundreds of thousands of transitional forms leading to the fossils of the Cambrian Explosion—biology's version of the Big Bang—none actually appear. And since Darwin's time, the problem has only gotten worse. The fossil record has greatly expanded, yet all the body plans of animals that exist today appear in the Cambrian rocks. Darwin said it best: "The distinctiveness of specific forms and their not being blended together by innumerable transitional links—is a very obvious difficulty."

APE-MEN. The illustration of a knuckle-dragging ape evolving through a series of imaginary transitional forms into modern-day man has appeared so many times in so many places that the picture has evolved into the proof. In light of the fanfare attending recent candidates nominated to flesh out the icons of evolution, we would do well to remember that past candidates have bestowed fame on their finders but have done little to distinguish themselves as prime exemplars in the process of human evolution. The discovery of *Darwinius masillae* several years ago is a classic case in point. It was dubbed the most important fossil discovery in 47 million years. The "mother of all monkeys." The scientific equivalent of discovering the Holy Grail. Like finding Noah's ark. In actuality, it proved to be little more than an in-house debate among evolutionists as to whether *Darwinius masillae* was the ancestor of lemurs or monkeys. The reality is this: the distance between an ape, which cannot read or write, and a descendant of Adam, who can compose a musical masterpiece or send a man to the moon, is the distance of infinity.

RECAPITULATION. Recapitulation—better known by the evolutionary phrase *ontogeny recapitulates phylogeny*—is the notion that in the course of an embryo's development (ontogeny), the embryo repeats (recapitulates) the evolutionary history of its species (phylogeny). Thus, at various points, an emerging human is said to be a fish, a frog, and then finally a fetus. In the words of evolutionary superstar Carl Sagan, "In human intrauterine development we run through stages very much like fish, reptiles, and non-primate mammals before we become recognizably human. The fish stage even has gill slits." Without so much as blushing, he communicated his contention that a first-trimester abortion does not constitute the painful killing of a human fetus but merely the termination of a fish or frog. Thus, in Sagan's world, *Roe v. Wade* provided the legal framework for the slaughter of multiplied millions of creatures rather than children. This idea, of course, is not science; it's science fiction. For more than a century, it has been well known that what *The Cosmos* series creator referred to as "gill slits" are essential parts of human anatomy. French geneticist Jerome LeJeune said it best when testifying to a US Senate subcommittee: "To accept the fact that after fertilization has taken place a new human has come into being is no longer a matter of taste or opinion. The human nature of the human being from conception to old age is not a metaphysical contention; it is plain experimental evidence."

CHANCE. One of the primary dilemmas of evolutionary theory is that it forces scientists to conclude that the cosmos—in all of its complexities—was created by chance. As biologist Jacques Monod, winner of the prestigious Nobel Prize, put it, "Pure chance, absolutely free but blind, is at the very root of the stupendous edifice of evolution." *Chance,* in this sense, refers to that which happens without purpose. Thus, chance implies the absence of both a design and a designer. Reflect on the absurdity of such a notion. Giving the evolutionary process every imaginable concession, arranging a simple protein molecule by chance is estimated to be one chance in 10^{161} (that's a 1 followed by 161 zeros). For a frame of reference, consider that there are only 10^{80} atoms in the entire known universe. If in time, a protein molecule was formed by chance, forming a second one would be infinitely more difficult. As such, the science of statistical probability underscores the stark reality that forming a protein molecule by random processes is not only improbable, it is impossible. And forming a cell or a chimp? Impossible beyond description.

EMPIRICAL SCIENCE. Rather than falling for the rhetoric and emotional stereotypes of modern-day evolutionists, lovers of truth must be united in their commitment to reason and empirical science. It doesn't take a rocket scientist to understand that every effect must have a cause greater than or equal to itself. In stark contrast, evolutionary theory attempts to make effects, such as organized complexity, greater than their causes. Moreover, in an age of scientific enlightenment, it is implausible to contend that nothing could produce everything, that life could spring from non-life, and that the life that sprang from non-life could produce metaphysical realities such as ethics and morals. From a purely logical point of view, it should be self-evident that nothing comes from nothing—nothing ever could.

In sum, philosophical naturalism—the worldview undergirding evolutionism—can provide only three explanations for the existence of the universe in which we live. First, the universe is merely an illusion. Furthermore, the universe sprang from nothing. Finally, the universe eternally existed. There is, however, one other possibility: "In the beginning, God created the heavens and the earth." In an age of empirical science, nothing could be more certain, clear, or correct.

In part adapted from *The Face That Demonstrates the Farce of Evolution*

All things came into being through Him,
and apart from Him nothing came into
being that has come into being.

JOHN 1:3 NASB

For further study, see Hank Hanegraaff, *Fatal Flaws: What Evolutionists Don't Want You to Know* (Nashville: Thomas Nelson, 2008).

Did humans evolve from hominids?

In the television premiere of *Ape Man: The Story of Human Evolution*, former CBS anchor Walter Cronkite declared that monkeys were his "newfound cousins." Cronkite went on to say: "If you go back far enough, we and the chimps share a common ancestor. My father's father's father's father, going back maybe a half million generations—about five million years—was an ape." Was Cronkite right? Do we and the chimps share a common ancestor? Or is this an illustration of the anti-knowledge surrounding ape-men?

First, whether in *Ape Man*, *National Geographic*, or *Time*, the ape-to-man icon has itself become the argument. Put another way, the illustration of a knuckle-dragging ape evolving through a series of imaginary transitional forms into modern man has appeared so many times in so many places that the picture has evolved into the proof. In light of the fanfare attending the most recent proof-candidates nominated by evolutionists to flesh out the icons of evolution, we would do well to remember that past candidates such as Lucy have bestowed fame on their finders but have done little to distinguish themselves as prime exemplars of human evolution.

Furthermore, as the corpus of hominid fossil specimens continues to grow, it has become increasingly evident that there is an unbridgeable chasm between hominids and humans in both composition and culture. Moreover, homologous structures (similar structures on different species) do not provide sufficient proof of genealogical relationships: common descent is simply an evolutionary assumption used to explain the similarities. To assume that hominids and humans are closely related because both can walk upright is tantamount to saying hummingbirds and helicopters are closely related because both can fly. Indeed, the distance between an ape, who cannot read or write, and a descendant of Adam, who can compose a musical masterpiece or send a man to the moon, is the distance of infinity (cf. Genesis 1:26–27).

Finally, evolution cannot satisfactorily account for the genesis of life, the genetic code, or the ingenious synchronization process needed to produce life from a single fertilized human egg. Nor can evolution satisfactorily explain how physical processes can produce metaphysical realities such as consciousness and spirituality. The insatiable drive to produce a "missing link" has substituted selling, sensationalism, and subjectivism for solid science. William Fix said it best: "When it comes to finding a new trooper to star as our animal ancestor, there's no business like bone business."

Is *Archaeopteryx* the missing link
between dinosaurs and birds?

henever I say that there are no transitions from one species to another, someone inevitably brings up *Archaeopteryx*. This happens so frequently that I've decided to coin a word for those times: *pseudosaur*. *Pseudo* means false and *saur* refers to a dinosaur or a reptile (literally, lizard). Thus, a pseudosaur is a false link between reptiles (such as dinosaurs) and birds. Myriad evidences demonstrate conclusively that *Archaeopteryx* is a full-fledged bird, not a missing link.

First, fossils of both *Archaeopteryx* and the kinds of dinosaurs *Archaeopteryx* supposedly descended from have been found in a fine-grained German limestone formation said to be Late Jurassic (the Jurassic period is said to have begun 190 million years ago and lasted 54 million years). Thus, *Archaeopteryx* is not a likely candidate as the missing link, since birds and their alleged ancestral dinosaurs thrived during the same period.

Furthermore, initial *Archaeopteryx* fossil finds gave no evidence of a bony sternum, which led paleontologists to conclude that *Archaeopteryx* could not fly or was a poor flyer. However, in April 1993, a seventh specimen was reported that included a bony sternum. Thus, there is no further doubt that *Archaeopteryx* was as suited for power flying as any modern bird.

HANK HANEGRAAFF

Finally, to say that *Archaeopteryx* is a missing link between reptiles and birds, one must believe that scales evolved into feathers for flight. Air friction acting on genetic mutation supposedly frayed the outer edges of reptilian scales. Thus, in the course of millions of years, scales became increasingly like feathers until, one day, the perfect feather emerged. To say the least, this idea must stretch the credulity of even the most ardent evolutionists.

These and other factors overwhelmingly exclude *Archaeopteryx* as a missing link between birds and dinosaurs. The sober fact is that *Archaeopteryx* appears abruptly in the fossil record, with masterfully engineered wings and feathers common in the birds observable today. Even the late Stephen Jay Gould of Harvard and Niles Eldridge of the American Museum of Natural History, both militant evolutionists, have concluded that *Archaeopteryx* cannot be viewed as a transitional form.

Adapted from *Fatal Flaws*

How serious are the consequences
of believing in evolution?

More consequences for society hinge on the cosmogenic myth of evolution than on any other. Among them are the sovereignty of self, the sexual revolution, and survival of the fittest.

First, the supposed death of God in the nineteenth century ushered in an era when humans proclaimed themselves sovereigns of the universe. Humanity's perception of autonomy led to sacrificing truth on the altar of subjectivism. Ethics and morals were no longer determined on the basis of objective standards but rather by the size and strength of the latest lobbying group. Rooted in no enduring reference point, societal norms were reduced to mere matters of preference.

Furthermore, the evolutionary dogma saddled society with the devastating consequences of the sexual revolution. We got rid of the Almighty and in return got adultery, abortion, and AIDS. Adultery has become commonplace as evolutionary man fixates on feelings rather than fidelity. Abortion has become epidemic as people embrace expediency over ethics. And AIDS has become pandemic as people clamor for condoms apart from commitment. Tragically, more people have died of AIDS than America has lost in all its wars combined. Despite the consequences, promiscuous sex continues to be glorified in the media, in movies, through music, and by Madison Avenue. Only one rule seems to endure: life has no rules (cf. Romans 1:28).

Finally, evolutionism has popularized such racist clichés as "survival of the fittest." In *The Descent of Man*, Darwin speculated "at some future period, not very distant as measured by centuries, the civilized races of man will almost certainly exterminate, and replace, the savage races throughout the world." In addition, Darwin subtitled his magnum opus *The Preservation of Favored Races in the Struggle for Life*. Indeed, for evolution to succeed, it is as crucial that the unfit die as that the fittest survive. Nowhere were the far-reaching consequences of such cosmogenic mythology more evident than in the pseudoscience of eugenics. Eugenics hypothesized that the gene pool was being corrupted by the less fit genes of inferior people. As a result, segments of our society—including Jews and blacks— were subjected to state-sanctioned sterilization. Thankfully, eugenics has faded into the shadowy recesses of history for now. The tragic consequences of the evolutionary dogma that birthed it, however, are yet with us today.

Is evolutionism racist?

irst, while not all evolutionists are racists, the theory of evolution is racist in the extreme. In *The Descent of Man*, Charles Darwin speculated, "At some future period, not very distant as measured by centuries, the civilized races of man will almost certainly exterminate, and replace, the savage races throughout the world." In addition, he subtitled his magnum opus *The Preservation of Favored Races in the Struggle for Life*. Thomas Huxley, who coined the term *agnostic* and was the man most responsible for advancing Darwinian doctrine, went so far as to say, "No rational man cognizant of the facts, believes that the average Negro is the equal, still less the superior, of the white man." Huxley was not only militantly racist but also lectured frequently against the resurrection of Jesus Christ in whom "[we] are all one" (Galatians 3:28).

Furthermore, for evolution to succeed, it is as crucial that the unfit die as that the fittest survive. Marvin Lubenow graphically portrays the ghastly consequences of such beliefs in his book *Bones of Contention*: "If the unfit survived indefinitely, they would continue to 'infect' the fit with their less fit genes. The result is that the more fit genes would be diluted and compromised by the less fit genes, and evolution could not take place." Adolf Hitler's philosophy that Jews were subhuman and that Aryans were supermen led to the extermination of six million Jews. In the words of Sir Arthur Keith, a militant anti-Christian physical anthropologist, "The German Führer, as I have consistently maintained, is an evolutionist; he has consciously sought to make the practice of Germany conform to the theory of evolution." It is significant to note that crusaders who used force to further their creeds in the name of God were acting in direct opposition to the teachings of Christ, while the worldview of Hitler was completely consistent with the teachings of Darwin. Indeed, Darwinism has provided the scientific substructure for some of the most significant atrocities in human history.

Finally, while the evolutionary racism of Darwin's day is politically incorrect today, current biology textbooks still promote vestiges of racism. For example, the inherently racist recapitulation theory* not only is common fare in science curricula but has been championed in our generation by such luminaries as Carl Sagan. This recapitulation theory persists despite the fact that modern studies in molecular genetics have demonstrated its utter falsity. The fact that recapitulation is inherently racist is underscored by no less an evolutionary authority than Stephen Jay Gould, who lamented that "recapitulation provided a convenient focus for the pervasive racism of white scientists" in the modern era.

Adapted from *Fatal Flaws*

God created man in His own image;
in the image of God He created him;
male and female He created them.

Genesis 1:27 nkjv

For further study, see Hank Hanegraaff, *Fatal Flaws: What Evolutionists Don't Want You to Know* (Nashville: W Publishing, 2003).

---

*Recapitulation theory—known by the evolutionary phrase *Ontogeny recapitulates phylogeny*—is the odd idea that in the course of an embryo's development, the embryo repeats or recapitulates the evolutionary history of its species.

Did God use evolution as
His method of creation?

Under the banner of "theistic evolution," a growing number of Christians maintain that God used evolution as His method for creation. This, in my estimation, is the worst of all possibilities. It is one thing to believe in evolution; it is quite another to blame God for it.

First, the biblical account of creation specifically states that God created living creatures according to their own "kinds" (Genesis 1:24–25). As confirmed by science, the DNA for a fetus is not the DNA for a frog, and the DNA for a frog is not the DNA for a fish. Rather, the DNA of a fetus, frog, or fish is uniquely programmed for reproduction after its own kind. Thus, while Scripture and science allow for *micro*evolution (transitions within a "kind"), they do not allow for *macro*evolution (amoebas evolving into apes or apes evolving into astronauts).

Furthermore, evolution is the cruelest, most inefficient system for creation imaginable. Perhaps Nobel Prize–winning evolutionist Jacques Monod put it best: "The struggle for life and elimination of the weakest is a horrible process, against which our whole modern ethic revolts." Indeed, said Monod,

"I am surprised that a Christian would defend the idea that this is the process which God more or less set up in order to have evolution."

Finally, *theistic evolution* is a contradiction in terms—like the phrase *flaming snowflakes*. God can no more direct an undirected process than He can create a square circle. Yet this is precisely what theistic evolution presupposes.

Evolutionism is fighting for its very life. Rather than prop it up with theories such as theistic evolution, thinking people everywhere must be on the vanguard of demonstrating its demise.

From one man he made every nation of men, that they should inhabit the whole earth; and he determined the times set for them and the exact places where they should live. God did this so that men would seek him and perhaps reach out for him and find him, though he is not far from each one of us.

ACTS 17:26–27

For further study, see "What is the F-A-R-C-E of evolution?" (p. 104) and Jay W. Richards, ed., *God and Evolution: Protestants, Catholics, and Jews Explore Darwin's Challenge to Faith* (Seattle: Discovery Institute Press, 2010).

Is intelligent design really science?

Richard Dawkins, formerly Oxford's professor of the Public Understanding of Science and arguably the best-known Darwinist on the planet, claims that those who do not believe in evolution are "ignorant, stupid or insane." But in place of rhetoric and emotional stereotypes, intelligent design (ID) proponents actually propose reason and empirical science.

First, ID proponents are willing to follow scientific evidence wherever it leads. ID theorists neither presuppose nor preclude supernatural explanations for the phenomena they encounter in an information-rich universe. As such, the ID movement rightly practices open-minded science.

Furthermore, ID begins with the common scientific principle that intelligent design is detectable wherever there is specified, organized complexity (i.e., "information"). This design principle is central to many scientific fields, including archaeology, forensic pathology, crime scene investigation, cryptology, and the search for extraterrestrial intelligence. When applied to information-rich DNA, irreducibly complex biochemical systems, the Cambrian Explosion in the fossil record, and the fact that earth is perfectly situated in the Milky Way for both life and scientific discovery, the existence of an intelligent designer is the most plausible scientific explanation.

Finally, although its conclusions are not worldview-neutral, ID lends no more support to Christian theism than Darwinian evolution lends to atheism. Thus, the appropriateness of ID for public education ought to be judged on the basis of the theory's explanatory power, not on its metaphysical implications.

> *Since the creation of the world His*
> *invisible attributes are clearly seen, being understood*
> *by the things that are made, even His eternal power*
> *and Godhead, so that they are without excuse.*
> Romans 1:20 nkjv

For further study, see William Dembski, *The Design Revolution* (Grand Rapids: IVP, 2004); see also Francis J. Beckwith, "Intelligent Design in the Schools: Is It Constitutional?" *Christian Research Journal* 25, 4 (2003), available through the Christian Research Institute at www.equip.org.

BIBLICAL INTERPRETATION

What are the L-I-G-H-T-S on your path to mining the Bible for all its wealth?

God has spoken! As such the Bible is divine rather than merely human in origin. If indeed this is so, it is crucial to understand what He has said. And that involves learning to mine the Bible for all its wealth. To do so is both a science and an art. It is a science in that certain rules apply; it is an art in that the more often you apply the rules, the better you get at it. These rules can be easily remembered using the acronym L-I-G-H-T-S.

LITERAL. To interpret the Bible literally is to interpret it as literature. Simply put, this means we are to read the Bible just as we read other forms of communication: in its most obvious and natural sense.

ILLUMINATION. "We have not received the spirit of the world," said Paul, "but the Spirit who is from God, that we may understand what God has freely given us" (1 Corinthians 2:12). The Spirit of truth provides us insights that both permeate the mind and *illumination* that penetrates the heart.

GRAMMAR. As the father of twelve children, I can testify firsthand to what scientific research has recently begun to validate—humans are hardwired for *grammar* from birth. It shouldn't surprise us, then, that the basic principles of language that we unconsciously absorb in early childhood and consciously internalize from grade school onward are foundational to discovering the language of God.

HISTORY. The biblical text is best understood when we are familiar with the customs, culture, and historical context of biblical times. Familiarity with the historical context of the books of the Bible, along with some plain old common sense, will serve you well in your quest to mine the Bible for all its wealth.

TYPOLOGY. A *type* is a person, event, or institution in the redemptive history of the Old Testament that prefigures a corresponding but greater reality in the New Testament. The greater reality to which a type points, and in which it finds its fulfillment, is referred to as an *antitype*. Eschatology is the thread that weaves the tapestry of Scripture into a glorious pattern; typology is the fabric out of which the thread is spun.

SCRIPTURAL SYNERGY. Simply stated, the whole of Scripture is greater than the sum of its individual passages. We cannot comprehend the Bible as a whole without comprehending its individual passages, and we cannot comprehend its individual passages apart from comprehending the Bible as a whole. We must always bear in mind that all Scripture, though communicated through various human instruments, has one single Author. And that Author never contradicts Himself.

Familiarity with the *literal*, *illumination*, *grammatical*, *historical*, *typology*, and *synergy* principles is imperative in the quest to know the Lover of our souls.

Be diligent to present yourself approved to God
as a workman who does not need to be ashamed,
accurately handling the word of truth.

2 Timothy 2:15 nasb

LITERAL

ILLUMINATION

GRAMMAR

HISTORY

TYPOLOGY

SCRIPTURAL SYNERGY

For further study, see "What does it mean to interpret the Bible literally?" (p. 125) and Hank Hanegraaff, *Has God Spoken? Memorable Proofs of the Bible's Divine Inspiration* (Nashville: Thomas Nelson, 2011), Part Four.

HANK HANEGRAAFF

What does it mean to interpret the Bible literally?

For more than a decade, popular TV personality Bill Maher has made a cottage industry out of ridiculing Christianity. Maher has gone so far as to dogmatically pontificate that the Bible was "written in parables. It's the idiots today who take it literally." Even a cursory reading reveals that Scripture is a treasury replete with a wide variety of literary styles ranging from poetry, proverbs, and psalms to historical narratives, didactic epistles, and apocalyptic revelations. To dogmatically assert that the Bible was written in parables and that those who read it *literally* must be "idiots" is, at best, an idiosyncratic form of fundamentalism and, at worst, a serious misunderstanding of the literal principle of biblical interpretation. In order to read the Bible for all its worth, it is crucial that we interpret it just as we would other forms of communication: in its most obvious and natural sense. As such, we must read it as literature, paying close attention to *form*, *figurative language*, and *fantasy imagery*.

First, in order to interpret the Bible literally we must pay special attention to what is known as *form* or genre. In other words, to interpret the Bible as literature, we must consider the kind of literature we are interpreting. Just as a legal brief differs in form from a prophetic oracle, so, too, there is a difference in genre between Leviticus and Revelation. This is particularly important when considering writings that are difficult to categorize, such as Genesis, which is largely a historical narrative interlaced with symbolism and repetitive poetic structure.

If Genesis were reduced to an allegory conveying merely abstract ideas about temptation, sin, and redemption devoid of any correlation with actual events in history, the very foundation of Christianity would be destroyed. If the historical Adam and Eve did not eat the forbidden fruit and descend into a life of habitual sin resulting in death, there is no need for redemption. On the other hand, if we consider Satan to be a slithering snake, we would not only misunderstand the nature of fallen angels, but we might also suppose that Jesus triumphed over the work of the devil by stepping on the head of a serpent (Genesis 3:15) rather than through His passion on the cross (Colossians 2:15).

A literalistic method of interpretation often does as much violence to the text as does a spiritualized interpretation that empties the text of objective meaning. A literal-at-all-costs method of interpretation is particularly troublesome when it comes to books of the Bible in which visionary imagery is the governing genre. For example, in Revelation, the apostle John sees an apocalyptic vision in which an angel swinging a sharp sickle gathers grapes into "the great winepress of the wrath of

God." The blood flowing out of the winepress rises as high as "the horses' bridles, for one thousand six hundred furlongs" (Revelation 14:19–20 NKJV). Interpreting such apocalyptic imagery in a woodenly literal sense inevitably leads to absurdity.

Furthermore, it is crucial to recognize that Scripture—particularly apocalyptic portions of Scripture—is replete with figurative language. Such language differs from literal language, in which words mean exactly what they say. Figurative language requires readers to use their imagination in order to comprehend what the author is driving at. Such imaginative leaps are the rule rather than the exception because virtually every genre of literature contains metaphorical language. In fact, we might well say that figurative language is the principal means by which God communicates spiritual realities to His children. In other words, God communicates spiritual realities through earthly, empirically perceptible events, persons, and objects—which might best be described as living metaphors.

A metaphor is an implied comparison that identifies a word or phrase with something that it does not literally represent. Far from minimizing biblical truth, metaphors serve as magnifying glasses that identify truth we might otherwise miss. This identification creates a meaning that lies beyond a woodenly literal interpretation and thus requires an imaginative leap in order to grasp what is meant. For example, when Jesus said, "I am the bread of life" (John 6:48 NKJV), He obviously was not saying that He was literally the *staff* of life (i.e., physical bread). Rather, He was metaphorically communicating that He is the *stuff* of life (i.e., the essence of true life). Biblical metaphors are never to be regarded as vacuous occasions for subjective flights of fantasy. On the contrary, biblical metaphors are always objectively meaningful, authoritative, and true.

Hyperbole is another figure of speech particularly prevalent in prophetic passages. In essence, hyperbole employs exaggeration for effect or emphasis. If you step onto a scale and exclaim, "O my goodness! I weigh a ton," you are obviously not intending to say that you literally weigh two thousand pounds. Similarly, when an NBA commentator looks up at the clock, sees a minute left, and says, "There's a world of time left in this game," he is using hyperbole to communicate that in the NBA a lot can happen in sixty seconds.

While hyperbole is commonly used in our culture, it is ubiquitous in the Bible. This is particularly true of prophetic passages. The prophet Isaiah used hyperbolic language when he predicted judgment on Babylon: "See, the day of the LORD is coming—a cruel day, with wrath and fierce anger—to make the land desolate and destroy the sinners within it. *The stars of heaven and their constellations will not show their light. The rising sun will be darkened and the moon will not give its light*" (Isaiah 13:9–10). To those unfamiliar with biblical language, these words might well have been taken to mean that the end of the world was at hand. In reality, Isaiah was prophesying that the Medes were about to put an end to the glories of the Babylonian empire.

As evidence one need only read the preceding verses that are packed with prophetic hyperbole: "Wail, for the day of the LORD is near; it will come like destruction from the Almighty. Because of this, *all hands will go limp, every man's heart will melt*. Terror will seize them, pain and anguish will grip them; they will writhe like a woman in labor. They will look aghast at each other, *their faces aflame*" (vv. 6–8). Even the most pedantic literalist intuitively recognizes that Isaiah was not intending to infer that all hands will literally go limp and that every heart will literally melt. Nor is he literalistically predicting that every Babylonian face will be on fire any more than John was using wooden literalism to prophesy that the two witnesses in Revelation will literally emit flames of fire from their mouths (Revelation 11:5).

Finally, it is crucial to correctly interpret fantasy imagery in apocalyptic passages—images such as an enormous red dragon with seven heads and ten horns (Revelation 12:3); locusts with human faces, women's hair, and lions' teeth (9:7); and a beast that resembled a leopard, but with feet like a bear and a mouth like a lion (13:2). What is distinct about such fantasy images is that they do not correspond to anything in the real world. But while fantasy images are unreal, they provide a realistic viewpoint from which to ponder reality.

Fantasy imagery, of course, is fraught with danger. That danger, however, lies not in its use but in its abuse. In Revelation 12, the apostle John described "an enormous red dragon with seven heads and ten horns and seven crowns on his heads. His tail swept a third of the stars out of the sky and flung them to the earth" (vv. 3–4). Many Christians abuse such imagery by interpreting it in a woodenly literalistic fashion, thus missing the point of the passage. Not only would a single star—let alone one-third of the stars—obliterate earth, but dragons are the stuff of mythology, not theology. Thus, the danger does not lie in the use of fantasy imagery but in uncritically impregnating these images with unbiblical notions.

While the Scriptures must indeed be read as literature, you and I must ever be mindful that the Bible is also far more than literature. The Scriptures are uniquely inspired by the Spirit. As Peter put it, "no prophecy of Scripture came about by the prophet's own interpretation. For prophecy never had its origin in the will of man, but men spoke from God as they were carried along by the Holy Spirit" (2 Peter 1:20–21). We must therefore fervently pray that the Spirit, who inspired the Scriptures, illumines our minds to what is in the text.

For further study, see Hank Hanegraaff, *The Apocalypse Code: Find Out What the Bible Really Says About the End Times . . . and Why It Matters Today* (Nashville: W Publishing Group, 2007).

What is the significance of biblical typology?

A *type* (from the Greek word *typos*) is a person, event, or institution in the redemptive history of the Old Testament that prefigures a corresponding but greater reality in the New Testament. A type is thus a copy, a pattern, or a model that signifies an even greater reality yet to come. The greater reality to which a type points and in which it finds its fulfillment is referred to as an *antitype*. The writer of Hebrews specifically employed the word *antitype* to refer to the greatness of the heavenly sanctuary of which the Holy Land, the Holy City, and the holy temple are merely types or shadows (9:23–24).

First, in Hebrews, as in the rest of the New Testament, the Old Testament history of Israel was interpreted as a succession of types that find ultimate fulfillment in the life, death, and resurrection of our Lord. As such, far from being peripheral, typology is central to a proper interpretation of the infallible Word of God. Indeed, throughout the New Testament, Jesus is revealed as the antitype of the Hebrew prophets through His preaching of repentance, His ministry of healing, His concern for the poor and the social outcasts, and His death near

Jerusalem (Luke 13:33). This, of course, is not to confuse the biblical principle of typology with an allegorical method of biblical interpretation that ignores or rejects the historical nature of the Old Testament narratives. On the contrary, typology is firmly rooted in historical fact and always involves historical correspondence.

Furthermore, biblical typology—as evidenced in the writings of the New Testament—always involves a heightening of the type in the antitype. It is not simply that Jesus replaces the temple as a new but otherwise equal substitute. No, Jesus is far greater than the temple! It is not as though Jesus is simply another in the line of prophets with Moses, Elijah, Isaiah, and Jeremiah. No, Jesus is much greater than the prophets! The new covenant is not a mere plan B that God instituted as a parenthesis between two phases of His redemptive work with Israel. The new covenant is far greater than the old covenant: the new is "a better covenant" (Hebrews 7:22) rendering the old "obsolete" (Hebrews 8:13)! Just as Joshua was a type of Jesus who led the true children of Israel into the eternal land of promise, so King David was a type of the "King of kings and Lord of lords," a type of Jesus who will forever rule and reign from the New Jerusalem in faithfulness and in truth (Revelation 19:16). In each case, the lesser is fulfilled and rendered obsolete by the greater.

Finally, it is important to point out that antitypes themselves may also function as types of future realities. Communion, for example, is the antitype of the Passover meal. Each year the Jews celebrated—and still celebrate—Passover in remembrance of God's sparing the firstborn sons in the homes of the Israelite families that were marked by the blood of the Passover lamb (Luke 22; cf. Exodus 11–12). Jesus' celebration of the Passover meal with His disciples on the night of His arrest symbolically pointed to the fact that He is the ultimate Passover Lamb "who takes away the sin of the world!" (John 1:29). Though the Last Supper and the corresponding sacrament of communion serve as the antitype of the Passover meal, they also point forward to their ultimate fulfillment in "the wedding supper of the Lamb" (Revelation 19:9; cf. Luke 22:15–18). On that glorious day the purified bride—true Israel—will be united with her Bridegroom in the new heaven and the new earth (Revelation 21:1–2). Thus, the fulfillment of the promise is itself a guarantee of the final consummation of the kingdom of God.

In sum, *eschatology* is the thread that weaves the tapestry of Scripture into a glorious pattern; *typology* is the material out of which that thread is spun.

For further study, see Hank Hanegraaff, *The Apocalypse Code: Find Out What the Bible Really Says About the End Times . . . and Why It Matters Today* (Nashville: Thomas Nelson, 2007).

What is the mystery of the A-G-E-S?

God's purpose now and to the ages of ages is to perfect a bride. This is the mystery of the ages. "A great multitude that no one can count, from every nation, tribe, people and language" cry out, "Salvation belongs to our God, who sits on the throne, and to the Lamb" (Revelation 7:9–10). Even the angels desire to deepen their vision of the glories God has in store for creation (1 Peter 1:12). Thus, as one body we sing in doxology, "Glory to the Father and to the Son and to the Holy Spirit, both now and forever and to the *ages of ages*." Indeed, the very word A-G-E-S is an apt reminder of the *ancient creeds*, the *gospel*, the *essentials* for which the martyrs shed their blood, and the *Scriptures*, which in symphony disclose the mystery of the ages.

ANCIENT CREEDS. The Apostles' Creed points to the one God, Maker of heaven and earth, who is revealed through "the profound mystery" of "Christ and the church" (Ephesians 5:32). For its part, the Nicene Creed—arguably the most important of the ancient creeds—combats ancient heresies such as Arianism that sought to undermine the divine Christ in whom we are one. The Chalcedonian Creed refuted heresies challenging the two natures of Christ by which the church is both redeemed and represented. The Athanasian Creed codifies the truth concerning the Triadic One and affirms Christ's incarnation, resurrection, ascension, and second appearing. Together, these ancient creeds combat heresy, distinguish between essential and secondary doctrines, and unveil "the mystery which has been hidden from ages and from generations, but now has been revealed to His saints. To them God willed to make known what are the riches of the glory of this mystery among the Gentiles: which is Christ in you, the hope of glory" (Colossians 1:26–27 NKJV). Now and forever and to the ages of ages, "there is neither Jew nor Greek, there is neither slave nor free, there is neither male nor female; for you are all one in Christ Jesus" (Galatians 3:28 NKJV).

GOSPEL. Like the ancient creeds, the gospel reveals the mystery "that through the gospel the Gentiles are heirs together with Israel, members together of one body, and sharers together in the promise in Christ Jesus" (Ephesians 3:6). This good news is at the heart of the Christian faith. Communicating it must become as second nature as reciting the ancient creeds. The gospel begins with the recognition that "all have sinned and fall short of the glory of God" (Romans 3:23). Apart from this realization, there is no need for the declaration that Christ, not Caesar, is Savior and Lord. As such, the gospel entails repentance. Jesus said, "Repent and believe the good news!" (Mark 1:15). True belief involves a willingness to receive—to trust in and depend on—Jesus Christ alone.

ESSENTIALS. The mystery of the ages is rendered meaningless if it does not rest on the firm foundation of essential Christian doctrine. From the deity of Christ to the certainty that He will appear a second time to judge the living and the dead, essential Christian doctrine is foundational to the faith delivered to the saints once for all (Jude v. 3).

All other religious systems compromise, confuse, or contradict these essentials. Muslims, for example, dogmatically denounce the doctrine of Christ's unique deity as the unforgivable sin of shirk—of putting something created on the same level as the Creator. They readily affirm the sinlessness of Christ, but adamantly deny His sacrificial death upon the cross and subsequent resurrection. While we may debate nonessentials without dividing over them, there must be unity when it comes to the essential Christian doctrine. Hence the maxim: *In essentials, unity; in nonessentials, liberty; and in all things, charity.*

SCRIPTURE. At one time the mystery of the ages was so buried in layers of tradition that it was unfathomable to Peter that anyone could be of Christ apart from full assimilation into Judaism. To penetrate his hardened heart, thrice God showed Peter a vision of clean and unclean food. Thereafter Peter unpacked the mystery to those assembled in the house of Cornelius: "God has shown me that I should not call any man impure or unclean" (Acts 10:28). Indeed, said Peter, "I now realize how true it is that God does not show favoritism but accepts men from every nation who fear him and do what is right" (Acts 10:34–35). This, then, is the mystery of the ages: irrespective of genealogy or gender, "if you belong to Christ, then you are Abraham's seed, and heirs according to the promise" (Galatians 3:29). In sum, Scripture from first to last reveals one chosen people who form one covenant community connected by the cross and beautifully symbolized by the apostle Paul as one cultivated olive tree (Romans 11:11–24).

Now to Him who is able to establish you according to my gospel and the preaching of Jesus Christ, according to the revelation of the mystery kept secret since the world began but now made manifest, and by the prophetic Scriptures made known to all nations, according to the commandment of the everlasting God, for obedience to the faith—to God, alone wise, be glory through Jesus Christ forever. Amen.

ROMANS 16:25–27 NKJV

ANCIENT CREEDS

GOSPEL

ESSENTIALS

SCRIPTURE

For further study, see Hank Hanegraaff, *The Apocalypse Code: Find Out What the Bible Really Says about the End Times . . . and Why It Matters Today* (Nashville: W Publishing Group, 2007).

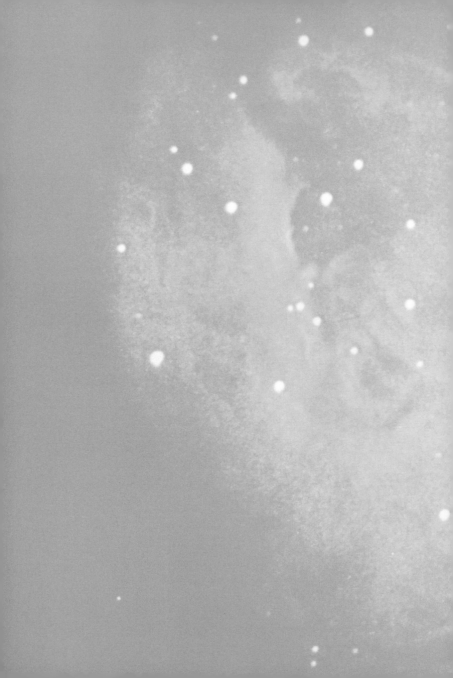

THE BIBLE: ITS RELIABILITY
AND ITS MESSAGE

How do we know that the Bible is divine rather than merely human in origin?

To defend the faith, we must be equipped to demonstrate that the Bible is divine rather than human in origin. When we accomplish this, we will be able to answer a host of other objections by simply appealing to Scripture.

To begin with, the Bible has stronger manuscript support than any other work of classical history—including Homer, Plato, Aristotle, Caesar, and Tacitus. Equally amazing is the fact that the Bible has been virtually unaltered since the original writing, as is attested by scholars who have compared the earliest manuscripts with manuscripts written centuries later. Additionally, the reliability of the Bible is affirmed by the testimony of its authors, who were eyewitnesses—or close associates of eyewitnesses—to the recorded events, as well as by secular historians who confirm the many events, people, places, and customs chronicled in Scripture.

Furthermore, archaeology is a powerful witness to the accuracy of the New Testament documents. Repeatedly, comprehensive archaeological fieldwork and careful biblical interpretation affirm the reliability of the Bible. Archaeological finds have, for instance, corroborated biblical details surrounding the trial that

HANK HANEGRAAFF

led to the fatal torment of Jesus Christ: Pontius Pilate did order Christ's crucifixion, and Caiaphas was the high priest who presided over the religious trials of Christ. It is telling when secular scholars must revise their biblical criticisms in light of solid archaeological evidence.

Finally, the Bible records prophecies of actual events that could not have been known or predicted by mere chance or common sense. For example, the book of Daniel (written before 530 BC) accurately foretold the progression of kingdoms from Babylon through the Median and Persian empires to the further persecution and suffering of the Jews under Antiochus IV Epiphanes with his desecration of the temple, his untimely death, and freedom for the Jews under Judas Maccabeus (165 BC). It is statistically preposterous that any or all of the Bible's specific, detailed prophecies could have been fulfilled by chance, good guessing, or deliberate deceit.

In part adapted from Resurrection and The Face That Demonstrates the Farce of Evolution

All Scripture is given by inspiration of God, and is profitable for doctrine, for reproof, for correction, for instruction in righteousness.

2 TIMOTHY 3:16 NKJV

For further study, see Lee Strobel, *The Case for Christ: A Journalist's Personal Investigation of the Evidence for Jesus* (Grand Rapids: Zondervan, 1998).

Is the Bible a reliable authority for faith and practice? (M-A-P-S)

The acronym M-A-P-S will place in your mind the four-part line of reasoning by which you can be certain the Bible is a reliable authority for faith and practice. Since most Bibles contain maps revealing that its words are rooted in history and physical evidence, this acronym should prove a meaningful association.

MANUSCRIPTS. The Bible has stronger manuscript support than any other work of classical history—including Homer, Plato, Aristotle, Caesar, and Tacitus. Equally amazing is the fact that the Bible has been virtually unaltered since the original writing, as is attested by scholars who have compared the earliest extant manuscripts with manuscripts dated centuries later. Moreover, the wisdom of God is evident through the way He protected the biblical text from tampering or ecclesiastical chicanery. By the time ecclesiastical power was centralized, the biblical manuscripts were long since copied, distributed, and buried in the sands of time. Nearly six thousand New Testament Greek manuscripts have now been uncovered. Not only is there a relatively short time interval between the earliest papyrus and parchment copies of the New Testament and their autographs (original writings), but there is also less than a generation between those autographs and the events they chronicle. The quantity and quality of manuscripts assure us that the message and intent of the original autographs have been passed on to the present generation without compromise.

ARCHAEOLOGY. The archaeologist's spade demonstrates time and time again that, in direct contrast to pagan mythology—from Mormonism to Mithras—the people, places, and particulars found in sacred Scripture have their roots in history and evidence. One of the best-known examples concerns the books of Luke and Acts. Sir William Ramsay, a biblical skeptic, trained as an archaeologist, set out to disprove the historical reliability of this portion of the New Testament. But through his painstaking archaeological trips to the Mediterranean, he became converted as, one after another, the historical allusions of Dr. Luke proved accurate. Recent archaeological finds have corroborated biblical details surrounding the trial that led to the fatal torment of Jesus Christ—including Pontius Pilate, who ordered Christ's crucifixion, as well as Caiaphas, the high priest who presided over the Jewish leaders' trials of Christ. It is telling when secular scholars must revise their biblical criticisms in light of solid archaeological and historical evidence. (See "Does what was once concealed in soil correspond to what is revealed in Scripture? (S-P-A-D-E)" on p. 146.)

PROPHECY. Biblical prophecy is not designed to help us pin the tail on an antichrist or pinpoint a future tribulation. Rather, prophetic stars in the constellation of biblical prophecy provide powerful proof that the Bible is divine rather than merely human in origin. In the words of the Almighty, "I told you these things long ago; before they happened I announced them to you so that you could not say, 'My idols did them; my wooden image and metal god ordained them'" (Isaiah

48:5). Or, in the words of Jesus, "I have told you before it happens, so that when it happens, you may believe" (John 14:29 NASB). Counterfeit prophets have one thing in common: they are consistently wrong. In illumined contrast, genuine prophets are infallibly correct, and, unlike the pretenders, their prophetic prowess cannot be pawned off to good luck, good guessing, or deliberate deceit. Daniel provides a classic case in point. Writing six centuries before Christ, he accurately predicted a progression of kingdoms from Babylon through the Median and Persian empires, to the persecution and suffering of the Jews under the Old Testament antichrist Antiochus IV Epiphanes and his desecration of the temple, and finally to freedom for the Jews under Judas Maccabeus (165 BC).

SCRIPTURAL SYNERGY. Simply stated, *scriptural synergy* means that the whole of Scripture is greater than the sum of its individual passages. We cannot comprehend the Bible as a whole without comprehending its individual parts, and we cannot comprehend its individual parts without comprehending the Bible as a whole. As such, individual passages of Scripture are synergistic rather than deflective with respect to the whole of Scripture. Indeed, the Bible contains myriad books, written by many authors, in multiple languages, over more than a millennium, on a multitude of different subjects, yet it remains unified and consistent throughout. How is that possible? The individual writers had no idea that their message would eventually be assembled into one Book, yet each work fits perfectly into place with a unique purpose as a synergistic component of the whole. The synergistic harmony of the Bible is a powerful testimony and an enduring reminder that God has spoken, that these are His words. Clearly, scriptural synergy is a powerful indicator of the trustworthiness of Scripture.

The next time someone denies the reliability of the Bible, remember the acronym M-A-P-S, and you will be ready to give "the reason for the hope that you have" (1 Peter 3:15). *Manuscripts*, *Archaeology*, *Prophecy*, and *Scriptural synergy* not only chart a secure course through the turnpikes of skepticism but also demonstrate conclusively that the Bible is divine rather than merely human in origin.

In part adapted from *Has God Spoken?*

Scripture cannot be broken.

JOHN 10:35 NKJV

For further study, see Hank Hanegraaff, *Has God Spoken? Memorable Proofs of the Bible's Divine Inspiration* (Nashville: Thomas Nelson, 2011).

Does what was once concealed in soil correspond to what is revealed in Scripture? (S-P-A-D-E)

L ike the Book of Mormon, the Bible has been roundly denounced as a cleverly invented story. Unlike the Book of Mormon, however, the Bible is buttressed by history and physical evidence. While the archaeologist's S-P-A-D-E continues to mount up evidence against the Book of Mormon, it has piled up proof upon proof for the trustworthiness of Scripture.

S TELES AND STONES. In demonstrating that what was concealed in the soil corresponds to what is revealed in the Scriptures, the Merneptah and the Tel Dan Steles come immediately to mind, as do the Moabite and the Pilate Stones. With "Israel is laid waste, its seed is not" etched into it, the Merneptah Stele presents as formidable a challenge to exodus deniers as the Tel Dan Stele does to those pontificating that the biblical account of King David is no more factual than tales of King Arthur. As *Time* rightly observed, the skeptics' claim that King David never existed is now hard to defend: "House of David" is inscribed on the Tel Dan Stele. The Moabite Stone honors the victory of King Mesha of Moab over Israel, mentioning Yahweh, House of David, Omri, and Nebo and therefore making it difficult to contend

146 HANK HANEGRAAFF

that these biblical kings and places are the stuff of myth. Likewise, the Pilate Stone demonstrates in spades that Pilate was the Roman authority in Judea when Christ was crucified.

POOLS AND FOOLS. Until quite recently, skeptics viewed the existence of the pools John referred to in his gospel to be little more than *a religious conceit,* a predilection on the part of Christians to believe that what they think is true *is* true solely because they *think* it's true. Only fools believed in John's pools. All of that changed in June 2004 when workers in the Old City of Jerusalem unearthed the place where Jesus cured the man born blind. Today, you can step into the very Pool of Siloam in which the blind man "washed, and came back seeing" (John 9:7 NASB). Likewise, you can rest your arms on the guardrail overlooking the excavated ruins of the pool of Bethesda, where Jesus cared for the physical and spiritual needs of a man who suffered there for thirty-eight years (John 5). And you can stand amazed that what was once secreted in soil accurately reflects that which is sealed in Scripture.

ASSYRIAN EMPIRE. From six hundred years before Christ until eighteen hundred years after Him, Assyria and its chief city, Nineveh, lay entombed in the dustbin of history. Then the stones cried out again. In 1845, Henry Austen Layard began digging along the Tigris River and unearthed Nineveh, the diamond of Assyria, embedded in the golden arc of the Fertile Crescent, midway between the Mediterranean and Caspian Seas. Among the stunning archaeological gems discovered there were Sennacherib's Prism, which corroborates the Bible's account of Sennacherib's assault on the Southern Kingdom of Judah

(2 Kings 18–20); the Black Obelisk of Shalmaneser, showing archaeology's oldest depiction of an Israelite, Jehu the king of Israel, giving a tribute of gold and silver to the Assyrian king; and the palace of Sargon, previously known only by a single reference in sacred Scripture (Isaiah 20:1). Together, Sennacherib's Prism, Shalmaneser's Black Obelisk, and the ruins of Sargon's Palace provide weighty testimony to the reliability of the biblical record.

DEAD SEA SCROLLS. In 1947, the shattering of parchment-preserving pottery led to one of the greatest archaeological discoveries of modern times. With the discovery of the Dead Sea Scrolls, we now have a virtual first-century Hebrew Old Testament library available at the click of a twenty-first-century mouse. Not only so, but the Dead Sea Scrolls predate the earliest extant Hebrew text—Masoretic—by a full millennium. As such, everyone from scholar to schoolchild can determine whether the Old Testament Scriptures have been corrupted by men or miraculously preserved by God. Additionally, the Dead Sea Scrolls provide significant insight into the text of the Old Testament and add considerable clarity to the text of the New Testament. (See "How do the Dead Sea Scrolls buttress God's preservation of Scripture? (S-I-G-N-S)" on p. 157.)

EPIC OF GILGAMESH. Until the late nineteenth century, the masses presumed the great primordial deluge to be relegated to the text of Scripture. That began to change in 1853 when Hormuzd Rassam discovered the palace of Assurbanipal. There, among the treasures of Assyria's last king, he uncovered clay tablets on which was recorded the Epic of Gilgamesh and its independent confirmation of a vast flood in ancient Mesopotamia, complete with a Noah-like figure and an ark. While the Epic views the waters of the flood through the opaque lens of paganism, it lends significant credence to the actual event. It is likewise a reminder that the reality of a great deluge is impressed on the collective consciousness of virtually every major civilization from the Sumerian epoch to the present age.

The archaeologist's S-P-A-D-E demonstrates time and time again that, in direct contrast to pagan mythology—from Mormonism to Mithras—the people, places, and particulars found in sacred Scripture have their roots in history and evidence. What was concealed in the soil corresponds to what is revealed in the Scriptures.

In part adapted from *Has God Spoken?*

> *When [Jesus] had said these things, He spat on the ground and made clay with the saliva; and He anointed the eyes of the blind man with the clay. And He said to him, "Go, wash in the pool of Siloam" (which is translated, Sent). So he went and washed, and came back seeing.*
> JOHN 9:6–7 NKJV

of a mere tittle—a microscopic appendage at the end of a Hebrew letter—to be an affront to the holiness of their Creator. New Testament counterparts, likewise, engaged in their craft with care. The contention that careless, capricious copyists created cartloads of contaminated copies simply does not correspond to reality.

ORAL CULTURE. It is often contended that biblical accounts ranging from the exodus of the Jews to the extraordinary miracles of Jesus were not only recorded long after the fact but also recklessly embellished. This, however, is hardly the case. Why? Because the biblical accounts were not only recorded early—by eyewitnesses—but they were recorded in an oral culture in which people practiced the principles of memory. As such, they left us a cultivated oral tradition communicated in memorable prose. In sharp contrast to the present, past generations chose oral transmission as the principle means by which to pass along historical truths. This, of course, does not imply the ancients did not employ written records. Instead, it is to put the emphasis on the right syllable: manuscript repositories augmented mental recall, not vice versa.

PAPYRUS AND PARCHMENT. The original writings of the prophets and apostles are forever immortalized in a supernaturally preserved corpus of biblical manuscripts, some made of papyrus; others, of parchment. Cumulatively, the sheer volume of manuscripts undergirding sacred Scripture dwarfs that of any other work of classical history. Consider, for example, Homer's *Iliad*. While its manuscript numbers are singularly impressive—1,757 copies—this pales in comparison to the almost 6,000 Greek manuscript fragments undergirding the New Testament. In the words of distinguished Greek scholar F. F. Bruce,

"There is no body of ancient literature in the world that enjoys such a wealth of textual attestation as the New Testament." Not only is there a relatively short time interval between the earliest extant papyrus and parchment copies and their autographs (original writings), but there is less than a generation between the autographs and the events they chronicle. The quantity and quality of papyrus and parchment manuscripts assure us that the message and intent of the original autographs have been passed on to the present generation without compromise.

INTERNAL EVIDENCE. The eyewitness testimony of its authors is surpassingly powerful internal evidence to the absolute and irrevocable trustworthiness of Scripture. As Peter reminded his hearers, "We did not follow cleverly invented stories when we told you about the power and coming of our Lord Jesus Christ, but we were *eyewitnesses* of his majesty" (2 Peter 1:16). Luke, likewise, said that he gathered *eyewitness* testimony and "carefully investigated everything" (Luke 1:3). Internal evidence points to the reality that far from being inventors of internally inconsistent stories about Jesus, the gospel writers were inspired to faithfully narrate the core set of facts by which they had been radically transformed. While it is conceivable that they would have faced torture, vilification, and even cruel deaths for what they fervently believed to be true, it is inconceivable that they would have been willing to die for cleverly invented stories that they knew to be lies.

EXTERNAL EVIDENCE. *Internal* evidence is sufficient to establish the biblical manuscripts as authentic, reliable, and complementary. *External* evidence, however, provides remarkable corroborating confirmation. From early external evidence provided by such credible

How do the Dead Sea Scrolls buttress God's preservation of Scripture? (S-I-G-N-S)

W
ith the discovery of the Dead Sea Scrolls (DSS), we now have a virtual first-century Hebrew Old Testament library available at the click of a twenty-first-century mouse. Not only that, but the DSS (c. 100 BC) predate the earliest extant Hebrew text—the Masoretic—by a full millennium. As such, everyone from scholar to schoolchild can determine whether the Old Testament Scriptures have been corrupted by men or miraculously preserved by God. S-I-G-N-S of their miraculous preservation can be found in the *Samuel scroll, Isaiah scroll, Goliath stature, "N" verse,* and *Salem's king.*

SAMUEL SCROLL. Discovered in Cave 4 in September 1952, the Samuel Scroll not only demonstrates that the text of Samuel has been faithfully preserved over the span of a thousand years, but adds color commentary and corroboration concerning people and practices chronicled in the biblical text.

ISAIAH SCROLL. Like the Samuel Scroll, the Great Isaiah Scroll demonstrates that God has miraculously preserved His Word over time. Consider the brightest star in the constellation of Isaiah prophecies—Isaiah 53. When compared to the Masoretic text, there are seventeen differences. While at first blush that might sound significant, ten were differences in spelling, four a matter of style, and three involve the Hebrew letters for *light*. None alter the substance of the text.

GOLIATH STATURE. In most modern translations, following the extant Hebrew text, Goliath is said to be six cubits and a span, or over nine feet tall (1 Samuel 17:4). The Septuagint (the Greek version of the Old Testament), however, renders Goliath "four cubits and a span," approximately six feet six inches tall. As a result of the DSS, it is now apparent that the exaggerated height of Goliath was the result of a corruption of the original account of 1 Samuel.

"N" VERSE. Discovery of the DSS solved a mystery that had long puzzled translators. Psalm 145, laid out as an alphabetical Hebrew acrostic poem, is missing a verse. In the Hebrew, all the letters in the acrostic are sequentially accounted for—except the letter *N*. Thus, the mystery: What happened to the *N* verse in the Hebrew acrostic? The mystery was solved when the Psalms Scroll was discovered in February 1956 in Cave 11, replete with the words "Ne'eman [faithful] is God in all his words, and gracious in all his deeds."

SALEM'S KING. From an earthly perspective, Abraham was the king of Salem (Jerusalem), the very region in which God called him to establish a righteous nation of kings and priests. However, from a heavenly perspective, it is Melchizedek who is Salem's king. Scripture designates Melchizedek as "king of righteousness" and

What are the prophetic
S-T-A-R-S in the constellation
of biblical prophecy?

P rophetic stars in the constellation of biblical prophecy are powerful proofs that the Bible is divine rather than merely human in origin. In the words of the Almighty, "I told you these things long ago; before they happened I announced them to you" (Isaiah 48:5). Counterfeit prophecy stars are consistently wrong. In illuminated contrast, genuine S-T-A-R-S are infallibly correct.

S UCCESSION OF NATIONS. One of the most significant demonstrations that God has spoken is the undeniable reality that Daniel, writing six centuries before the advent of Christ, was empowered by almighty God to do what no soothsayer or astrologer could. With awe-inspiring precision, he predicted a succession of nations from Babylon through the Median and Persian empires. He also foretold the persecution and suffering of the Jews under the second-century Greco-Syrian beast Antiochus IV Epiphanes, including the despot's desecration of the Jerusalem temple, his untimely death, and freedom for the Jews under Judas Maccabaeus. Moreover, as Daniel looked down the corridor of time, he got a glimpse of a kingdom that will itself endure forever. Truly, the succession of nations immortalized by Daniel is a spectacular star in the constellation of biblical prophecy.

TYPOLOGICAL PROPHECY. Predictive prophecy is fairly straight-forward. Micah 5:2—"Bethlehem Ephrathah, . . . out of you will come for me one who will be ruler over Israel"—is a predictive prophecy directly and specifically fulfilled in the birth of Christ in Bethlehem. Typological prophecy is more complex in that it involves *a divinely intended pattern of events encompassing both historical correspondence and intensification.* When Matthew says that the virgin birth of Jesus is the fulfillment of Isaiah's prophecy (Matthew 1:22–23 and Isaiah 7:14), he is speaking of typological rather than predictive fulfillment. Only when the elegance of typology is comprehended can the mystery of Scripture be fully apprehended.

ABOMINATION OF DESOLATION. The prophesied abomination of desolation by which the temple was desecrated in the Old Testament (167 BC) and destroyed in the New (AD 70) is at once a bloody scar and a brilliant star enlightening our minds to the divine nature of the Scriptures. Still, its light has been darkened and its meaning diminished by modern-day prophecy pundits bent on pinning the tail on a twenty-first-century antichrist. While Zionist zeal threatens to light the fuse of Armageddon, we can be absolutely certain that the prophecies of Daniel and Jesus already blaze as stars in the constellation of fulfilled prophecy demonstrating that the Bible is infallibly correct.

RESURRECTION. Resurrection is the brightest star in the constellation of biblical prophecy. While all prophecies invoke

OLD TESTAMENT ISSUES

Who was Cain's wife?

One of the most common objections to the Genesis account of creation concerns the reference to Cain's wife in Genesis 4:17. Unless God supernaturally created a wife for Cain as He had for Adam, Cain would have had to engage in incest with one of his sisters.

First, we should note that Adam lived almost a thousand years (Genesis 5:5) and fulfilled God's charge to "be fruitful and increase in number" (Genesis 1:28). Thus, while Scripture does not tell us where Cain got his wife, the logical implication is that he married either a sister or a niece.

Furthermore, because genetic imperfections accumulated gradually over time, there was no prohibition against what we call incest in the earliest stages of human civilization. The Levitical law against incestuous relationships was given by God thousands of years after Cain at the time of Moses. Thus, familial relationships were preserved and birth defects were prevented (Leviticus 18:6, 9).

Finally, the speculation that God may have created a wife for Cain as He had for Adam is completely *ad hoc*. The consistent teaching of Scripture is that "from one man [God] made every nation of men, that they should inhabit the whole earth; and he determined the times set for them and the exact places where they should live. God did this so that men would seek him and perhaps reach out for him and find him; though he is not far from each one of us" (Acts 17:26–27).

> *Cain knew his wife, and she*
> *conceived and bore Enoch.*
> GENESIS 4:17 NKJV

For further study, see Gleason Archer, *Encyclopedia of Bible Difficulties* (Grand Rapids: Zondervan, 1982).

Does the Bible promote polygamy?

Polygamy—the practice of one man having multiple wives—was common in antiquity. Though practiced in the Old Testament, polygamy was never God's perfect plan.

First, the ideal pattern of monogamous marriage of one woman and one man was established early in Genesis: "A man will leave his father and mother and be united to his wife, and they will become one flesh" (2:24). Moreover, this very passage was quoted by both Jesus and Paul in defense of the sacredness and exclusivity of monogamous marriage (Matthew 19:3–9; 1 Corinthians 6:15–17; cf. 1 Corinthians 7:2).

Furthermore, the Bible explicitly condemns the polygamy of Old Testament kings (Deuteronomy 17:17). Likewise, New Testament elders and deacons are called to be "the husband of but one wife" (1 Timothy 3:2, 12; Titus 1:6). Just as the requirements for church leaders set the standards of morality and spiritual maturity for all believers, so, too, the admonition against polygamy for the kings of Israel demonstrated the danger of this practice for all.

Finally, God's disdain for polygamy is seen in its consequences. The Old Testament clearly reveals the familial strife and temptations that accompany the practice. Solomon is the quintessential example of one whose legacy of faithfulness was compromised because of his polygamous behavior. Despite his world-renowned wisdom, Solomon's peaceful and prosperous rule ended in idolatrous scandal and civil strife, for "his wives turned his heart after other gods" (1 Kings 11:4).

Monogamy—not polygamy—is God's perfect plan.

> *"Have you not read that He who made them at the beginning 'made them male and female,' and said, 'For this reason a man shall leave his father and mother and be joined to his wife, and the two shall become one flesh'? So then, they are no longer two but one flesh. Therefore what God has joined together, let not man separate."*
>
> MATTHEW 19:4–6 NKJV

For further study, see Gleason Archer, *Encyclopedia of Bible Difficulties* (Grand Rapids: Zondervan, 1982).

Was Jonah swallowed by a whale?

The book of Jonah contains the familiar story of a prophet named Jonah who was preserved for three days and three nights in the belly of a large fish (1:17). Though skepticism has led many to allegorize this fish tale, there are good reasons to interpret it as an actual historical account.

First, details and descriptions in the narrative defy allegorization. The book of Jonah is written in the genre of historical narrative. The brief mention of the fish does not detour literarily from that genre, from the descriptions of Jonah's journey to Joppa, his payment of the fare, his conversations with the sailors during the storm, and his eventual trip to Nineveh.

Furthermore, the Christian worldview presupposes the miraculous. The universe itself is an effect that presupposes a cause equal to or greater than itself. Just as the uncaused First Cause created the universe, so the uncaused First Cause is capable of supernaturally intervening in the universe He created. Because God created the universe *ex nihilo* ("out of nothing"), preserving Jonah in the belly of a great fish poses no problem whatsoever.

Finally, when we hear a miraculous account of this magnitude, we would do well to seek a second opinion. In the case of

Jonah, corroboration is provided by no less an authority than Jesus Christ. Our Lord not only referred to Jonah's preservation for "three days and three nights in the belly of a fish" as a miracle, He used it as the basis for prophesying that He too would be preserved for "three days and three nights in the heart of the earth" (Matthew 12:40). As such, Jonah's marine rescue is a type of Jesus' miraculous resurrection.

> *"For as Jonah was three days and three nights in the belly of the great fish, so will the Son of Man be three days and three nights in the heart of the earth."*
>
> MATTHEW 12:40 NKJV

For further study, see Walter C. Kaiser Jr., Peter H. Davids, F. F. Bruce, and Manfred T. Brauch, eds., *Hard Sayings of the Bible* (Downers Grove, IL: InterVarsity Press, 1996).

How could a good God sanction the stoning of a disobedient child?

The Mosaic law included the following provision for dealing with a disobedient son: "His father and mother shall take hold of him and bring him to the elders at the gate of his town. They shall say to the elders, 'This son of ours is stubborn and rebellious. He will not obey us. He is a profligate and a drunkard.' Then all the men of the town shall stone him to death. You must purge the evil from among you" (Deuteronomy 21:19–21). At first glance such language jars modern moral sensibilities. A closer examination, however, turns such moral pretension on its head.

First and foremost, the son in question should not be thought of as an adolescent guilty of nothing more than slamming doors or stubbornly asserting his independence. Rather, the son described above is old enough to be morally culpable of extravagantly wicked behavior that threatens the health and safety of the entire community. The prescribed punishment is not for adolescent defiance but for adult degeneracy.

Furthermore, the parents' desire to spare their own son serves as a built-in buffer against an unwarranted or frivolous enforcement of this law. Likewise, the elders' ratification of the parents' plan precludes a precipitous judgment on their part. This standard of evidence prescribed by the Mosaic law exceeds that of modern jurisprudence.

Finally, for modern skeptics to claim the moral high ground over the ancient Scriptures is the height of hypocrisy. Rather than the civility of the Mosaic law, our culture reflects the carnality of Israel's neighbors who sacrificed their sons and daughters. Indeed, for over four decades, Western society has sanctioned the systematic slaughter of children who are guilty of nothing more than being unloved.

Looking at the historical context of Mosaic law reveals it to be wise, not wanton.

> *"Do I have any pleasure at all that the wicked*
> *should die?" says the Lord GOD, "and not that*
> *he should turn from his ways and live?"*
> EZEKIEL 18:23 NKJV

For further study, see Walter C. Kaiser Jr., Peter H. Davids, F. F. Bruce, and Manfred T. Brauch, (eds.), *Hard Sayings of the Bible* (Downers Grove, IL: InterVarsity Press, 1996); on related issues, see Hank Hanegraaff, "TV's *The West Wing* vs. The Bible," available through the Christian Research Institute at www.equip.org.

How can Christians legitimize
a God who orders the genocide
of entire nations?

The very notion that God would command the obliteration of entire nations is abhorrent to skeptics and seekers alike. In context, however, God's commands are perfectly consistent with His justice and mercy.

First, a text without a context is a pretext. God's commands to destroy the nations inhabiting the promised land of Canaan must never be interpreted in isolation from their immediate contexts. The command to "destroy them totally" (Deuteronomy 7:2) is contextualized by the words: "Do not intermarry with them . . . for they will turn your sons away from following me to serve other gods. . . . This is what you are to do to them: Break down their altars, smash their sacred stones, cut down their Asherah poles and burn their idols in the fire" (vv. 3–5). As such, the aim of God's command was not the obliteration of the wicked but the obliteration of wickedness.

Furthermore, God's martial instructions are qualified by His moral intentions to spare the repentant. As the author of Hebrews explains, "By faith the prostitute Rahab, because she welcomed the spies, was not killed with those who were disobedient" (11:31; cf. Jeremiah 18:7–10). Not only were Rahab and her family spared on account of her faith, but she was allowed to live among the Israelites (Joshua 6:25) and came to hold a privileged position in the lineage of Jesus Christ (Matthew 1:5). God's desire to spare the pagan city of Nineveh further illustrates the extent of His mercy for the repentant (see Jonah).

Finally, God unequivocally commanded Israel to treat the aliens living among them with respect and equality. Foreigners living among the Israelites celebrated Passover (Numbers 9:14; cf. 15:15), benefited from an agrarian system of welfare (Leviticus 19:9), and enjoyed full legal protection (Deuteronomy 1:16–17). Even descendants of Israel's enemies, the Edomites and the Egyptians, were allowed to enter the assembly of the Lord (Deuteronomy 23:7–8). In fact, God condemned oppression of aliens in the harshest possible language: "Cursed is the man who withholds justice from the alien, the fatherless or the widow" (Deuteronomy 27:19). Such concern for foreigners clearly demonstrates that mercy was to be shown to those who by faith repented of their idolatry and were thereby grafted into true Israel (cf. Romans 11:11–24).

How could Pharaoh be morally responsible if God hardened his heart?

T he apostle Paul explicitly stated that God hardened Pharaoh's heart (Romans 9:17–18). That, of course, raises this question: "If God determined to harden Pharaoh's heart, then how is God just in holding Pharaoh morally responsible for his sins?"

First, although God promised Moses that He would harden Pharaoh's heart (Exodus 4:21; 7:3), the Exodus account underscores the fact that Pharaoh was responsible for hardening his own heart: "But when Pharaoh saw that there was relief, he hardened his heart and would not listen to Moses and Aaron, just as the LORD had said" (Exodus 8:15; see also Exodus 7:13, 22; 8:19, 32; 9:7; cf. 9:34).

Furthermore, far from hardening Pharaoh's heart in a direct or deterministic fashion, God presented Pharaoh with ample opportunity and free choice to either repent or continue to rebel. Every time God showed Pharaoh mercy and removed a plague from Egypt, Pharaoh responded with stubborn disobedience. As such, God's mercy was the occasion for the hardening of Pharaoh's heart.

Finally, in dealing with this issue, the apostle Paul began with the presupposition that God judges all men justly (Romans 3:5–8). He emphasized the fact that people like Pharaoh are "prepared for destruction" because that is ultimately what they will for themselves. Every time God provides an opportunity to repent, too many people do as Pharaoh did: they harden their hearts in disobedience and unbelief.

When Pharaoh saw that the rain, the hail, and the thunder had ceased, he sinned yet more; and he hardened his heart, he and his servants. So the heart of Pharaoh was hard; neither would he let the children of Israel go, as the LORD had spoken by Moses.

EXODUS 9:34–35 NKJV

For further study, see Paul Marston and Roger Forster, *God's Strategy in Human History*, 2nd ed. (Wipf and Stock Publishers, 2000).

Does Isaiah 53:5 guarantee
our healing today?

The mantra "by his stripes we are healed" is repeated endlessly in Christian circles. However, these words extracted from Isaiah 53:5 focus on *spiritual* rather than *physical* healing.

First, a quick look at the context makes it clear that Isaiah had *spiritual* rather than *physical* healing in mind: Christ "was wounded for our *transgressions*, He was bruised for our *iniquities*; the chastisement for our peace was upon Him, and by His stripes we are healed" (Isaiah 53:5 NKJV). Peter built on this understanding of spiritual healing when he wrote, "[Jesus] himself bore our *sins* in his body on the tree, so that we might die to *sins* and live for righteousness; by his wounds you have been healed" (1 Peter 2:24).

Furthermore, while healing for the body is not referred to in Isaiah 53:5, it is referred to in the verse *immediately* preceding it. There Isaiah wrote, "Surely he took up our infirmities and carried our sorrows, yet we considered him stricken by God, smitten by him, and afflicted" (Isaiah 53:4). *Physical* healing here is not only clear in context, but it is also affirmed by the Gospels where it is given an important qualification:

"When evening came, many who were demon-possessed were brought to [Jesus], and he drove out the spirits with a word and healed all the sick. This was to fulfill what was spoken through the prophet Isaiah: 'He took up our infirmities and carried our diseases'" (Matthew 8:16–17). Thus, the healing Isaiah spoke of was *fulfilled* during the ministry of Christ, but his prophecy does not *guarantee* healing today.

Finally, I should note that in a real sense Christ's atonement on the cross *does* extend to *physical* healing. One day, "there will be no more death or mourning or crying or pain, for the old order of things has passed away" (Revelation 21:4). However, as Paul pointed out, "We hope for *what we do not yet have*, we *wait* for it patiently" (Romans 8:25). And as we wait, we will all experience sickness and suffering. Indeed, those who live before Christ returns will all die of their last disease—the death rate is one per person, and we're all going to make it!

Is baptism necessary for salvation?

T hose who suppose baptism is necessary for salvation frequently cite Peter's words in Acts 2:38—"Repent and be baptized"—as evidence that belief *plus* baptism results in salvation. Scripture clearly does not support this view.

First, as the book of Acts itself demonstrates, baptism is a *sign* of conversion, not the *means* of conversion. Indeed, Acts 10:47 describes believers who were indwelt by the Holy Spirit and therefore saved (see Romans 8:9) prior to being baptized. Moreover, when the thief on the cross placed his faith in Christ, Jesus said to him, "Today you will be with me in paradise" (Luke 23:43), even though the dying thief had no opportunity to be baptized.

Furthermore, the Bible as a whole clearly communicates that we are saved by faith and not by works (Ephesians 2:8–9). As Paul pointed out in Romans, our righteous standing before God is "by faith from first to last" (Romans 1:17). When the jailer asked the apostle Paul, "What must I do to be saved?" Paul responded, "Believe in the Lord Jesus, and you will be saved" (Acts 16:30–31).

Finally, although baptism is not the means by which we are saved, it is the means by which we are set apart. Through baptism we testify that we are no longer our own—we have been bought by Christ's blood and have been brought into the community of faith. Thus, in Acts 2:38, Peter was not suggesting that his hearers could not be saved apart from baptism; rather, he was saying that their genuine repentance would be evidenced by their baptism. As the reformer Martin Luther taught, it is not the absence of baptism but the despising of baptism that damns.

Indeed, behind the symbol of baptism is the substance of baptism: the blood of Jesus Christ that cleanses from sin. As water cleanses the skin from soil and sweat, so the blood of Jesus Christ cleanses the soul from the stain of sin.

> *You are all sons of God through faith in Christ Jesus. For as many of you as were baptized into Christ have put on Christ.*
> GALATIANS 3:26–27 NKJV

For further study, see Hank Hanegraaff, "Bringing Baptism into Biblical Balance," *Christian Research Journal*, vol. 19, no. 1 (1996), available through the Christian Research Institute at www.equip.org.

Does James teach salvation by works?

C ritics of the Bible have long argued that the book of James contradicts the rest of Scripture in its teaching "that a person is justified by what he does and not by faith alone" (2:24). Upon closer examination, however, the book of James—like the rest of Scripture—confirms that we are saved not by what we do but by what Jesus Christ has *done*.

First, in context, James actually taught that we are saved not by works but by the kind of faith that produces good works. As James put it, "What good is it, my brothers, if a man claims to have faith but has no deeds? Can such faith save him?" (2:14). The answer is no. "As the body without the spirit is dead, so faith without deeds is dead" (v. 26).

Furthermore, when James said a person is not justified by faith alone, he meant that a person is not justified by mental *assent* alone. Thus he said, "Show me your faith without deeds, and I will show you my faith by what I do. You believe that there is one God. Good! Even the demons believe that—and shudder" (vv. 18–19). In other words, demons believe in the sense of giving mental *assent* to the fact that there is only one true God, all the while failing to place their hope and trust in Him.

Finally, while James said that "a person is justified by what he does and not by faith alone" and Paul said "man is justified by faith apart from observing the law" (Romans 3:28), their words are in complete harmony. James was countering the false assertion that a *said faith* is a substitute for a *saving faith*, while Paul was countering the equally fallacious notion that salvation can be earned by observing the law. As the Reformers were wont to say, "Justification is by faith alone, but not by a faith that is alone."

> *Was not Abraham our father justified by works when he offered Isaac his son on the altar? Do you see that faith was working together with his works, and by works faith was made perfect?*
> JAMES 2:21–22 NKJV

Can a woman be saved through childbearing?

In his first letter to Timothy, Paul said that "women will be saved through childbearing" (2:15). If this is the case, there must be more than one way to be saved.

First, in the Jewish culture of Paul's day, it was believed that if women died in childbirth, it was a direct punishment for Eve's role in the fall. Thus, Paul may well have been assuring believers that women will be kept safe through the process of childbirth "if they continue in faith, love and holiness with propriety" (2:15). As such, Paul's words refuted the denigration of women both in the culture and in the church.

Furthermore, men and women alike are ultimately saved as a result of the most significant birth in the history of humanity. Thus, Paul may have also been alluding to the fact that just as "the woman [Eve] was deceived and became a sinner" (v. 14), so the woman Mary conceived and brought forth the Savior.

Finally, *salvation* here cannot mean salvation in the ultimate sense. If it did, women would not be saved by God's grace through faith. Unlike men, they would also have to bear children to know salvation. This not only is absurd, but it stands in direct opposition to the unambiguous teaching of Scripture (John 14:6; Ephesians 2:8–9; Galatians 3:28).

Remember, that which is cloudy must always be interpreted in the light of that which is clear.

> *By grace you have been saved through faith,*
> *and that not of yourselves; it is the gift of*
> *God, not of works, lest anyone should boast.*
> EPHESIANS 2:8–9 NKJV

For further study, see Philip H. Towner, *The Letters to Timothy and Titus* (Grand Rapids: Eerdmans Publishing Co., 2006), 233–37.

Is the New Testament canon
authoritative or authoritarian?

T he Bible has come under attack by liberal scholars who claim that the New Testament canon was determined by the winners of a supposed struggle for dominance in the early centuries of Christianity. As the following evidence reveals, however, the canon is not arbitrary or authoritarian, but divinely authoritative.

First, the entire New Testament canon was recorded *early* and thus was not subject to legendary contamination. Had any part of the canon been composed after AD 70, it would most certainly have mentioned the destruction of the very temple that had given the ancient Jews their theological and sociological identity. Additionally, because Matthew and Luke likely used Mark as a source and Luke composed his gospel prior to the writing of Acts, which was completed prior to Paul's martyrdom in the mid-60s, Mark may have been composed as early as the AD 40s, just a few years after the events recorded. Moreover, in 1 Corinthians 15 Paul reiterated a Christian creed that can be traced to within three to eight years of Christ's crucifixion. By contrast, the Gnostic gospels, including the Gospel of Thomas and the Gospel of Judas, are dated long after the close of the first century.

HANK HANEGRAAFF

Furthermore, the authority of the New Testament is confirmed by the *eyewitness* credentials of its authors. John wrote, "That which was from the beginning, which we have heard, which we have seen with our eyes, which we have looked at and our hands have touched—this we proclaim concerning the Word of life" (1 John 1:1). Likewise, Peter reminded his readers that the disciples "did not follow cleverly invented stories" but "were eyewitnesses of [Jesus'] majesty" (2 Peter 1:16). Moreover, the New Testament contains *embarrassing* details that no authoritarian association bent on dogmatic dominance would have adopted. For instance, the Gospels present the founding members of the movement as disciples who not only doubted but denied their Master.

Finally, *extrabiblical* evidence confirms the New Testament canon and knows nothing of early competing canons. Secular historians—including Josephus (before AD 100), the Roman historian Tacitus (around AD 120), the Roman historian Suetonius (AD 110), and the Roman governor Pliny the Younger (AD 110)—confirm the many events, people, places, and customs chronicled in the New Testament. Early church leaders such as Irenaeus, Tertullian, Julius Africanus, and Clement of Rome—all writing before AD 250—also shed light on the New Testament's historical accuracy. From such sources, we can piece together the highlights of the life of Christ independent of the New Testament canon. Moreover, Eusebius of Caesarea acknowledged the centrality of the canonical subsequent Jerusalem Council (Acts 15) clearly demonstrate both the inclusive nature of the church as well as the initial resistance of Jewish Christians to Gentile inclusion (see also Galatians 2:11–14). While the early Christians were certainly not anti-Semitic, at least some Jewish believers initially manifested the opposite prejudice. Far from being anti-Semitic, the New Testament simply records the outworking of redemptive history as foretold by the Jewish prophets who prophesied that one of Christ's companions would betray Him (Psalm 41:9; John 13:18). There is nothing subtle about the crucifixion narrative. The Jewish gospel writers explicitly state that it was their leaders who condemned Christ of blasphemy. They had no motive for fabricating a fictional Judas who would represent the quintessential Jew.

Finally, the whole of Scripture goes to great lengths to underscore that when it comes to faith in Christ, there is no distinction between Jew and Gentile (Galatians 3:28), and that Jewish people throughout the generations are no more responsible for Christ's death than anyone else. As Ezekiel put it, "The son will not share the guilt of the father, nor will the father share the guilt of the son" (Ezekiel 18:20). Truly, liberal scholars owe the world an apology for inventing an idiosyncratic brand of fundamentalism that foments bigotry and hatred by entertaining the absurd notion that the New Testament is anti-Semitic.

I am not ashamed of the gospel of Christ, for it is the power of God to salvation for everyone who believes, for the Jew first and also for the Greek.

ROMANS 1:16 NKJV

For further study, see Hank Hanegraaff, "The Search for Jesus Hoax," *Christian Research Journal* 23, 2 (2000), available through the Christian Research Institute at www.equip.org.

Does the Bible begin with two contradictory creation accounts?

S keptics dismiss the Bible from its very genesis. According to the *Skeptics Annotated Bible*, "In the first creation story, humans are created after the other animals. In the second story, humans are created before the other animals." Is this an indisputable contradiction or an indication of cynical bias?

First, what is often lost on skeptics is the genius of Genesis. For example, Genesis opens with a literary mnemonic by which we are daily reminded of God's creative prowess. The first six days outline a hierarchy of creation that culminates in humanity, its crowning jewel. As such, the history of creation is remembered and recalled through its association with a continuous seven-day cycle of life. Moreover, the account of the seven-day creation is a sevenfold pattern that contains a three-way parallel structure: day 1 light, day 4 luminaries; day 2 sky and sea, day 5 sky and sea creatures; day 3 land, day 6 land creatures. Rather than mining Genesis for all its wealth, fundamentalist fervor seems bent on forcing the language into a literalistic labyrinth from which nothing but nonsense can emerge.

Furthermore, even a cursory reading of Genesis 1 and 2 should be enough to discern that Moses had a different purpose in one than in the other. In the so-called first creation story, Moses presented a *hierarchy* of creation. In the "second story," he focused on the crowning jewels of God's creation who are designed to be in right relationship with both creation and Creator. With inspired brilliance, Moses interlaced his historical narrative with symbolism and repetitive poetic structure. He employed the powerful elements of story (characters, plot, tension, resolution) to set the foundation for the rest of redemptive revelation. The rest of Genesis is structured in such a way that it may be remembered using our ten fingers. With the fingers of one hand, we recall primeval history (Creation, Adam, Noah, Noah's sons, and Shem, father of the ancient Near East). With the other hand, we remember the patriarchs (Abraham, Ishmael, Isaac, Esau, and Jacob, who is called Israel).

Finally, just as when a theoretical physicist attempts to explain the nature of matter to a child, biblical language involves heavenly condescension. A skeptic reading Scripture might well suppose that the earth is stationary on the basis of Psalm 93:1—"the world is firmly established; it cannot be moved." Clearly, however, this is not the intent of the passage. A quick look at context reveals the deeper meaning: the kingdom of the "Lord [who] is robed in majesty" (hardly a comment on His clothing, v. 1) cannot be shaken by the pseudo-powers on earth. The point is that, apart from a basic understanding humanity. Additionally, calling Adam "the son of God" (3:38) and strategically placing the genealogy between Jesus' baptism and the desert temptation, Luke masterfully revealed Jesus as *Theanthropos*, the God-man. It is also instructive to note that while Luke's genealogy stretches from the first Adam to the Second, only mountain peaks in the lineage are accounted for. Thus, it is impossible to determine how many years elapsed between the creation of Adam and the birth of Jesus.

Finally, just as there are different emphases in the genealogies, so, too, there are different explanations for their dissimilarities. Matthew traced his genealogy through David's son Solomon, while Luke traced his genealogy through David's son Nathan. It may be that Matthew's purpose was to provide the legal lineage from Solomon through Joseph, while Luke's purpose was to provide the natural lineage from Nathan through Mary. It could also be that Matthew and Luke were both tracing Joseph's genealogy: Matthew, the legal line, and Luke, the natural line. As such, the legal line diverges from the natural in that Levirate law stipulated if a man died without an heir, his genealogy could legally continue through his brother (Deuteronomy 25:5–6). Obviously, the fact that there are a number of ways to resolve dissimilarities rules out the notion that the genealogies of Jesus in Matthew and Luke are contradictory.

Is the Caesar census a canonical corruption?

O n *Dateline NBC*'s *The Birth of Jesus* episode, Dr. John Dominic Crossan, cofounder of the once popular Jesus Seminar, called into question the historical veracity of Holy Scripture: "Luke tells us the story that at the time *Jesus was born,* Augustus had decreed a census of the whole earth. *Now, every scholar will tell you there was no such census ever.*"

Is Crossan correct? Is the canon corrupt? Did Dr. Luke make a colossal historical blunder that effectively discredits sacred Scripture? In an age when the historical reliability of the Bible is being questioned, it is crucial that Christians are equipped to demonstrate that Scripture is the *infallible* repository of redemptive revelation. So how do we respond to critics like Crossan? Is his pontification a defensible argument or merely a dogmatic assertion?

First, while Crossan made his statement with typical bravado, it turns out to be patently false. Caesar Augustus was famous for census taking. So famous, in fact, that this issue is no longer even debated among credible historians. The Jewish historian Josephus referred to a Roman taxation in AD 6, and considering the scope of the taxation, it is logical to assume that it took a long time to complete. Undoubtedly it began with remembered right after Jesus drove out the money changers the first time: "Zeal for your house will consume me" (John 2:17). Defiling the place in which the shekinah glory of God dwelt is no trifling matter. Moreover, as should be evident, not every action Jesus took was recorded: "If every one of them were written down, I suppose that even the whole world would not have room for the books that would be written" (John 21:25).

Finally, we should note the pattern of the gospel writers. Inevitably they present complementary details that serve to flesh out "the rest of the story." Far from *contradictory*, they are quite obviously *complementary*. If every gospel writer presented his account in precisely the same fashion, the critics could correctly cry, "*Collusion!*"

The very fact that a number of plausible resolutions can be forwarded negates the assertion that "the accounts are not reconcilable." Seeking to debunk the Bible has become a profitable cottage industry. But "what profit is it to a man if he gains the whole world, and loses his own soul?" (Matthew 16:26 NKJV).

Did John err in saying that Jesus' second miracle took place in Cana?

T he Internet is awash with alleged Bible contradictions. More often than not they can be traced back to the notorious Bart Ehrman, a religious studies professor who has made a cottage industry out of alleged contradictions. The question at hand is a classic case in point. Says Ehrman, "In John's Gospel, Jesus performs his first miracle, when he turns water into wine and we're told that 'this was the first sign that Jesus did' (John 2:11). Later in that chapter we're told that Jesus did 'many signs' in Jerusalem (John 2:23). And then, in chapter 4, he heals the son of a centurion, and the author says, 'This was the second sign that Jesus did' (John 4:54). Huh? One sign, many signs, and then the second sign?" Truthfully, what I have a hard time understanding is how a simple "problem" like this can stump a world-class scholar.

First, as is clearly communicated in the gospel of John, the first miraculous sign Jesus performed at Cana in Galilee was to change water into wine. Once again, class, the first miraculous sign (#1) that Jesus performed in *Cana in Galilee* was changing water into wine.

Furthermore, according to the gospel of John, the second

the kingdom. Indeed, Jesus said as much when He continued with, "Or what *parable* shall we use to describe it?" (v. 30). As with metaphors, the danger is to interpret extended similes in a strictly wooden and literal sense. The kingdom of God is obviously not like a mustard seed in every way. Nor does Jesus intend to make His parable "walk on all fours." A kingdom does not look like a mustard seed, nor is a mustard seed the smallest seed in the kingdom. Rather, the kingdom of God is like a mustard seed in the sense that it begins small and becomes large (cf. Daniel 2:31–45).

Finally, although the One who caused the universe to leap into existence (another figure of speech) by simply speaking would obviously know that an orchid seed is smaller than a mustard seed, an orchid seed would have been profoundly inept for the purpose of the parable. Jesus used the smallest seed familiar to a Palestinian farmer—a small seed that, unlike an orchid seed, grows to have "big branches that the birds of the air can perch in its shade" (Mark 4:32)—to illustrate that the kingdom of God began in obscurity but would one day fill the earth.

In sum, to avoid the dangers of the hyperliteralism of fundamentalist scholars on the left, it is crucial to read the Bible as literature, paying close attention to *form*. As we do, you and I must ever be mindful that the Bible is not *merely* literature. Instead, the Scriptures are uniquely inspired by the Spirit.

Thus, we must fervently pray that the Spirit, who inspired the Scriptures, illumines our minds as we learn to read the Bible for all its worth.

> *"To what shall we liken the kingdom of God? Or with what parable shall we picture it? It is like a mustard seed which, when it is sown on the ground, is smaller than all the seeds on earth; but when it is sown, it grows up and becomes greater than all herbs, and shoots out large branches, so that the birds of the air may nest under its shade."*
>
> MARK 4:30–32 NKJV

For further study, see "What does it mean to interpret the Bible literally?" (p. 125).

Did Jesus have a painfully short attention span?

In a book titled *Jesus, Interrupted*, one of the world's most famous Bible critics cites one of his favorite Bible contradictions. In John 13:36, Peter said to Jesus, "Lord, where are you going?" A few verses later, Thomas said, "Lord, we don't know where you are going" (14:5). And then, a few minutes later, at the same meal, Jesus upbraided His disciples, saying, "Now I am going to him who sent me, yet none of you asks me, 'Where are you going?'" (16:5). That leaves only two possibilities, according to author Bart Ehrman: "Either Jesus had a very short attention span or there is something strange going on with the sources for these chapters."

First, it is instructive to note that were I to take the professor in the woodenly literal sense that he takes the Bible, I would be doing him a grave injustice. It would be less than fair to suppose that he really thinks it possible that "Jesus had a very short attention span." Anyone who reads Ehrman's materials in context knows full well that he is convinced that John—whom he characterizes as a "lower-class, illiterate, Aramaic-speaking peasant"—did not write the gospel attributed to him and that the sources that were cobbled together to create the text are decidedly unreliable.

Furthermore, we must be careful not to fall for historical revisionists who, like Ehrman, attempt to persuade the gullible that John was illiterate and therefore could not have written the fourth gospel. John may have been "unlettered" in the sense that he was not educated beyond the primary schooling available to boys at that time, but he was clearly not illiterate. Not only is it an uncharitable stretch to demean John for his lack of a formal education, but this characterization neglects the reality that John continually "astonished" the Jewish teachers of the Law with his knowledge and wisdom (Acts 4:13) in much the same way as Jesus Himself had—though he, too, was without the requisite rabbinic training demanded by Ehrman.

Finally, allow me to underscore what is painfully obvious to anyone who engages Bart's so-called "problems with the Bible." Ehrmanites, it seems, are wholly incapable of comprehending the subtlety of sophisticated literary nuances. Peter and Thomas obviously uttered the words, "Where are you going?" with decidedly different drifts. As the venerable New Testament scholar R. C. H. Lenski has well said, "Peter's question in 13:36 was . . . only a selfish exclamation which would not hear of Jesus' going away alone. And the assertion of Thomas in 14:5 was nothing but an expression of discouragement and dullness of mind. So here Jesus is leaving, his going to his Sender means so much to the disciples, and yet none of them requests one word of this precious information." Put another way, while the using the presence of two animals as a way of depicting faithful Jews and faithful Gentiles, who through the mission and ministry of Messiah have come together as one body. Far from contradictory, the biblical imagery is complex and awe inspiring. Jesus did not ride into Jerusalem in a horse and chariot as a conquering king but on an animal that quite obviously signifies peace and humility. The message is not one that conveys earthly might but rather one that conveys the heavenly reality that the meek shall inherit the earth (Matthew 5:5).

Finally, while Matthew *did* say that the disciples "placed their cloaks on *them*, and Jesus sat on *them*" (Matthew 21:7), this is not to say that Jesus rode into Jerusalem sitting on two animals simultaneously as though His triumphal entry were akin to a clown act. A straightforward reading of the text is that the disciples placed their cloaks on two animals, and Jesus sat upon them, meaning the cloaks. Even if the word *them* is taken to refer to both animals, it would hardly be "absurd." When we say that the president rode into Washington in a motorcade, only the most entrenched literalist supposes that he was sitting in multiple vehicles simultaneously. *Absurdly*, therefore, does not apply to Matthew but to myopic fundamentalists bent on rendering the majestic tapestry of Scripture in wooden, literalistic fashion.

In contrast to spoofers, scholars look for a reliable *core* set of facts to validate historical narratives. If each of the gospel writers were to present their accounts in identical fashion, we would quite justifiably wonder about collusion. Instead, what we discover are complementary details that serve as fibers in an unparalleled tapestry. You've got to love it! God can speak through even the mouth of an ass.

> Now when they drew near Jerusalem, and came to Bethphage, at the Mount of Olives, then Jesus sent two disciples, saying to them, "Go into the village opposite you, and immediately you will find a donkey tied, and a colt with her. Loose them and bring them to Me. And if anyone says anything to you, you shall say, 'The Lord has need of them,' and immediately he will send them."
>
> All this was done that it might be fulfilled which was spoken by the prophet, saying:
>
> > "Tell the daughter of Zion,
> > 'Behold, your King is coming to you,
> > Lowly, and sitting on a donkey,
> > A colt, the foal of a donkey.'"
>
> So the disciples went and did as Jesus commanded them. They brought the donkey and the colt, laid their clothes on them, and set Him on them.
>
> MATTHEW 21:1–7 NKJV

For further study, see "How many times did Jesus cleanse the temple?" (pp. 213–214).

*Jesus said to him, "Assuredly, I say to you
that this night, before the rooster crows,
you will deny Me three times."*
Matthew 26:31–34 nkjv

For further study, see Hank Hanegraaff *Has God Spoken? Memorable Proofs of the Bible's Divine Inspiration* (Nashville: Thomas Nelson, 2011).

Did Jesus suffer agony on the cross, as per Mark, or not, as per Luke?

A few years ago, on the day before Good Friday, Comedy Central featured bestselling author Bart Ehrman making light of Christ's agony on the cross. To the delight of his audience, he and host Stephen Colbert ridiculed Mark and Luke for contradicting one another respecting the death of Christ: "In Mark's gospel, Jesus goes to his death in deep agony over what's happening to him and doesn't seem to understand what's happening to him." Conversely, "When you read Luke's gospel, he is not in agony at all."

First, to suggest that in Mark's account Jesus "doesn't seem to understand what is happening to him" is hardly humorous or accurate. As Mark made clear, Jesus knew precisely what would happen to Him and why. Jesus explained during the Last Supper: "This is my blood of the covenant, which is poured out for many" (14:24). Or, as He put it just prior to entering Jerusalem, the Son of Man came "to give his life as a ransom for many" (10:45). Jesus had in fact repeatedly predicted His suffering, death, and resurrection. To say otherwise is an insult to Christ and to common sense.

Furthermore, only a biblically illiterate studio audience

Was Jesus really in the grave for three days and three nights?

J esus specifically said, "As Jonah was three days and three nights in the belly of a huge fish, so the Son of Man will be three days and three nights in the heart of the earth" (Matthew 12:40). The Gospels also tell us that Jesus died on the day before the Sabbath—Friday—and rose on the day after the Sabbath—Sunday. How do we resolve this apparent contradiction?

First, in Jewish idiom any part of a day counted as a day-night unit. Thus, there is no need to demand that a literal seventy-two hours be accounted for. This way of speaking in reference to time is particularly evident in light of Jesus' own contention that He would rise *on* the third day, not *after* the third day and night had ended (Matthew 16:21; 17:23; 20:19; Luke 24:46; cf. Matthew 26:61; 27:40, 63–64).

Furthermore, the Gospels unanimously declare that Jesus died on the Day of Preparation; that is, Friday, the day leading up to the beginning of the Sabbath at sundown (Matthew 27:62; Mark 15:42; Luke 23:54; John 19:31, 42). The gospel writers demonstrate similar unanimity regarding the discovery of Jesus' resurrection early in the morning on the day following the Sabbath; that is, Sunday, the first day of the week (Matthew 28:1; Mark 16:1; Luke 24:1; John 20:1). Thus, to suggest—as some have—that Jesus died on Wednesday and rose on Saturday, or died on Thursday and rose on Sunday, directly contradicts the testimony of all four gospel writers.

Finally, once knowledge of ancient culturally informed modes of oral and literary expression replaces a naïve, literalistic interpretation of God's Word, the majestic harmony of Scripture shines through. Indeed, Jesus' sacrificial death and miraculous resurrection on the third day is the glorious archetypal fulfillment of Old Testament types including the Passover Lamb (Exodus 12; cf. 1 Corinthians 5:7), Jonah's preservation "for three days and three nights" (Jonah 1:17), and the restoration of Israel "on the third day" prophesied by Hosea (Hosea 6:2).

> *For I delivered to you as of first importance what I also received, that Christ died for our sins according to the Scriptures, and that He was buried, and that He was raised on the third day according to the Scriptures.*
>
> 1 CORINTHIANS 15:3–4 NASB

For further study, see Hank Hanegraaff, *Resurrection* (Nashville: Word Publishing, 2000).

by Peter Jennings in *The Search for Jesus*. We can safely conclude that far from being contradictory, the gospel accounts are clearly *complementary*; a consensus of credible scholars considers the *core* set of facts presented by the gospel writers to be authentic and reliable; and the unique perspectives provided by Matthew, Mark, Luke, and John preclude the possibility of *collusion*.

> *Then Peter, turning around, saw the disciple whom Jesus loved following, who also had leaned on His breast at the supper, and said, "Lord, who is the one who betrays You?" . . . This is the disciple who testifies of these things, and wrote these things; and we know that his testimony is true.*
>
> JOHN 21:20, 24 NKJV

For further study concerning alleged contradictions in the Bible, see Gleason L. Archer, *New International Encyclopedia of Bible Difficulties* (Grand Rapids: Zondervan, 1982); concerning evidences for Christ's resurrection, see Hank Hanegraaff, *The Third Day* (Nashville: W Publishing Group, 2003). Also see Hank Hanegraaff, "The Search for Jesus Hoax," available at www.equip.org.

Who did the women encounter at the empty tomb: a man, men, or angels?

In a book purporting to reveal "hidden contradictions in the Bible," the infamous professor Bart Ehrman is unable to figure out whether the women at Jesus' empty tomb saw "a man, as Mark says, or two men (Luke), or an angel (Matthew)." One is left to wonder why one of Professor Ehrman's students didn't pause to unpack the mystery for him.

First, wherever there are two angels, there is also one! The fact that Mark only referenced the angel ("man") who addressed the women shouldn't be problematic even for someone who has made a virtual art form out of exploiting "discrepancies" among the secondary details of the Gospels. The fact that Matthew only referenced one angel does not preclude the fact that two angels were present.

Furthermore, even though Luke did not specifically refer to the two men as angels, the fact that he described these beings as "men in clothes that gleamed like lightning" (Luke 24:4) should have been a dead giveaway. Moreover, as a historian addressing a predominantly Gentile audience, Luke no doubt measured his words carefully so as not to unnecessarily give rise to pagan superstitions.

Does the Bible claim Jesus is God?

Many biblical texts can be used to demonstrate that Jesus is God. Three, however, stand out above the rest. Not only are they clear and convincing, but their "addresses" are easy to remember as well—John *1*, Colossians *1*, and Hebrews *1*.

First, is *John 1*: "In the beginning was the Word, and the Word was with God, *and the Word was God*" (v. 1). Here we see that Jesus not only was in existence before the world began, but He is differentiated from the Father and explicitly called "God," indicating that He shares the same nature as His Father.

Furthermore, *Colossians 1* informs us that "all things were created by [Jesus]" (v. 16); He is "before all things" (v. 17); and "God was pleased to have all his fullness dwell in him" (v. 19). Only deity has the prerogative of creation, preexists all things, and personifies the full essence and nature of God.

Finally, *Hebrews 1* overtly tells us that—according to God the Father Himself—Jesus is God: "About the Son he [the Father] says, 'Your throne, O God, will last for ever and ever'" (v. 8). Not only is the entirety of Hebrews 1 devoted to demonstrating the absolute deity of Jesus, but in verses 10–12 the inspired writer quoted a passage from Psalm 102 referring to Yahweh and directly applied it to Christ. In doing so, the

Scripture specifically declared Jesus ontologically equal with Israel's God.

Many similar texts could be added to this list. For example, in *Revelation 1*, the Lord God says, "I am the Alpha and the Omega, who is, and who was, and who is to come, the Almighty" (v. 8). In the last chapter of Revelation, Jesus applied these same words—*Alpha* and *Omega*—to Himself! Additionally, in *2 Peter 1*, Jesus is referred to as "our God and Savior Jesus Christ" (v. 1). In these passages and a host of others, the Bible explicitly claims that Jesus *is* God.

> *We should live soberly, righteously, and godly in the present age, looking for the blessed hope and glorious appearing of our great God and Savior Jesus Christ.*
> TITUS 2:12–13 NKJV

For further study, see Hank Hanegraaff, *Resurrection* (Nashville: Word Publishing, 2000).

the dead (John 2:19); and He alluded to His *omnipresence* by promising He would be with His disciples "to the very end of the age" (Matthew 28:20). Not only so, but Jesus said to the paralytic in Luke 5:20, "Friend, your sins are forgiven." In doing so, He claimed a prerogative—forgiving a person's sin—reserved for God alone. In addition, when Thomas worshipped Jesus, saying, "My Lord and my God!" (John 20:28), Jesus responded with commendation rather than condemnation.

Throughout the Gospels, Jesus claimed with both His words and His deeds to be God.

> *Do not be afraid; I am the First and the*
> *Last. I am He who lives, and was dead,*
> *and behold, I am alive forevermore.*
> Revelation 1:17–18 NKJV

For further study, see Millard J. Erickson, *The Word Became Flesh: A Contemporary Incarnational Christology* (Grand Rapids: Baker Book House, 1996).

What credentials back up Jesus' claim to deity?

J esus not only claimed to be God but also provided many convincing proofs that He indeed was divine.

First, Jesus demonstrated that He was God in human flesh by manifesting the credential of sinlessness. While the Qur'an exhorts Muhammad to seek forgiveness for his sins, the Bible exonerates Messiah, saying Jesus "had no sin" (2 Corinthians 5:21). And this is not a singular statement. John declared, "In him is no sin" (1 John 3:5), and Peter said that Jesus "committed no sin, and no deceit was found in his mouth" (1 Peter 2:22). Jesus Himself went so far as to challenge His antagonists asking, "Can any of you prove me guilty of sin?" (John 8:46).

Furthermore, Jesus demonstrated supernatural authority over sickness, the forces of nature, fallen angels, and even death itself. *Matthew 4* records that Jesus went throughout Galilee teaching, preaching, "and healing every disease and sickness among the people" (v. 23). *Mark 4* documents Jesus rebuking the wind and the waves saying, "Quiet! Be still!" (v. 39). In *Luke 4*, Jesus encountered a man possessed by an evil spirit and commanded the demon to "Come out of him!" (v. 35). And in *John 4*, Jesus told a royal official whose son was close to death, "Your son will live" (v. 50). And all four Gospels record how Jesus demonstrated ultimate power over death through the immutable fact of His resurrection.

Finally, the credentials of Christ's deity are seen in the lives of countless men, women, and children. Each day people of every tongue and tribe and nation experience the resurrected Christ by repenting of their sins and receiving Jesus as Lord and Savior of their lives. Thus, they not only come to know about Christ evidentially, but experientially Christ becomes more real to them than the very flesh upon their bones.

Adapted from *The Third Day*

When John had heard in prison about the works of Christ, he sent two of his disciples and said to Him, "Are You the Coming One, or do we look for another?"

Jesus answered and said to them, "Go and tell John the things which you hear and see: The blind see and the lame walk; the lepers are cleansed and the deaf hear; the dead are raised up and the poor have the gospel preached to them."
MATTHEW 11:2–5 NKJV

For further study, see William Lane Craig, *Reasonable Faith: Christian Truth and Apologetics*, rev. ed. (Wheaton, IL: Crossway Books, 1994), chapters 7 and 8.

Resurrection: What are memorable keys to the greatest F-E-A-T in history?

he physical resurrection of Jesus Christ constitutes the very capstone of our faith. Without it, Christianity crumbles. As such, those who take the sacred name of Christ upon their lips must be prepared to defend its historicity. To make the process memorable, I've developed the acronym F-E-A-T. It will serve as an enduring reminder that the resurrection of Jesus Christ is the greatest *feat* in the annals of recorded history. Each letter will serve to remind you of an undeniable fact of the resurrection.

FATAL TORMENT. The fatal suffering of Jesus Christ as recounted in the New Testament is one of the most well-established facts of ancient history. Even in today's modern age of scientific enlightenment, there is virtual consensus among New Testament scholars—both conservative and liberal—that Christ suffered fatal torment. Believing Jesus swooned—rather than suffered fatal torment—stretches credulity. It means Christ survived six trials, suffered scourging, survived seven-inch iron spikes, survived a spear wound in His side and then single-handedly rolled away an enormously heavy tombstone, subdued armed guards, strolled around on pierced feet, and seduced His disciples into communicating the myth that He had conquered death while living out the remainder of a pathetic life in obscurity.

EMPTY TOMB. As with Christ's fatal torment, liberal and conservative New Testament scholars alike agree that the body of Jesus was buried in the private tomb of Joseph of Arimathea. As a member of the Jewish court that convicted Jesus, Joseph of Arimathea is unlikely to be Christian fiction. And considering that females in ancient Judaism were routinely considered little more than chattel, the empty tomb accounts provide powerful evidence that the gospel writers valued truth over cultural correctness. Not only so, but the earliest Jewish response to the resurrection presupposes the empty tomb; and in the centuries following the resurrection, the fact of the empty tomb was forwarded by Jesus' friends and foes alike. As the late liberal scholar John A. T. Robinson of Cambridge conceded, the burial of Christ "is one of the earliest and best attested facts about Jesus." Christianity simply could not have endured an identifiable tomb containing the remains of Messiah.

APPEARANCES. One thing can be stated with iron-clad certainty: the apostles did not merely propagate Christ's teachings; they were absolutely certain that He had appeared to them in the flesh after His crucifixion, death, and burial. Although two thousand years removed from the actual event, we too can be absolutely confident in Christ's post-resurrection appearances. In 1 Corinthians 15:3–7, the apostle Paul reiterated a Christian creed that scholars of all stripes conclude can be dated to mere months after Messiah's murder. The creed, which unambiguously affirms Christ's post-resurrection appearances, is free from legendary contamination and, ultimately, is grounded in eyewitness testimony. No doubt the most amazing post-resurrection appearance involves Jesus' half-brother James. Before Christ's appearances, James was embarrassed by all that his half brother represented. Afterward, he was willing to die for the notion that his half brother was God. The question that inevitably arises is this: What would it take for someone to willingly die for the notion that one of his family members is God? The answer can be nothing other than the post-resurrection appearances of Messiah.

TRANSFORMATION. What happened as a result of the resurrection is unique in human history. In a span of a few hundred years, a small band of seemingly insignificant believers succeeded in turning an entire empire upside down. Within days of encountering the resurrected Christ, not merely twelve, but thousands of people willingly surrendered their spiritual and sociological traditions. The Sabbath was transformed into a *first-day-of-the-week* celebration of the *rest* we have through Christ who delivers us from sin and the grave. Not only so, but after the resurrection, followers of Christ suddenly stopped making animal sacrifices. They recognized the new covenant as better than the old covenant because the blood of Jesus Christ was better than the blood of animals. The Jewish rite of Passover was radically transformed as well. In place of the Passover meal, believers began partaking of the Eucharist. In like fashion, baptism took on new meaning. Prior to the resurrection, converts to Judaism were baptized in the name of Yahweh, God of Israel. After the resurrection, converts to Christianity were baptized in the name of Jesus. In doing so, believers equated Jesus with Israel's God.

ascension points to the greater truth that He is now glorified in the presence of God and that our glorification is divinely guaranteed as well.

> Now when [Jesus] had spoken these things, while [His followers] watched, He was taken up, and a cloud received Him out of their sight. And while they looked steadfastly toward heaven as He went up, behold, two men stood by them in white apparel, who also said, "Men of Galilee, why do you stand gazing up into heaven? This same Jesus, who was taken up from you into heaven, will so come in like manner as you saw Him go into heaven."
>
> ACTS 1:9–11 NKJV

For further study, see Hank Hanegraaff, *AfterLife: What You Need to Know About Heaven, the Hereafter, and Near-Death Experiences* (Brentwood, TN: Worthy, 2013).

Was Christianity influenced by ancient pagan mystery religions?

A common refrain sung by those determined to demolish the biblical Jesus in the court of public opinion is that His life, death, burial, and resurrection are myths borrowed from ancient pagan mystery religions. Once reverberating primarily through the bastions of private academia, this refrain is now also commonly heard in public arenas.

The first prevailing myth widely circulated in this regard is that the similarities between Christianity and the mystery religions are striking. Purveyors of this mythology employ biblical language and then go to great lengths to concoct commonalities. Take, for example, the alleged similarities between Christianity and the cult of Isis. The god Osiris was supposedly murdered by his brother and buried in the Nile. The goddess Isis recovered the cadaver, only to lose it once again to her brother-in-law who cut the body into fourteen pieces and scattered them around the world. After finding the parts, Isis "baptized" each piece in the Nile River and Osiris was "resurrected."

The alleged similarities as well as the terminology used to communicate them are greatly exaggerated. Parallels between the "resurrection" of Osiris and the resurrection of Christ are an

Is the virgin birth miracle or myth?

odernity has left many people with the false impression that the virgin birth is nothing more than ancient superstition. In an op-ed piece published by the *New York Times*, columnist Nicholas Kristof used the virgin birth of Jesus to shamelessly promote the Enlightenment's false dichotomy between faith and reason. In his words, "The faith in the Virgin Birth reflects the way American Christianity is becoming less intellectual and more mystical over time." Kristof ends his piece with the following patronizing comment: "The heart is a wonderful organ, but so is the brain." Those who have a truly open mind, however, should resist rejecting the virgin birth *a priori* (prior to examination).

First, miracles are not only possible, but they are necessary in order to make sense of the universe in which we live. According to modern science, the universe not only had a beginning, but it is unfathomably fine-tuned to support life. Not only so, but the origin of life, information in the genetic code, irreducible complexity in biological systems, and the phenomenon of the human mind pose intractable difficulties for merely natural explanations. Thus, reason forces us to look beyond the natural world to a supernatural Designer who miraculously intervenes in the affairs of His created handiwork. In other words, if we are willing to believe that God created the heavens and the earth (Genesis 1:1), we should have no problem accepting the virgin birth.

Furthermore, we are compelled by reason and evidence to acknowledge that the Bible is divine rather than merely human in origin. The miraculous preservation of God's Word via manuscripts and archaeology, together with prophecy, provides a cumulative case for the reliability of Scripture. Thus, we may legitimately appeal to the Word of God itself as supernatural evidence for the virgin birth. Moreover, Christ, who demonstrated that He was God in human flesh through the supernatural fact of His resurrection, pronounced the Scriptures infallible (John 10:35; 14:24–26; 15:26–27; 16:13; Hebrews 1:1–2). And if Christ affirmed the biblical record of the virgin birth, no one should have the temerity to contradict His claim.

Finally, while it is popular to suggest that the gospel writers borrowed the virgin birth motif from pagan mythology, the facts say otherwise. Stories of gods having sexual intercourse with women—such as the sun god Apollo becoming a snake and impregnating the mother of Augustus Caesar—hardly parallel the virgin birth account. What is more, given the strict monotheistic worldview of New Testament authors, it should stretch credulity beyond the breaking point to suppose they

Finally, if viewing an image necessarily leads to idolatry, then the incarnation of Christ was the greatest temptation of all. Yet Jesus thought it appropriate for people to look on Him and worship Him as God (Matthew 28:9; Luke 24:52). That worship, however, was to be directed to His Person, not His appearance. Indeed, idolatry lies not in the making of images but in the worship of man-made images in place of the "image of the invisible God" (Colossians 1:15).

> *As we have borne the image of the man of dust, we*
> *shall also bear the image of the heavenly Man.*
>
> 1 CORINTHIANS 15:49 NKJV

For further study on a related issue, see "Should Christians celebrate Christmas?" (p. 394).

Was Isaiah thinking about Jesus when he prophesied the virgin birth?

L ooking back at the Old Testament through the lens of the New, it is easy to assume that Isaiah understood the messianic meaning of his prophecy. However, those who believe that the Bible is the infallible repository of redemptive revelation must be willing to test all things in light of Scripture and hold fast to that which is good (1 Thessalonians 5:21).

First, the prophecy in Isaiah 7:14—"the virgin will be with child and will give birth to a son, and will call him Immanuel"— was fulfilled in Isaiah 8. As Isaiah made clear, this prophecy was fulfilled when Isaiah "went to the prophetess, and she conceived and gave birth to a son" named Maher-Shalal-Hash-Baz (8:3). In context, Judah was "shaken" as two powerful kingdoms sought the nation's demise (7:1–2). God, however, promised that the birth of Maher-Shalal-Hash-Baz was a sign that Judah would be spared. In the words of Isaiah, "Before the boy knows enough to reject the wrong and choose the right, the land of the two kings you dread will be laid waste" (7:16; cf. 8:4).

Furthermore, though Isaiah's wife, unlike Mary, was not a virgin when she gave birth, she nonetheless was the near-future fulfillment of Isaiah's prophecy. *Virgin (almah)* was simply a

9:5, Paul defended his right to have a wife by appealing to the fact that Peter and other apostles had wives: "Don't we have the right to take a believing wife along with us, as do the Lord's brothers and Cephas?" If Jesus had been married, it is unthinkable that Paul would have neglected to appeal to Jesus as the ultimate precedent. For this reason Paul Maier, professor of ancient history at Western Michigan University, aptly refers to 1 Corinthians 9:5 as "the graveyard of the married-Jesus fiction."

> *"All cannot accept this saying, but only those to*
> *whom it has been given: For there are eunuchs*
> *who were born thus from their mother's womb,*
> *and there are eunuchs who were made eunuchs*
> *by men, and there are eunuchs who have made*
> *themselves eunuchs for the kingdom of heaven's sake.*
> *He who is able to accept it, let him accept it."*
>
> MATTHEW 19:11–12 NKJV

For further study, see Hank Hanegraaff and Paul L. Maier, *The Da Vinci Code: Fact or Fiction?* (Wheaton, IL: Tyndale House, 2004), 15–21.

Is the incarnation logically incoherent?

ike the Trinity, the doctrine of the incarnation is often considered to be logically incoherent. While many issues surrounding the incarnation, such as the precise modes of interaction between Christ's divine nature and His human nature, may transcend our human understanding, the doctrine of the incarnation does not transgress the laws of logic.

First, to understand the logical coherence of the incarnation, one must first consider the *imago Dei* (image of God). Because God created humanity in His own image (Genesis 1:27), the essential properties of human nature (rationality, will, moral character, and the like) are not inconsistent with His divine nature. Though the notion of God becoming a clam would be absurd, the reality that God became a man is not.

Moreover, it is crucial to point out that though the God-man is *fully* human, He is not *merely* human. And though the divine Son of God took on all the essential properties of human nature, He did not take on that which is nonessential (e.g., sinful inclinations). Indeed, as Adam was created without a proclivity toward sin, so the Second Adam (Jesus) was untainted by original sin. And like His moral perfection, Jesus' other divine attributes (omniscience, omnipotence, omnipresence, and so forth) were not undermined in the incarnation.

*In the beginning was the Word, and the Word
was with God, and the Word was God. . . . And
the Word became flesh and dwelt among us,
and we beheld His glory, the glory as of the only
begotten of the Father, full of grace and truth.*

JOHN 1:1, 14 NKJV

For further study, see Ronald H. Nash, *Is Jesus the Only Savior?* (Grand Rapids: Zondervan, 1994), 84–91; for the definitive philosophical work on this topic, see Thomas V. Morris, *The Logic of God Incarnate* (Ithaca, NY: Cornell University Press, 1986).

If God cannot be tempted, how could Jesus be tempted?

On the one hand Scripture tells us that "God cannot be tempted by evil" (James 1:13). On the other, it informs us that during His wilderness sojourn, Jesus *was* tempted by the evil one (Matthew 4:1–11). Could Jesus be tempted—or couldn't He?

First, for sin to take place, there must be a sinful inner response to a seductive suggestion to sin. Although Satan appealed to Jesus' natural human desires (e.g., hunger), our Lord did not fantasize in response to Satan's suggestion. To mull over Satan's suggestion even for a moment would have constituted sin. And had Jesus sinned, He could not have been our Savior.

Furthermore, although Christ did not have any sinful proclivities that inclined Him toward evil, Satan's temptations were nonetheless as real as the very flesh upon Jesus' bones. Even those who are born into sin can identify with being tempted to do something they are utterly disinclined to do. By way of analogy, most mothers would never consider killing their children even if offered a life free from suffering in return. Nonetheless, the natural desire to avoid suffering would render such a temptation genuine.

Finally, in saying "God cannot be tempted by evil," James focused on God as the self-sufficient Sovereign of the universe. As such, God has no unmet needs. Conversely, the accounts of Jesus' wilderness temptation focus on God-Incarnate who experienced all the essential physical and psychological needs commensurate with humanity—including hunger, fatigue, and the desire for self-preservation. Thus, the biblical truths that God cannot be tempted and yet Christ *was* tempted are complementary, not contradictory.

> *We do not have a High Priest who cannot*
> *sympathize with our weaknesses, but was in all*
> *points tempted as we are, yet without sin.*
> HEBREWS 4:15 NKJV

For further study, see Adam Pelser, "Genuine Temptation and the Character of Christ," *Christian Research Journal* 30, 2 (2007), available through the Christian Research Institute at www.equip.org.

How can the eternal Son of God be "the firstborn over all creation"?

In his letter to the Colossians, Paul called Jesus Christ "the firstborn over all creation" (Colossians 1:15). How can Christ be both the eternal Creator of all things and yet Himself be the *firstborn*?

First, in referring to Christ as the firstborn, Paul had in mind preeminence. This usage is firmly established in the Old Testament. For example, Ephraim is referred to as the Lord's "firstborn" (Jeremiah 31:9) even though Manasseh was born first (Genesis 41:51). Likewise, David was appointed the Lord's "firstborn, the most exalted of the kings of the earth" (Psalm 89:27) despite being the youngest of Jesse's sons (1 Samuel 16:10–13). While neither Ephraim nor David was the first one born in his family, both were firstborn in the sense of preeminence or prime position.

Furthermore, Paul referred to Jesus as the firstborn *over* all creation not the firstborn *in* creation: Jesus "is before *all things*, and in him *all things* hold together" (Colossians 1:17). The force of Paul's language is such that the cult of the Jehovah's Witnesses, who ascribe to the ancient Arian heresy that the Son is not preexistent and coeternal with the Father, have been forced to insert the word *other* (e.g., "all other things") in their deeply flawed New World Translation of the Bible in order to demote Christ to the status of a created being.

Finally, as the panoply of Scripture makes plain, Jesus is the eternal Creator who spoke and the limitless galaxies leapt into existence. In John 1, He is overtly called "God" (v. 1), and in Hebrews 1, He is said to be the one who "laid the foundations of the earth" (v. 10). And in the very last chapter of the Bible, Christ referred to Himself as "the Alpha and the Omega, the First and the Last, the Beginning and the End" (Revelation 22:13). Indeed, the whole of Scripture precludes the possibility that Christ could be anything other than the preexistent Sovereign of the universe.

He is the image of the invisible God, the firstborn over all creation. For by Him all things were created that are in heaven and that are on earth, visible and invisible, whether thrones or dominions or principalities or powers. All things were created through Him and for Him.

COLOSSIANS 1:15–16 NKJV

For further study, see Robert L. Reymond, *Jesus, Divine Messiah* (Tain, Ross–shire, Scotland: Christian Focus Publications, 2003) at www.equip.org.

Why does the Apostles' Creed say that Jesus "descended into hell"?

T he Apostles' Creed is no doubt the most precise and poetic summary of the Christian faith in existence. The phrase *he descended into hell*, however, continues to be controversial. Some Christians remove it, others reinterpret it, and still others simply refuse to recite it.

First, it is instructive to understand how the Apostles' Creed morphed into existence. Prior to crystallization as a creedal confession in public worship, it was recited at baptism. Then, in the second century, such recitations were systematized to counter Gnostic heresies. But not until long after the fourth century was the clause *he descended into hell* appended to the confession— and perhaps not officially until the eighth century. Because the phrase in question did not appear in the Apostles' Creed until late, it cannot be credibly argued that it was the profession of early church fathers, much less the apostles.

Furthermore, the phrase in question resulted principally from a misinterpretation of 1 Peter 3:19–20 that says Jesus "went and preached to the spirits in prison who disobeyed long ago when God waited patiently in the days of Noah while the ark was being built." In context there is nothing to commend the idea that Jesus went to hell between His death and resurrection in order to preach to demonic spirits or to scoffers who disobeyed while the ark was being built. Instead, just as the Spirit of Jesus preached through Noah to the people of his day—who were then in the flesh, but at the writing of Peter's epistles were disembodied spirits incarcerated in the prison house of hades—so, too, in the days preceding the fall of Jerusalem, the Spirit of Jesus was preaching through Peter and the persecuted to a pagan world drowning in dissipation.

Finally, the phrase *he descended into hell* may well have been included in the creed due to a misapprehension respecting *hades* and *hell*. As is the case today, Christians have not always been cognizant of the biblical distinction between hades, depicted as a "place of torment" by our Lord in Luke 16:28, and hell, described by John in passages such as Revelation 20. As horrifying as hades is, it is but an earnest of Gehenna (hell), to which the rich man will be sentenced when Jesus appears a second time. As such, the apostle John described the horror of hades being thrown into the lake of fire (hell), as "the second death" (Revelation 20:14).

In any case, the canon, not the creed, is the final court of arbitration. In Scripture, Jesus said to the thief also dying on a cross: "I tell you the truth, today you will be with me in paradise" (Luke 23:43). As such, the phrase *he descended into hell* is a mistaken tradition, a misunderstanding of Scripture, and a misapprehension of the meaning of words.

In part adapted from *AfterLife*

I believe in God, the Father Almighty,
the Maker of heaven and earth,
and in Jesus Christ, His only Son, our Lord:
Who was conceived by the Holy Ghost,
born of the virgin Mary,
suffered under Pontius Pilate,
was crucified, dead, and buried;
He descended into hell.
The third day He arose again from the dead;
He ascended into heaven,
and sitteth on the right hand of God the Father
 Almighty;
from thence He shall come to judge the quick
 and the dead.
I believe in the Holy Ghost;
the holy catholic church;
the communion of saints;
the forgiveness of sins;
the resurrection of the body;
and the life everlasting.
Amen.

—Apostles' Creed

What distinguishes Christianity
from other religions?

C hristianity is unique among the religions of the world for several reasons.

First, unlike other religions, Christianity is rooted in history and evidence. Jesus of Nazareth was born in Bethlehem in Judea during the reign of Caesar Augustus and was put to death by Pontius Pilate, a first-century Roman governor. The testimony of His life, death, and resurrection is validated both by credible eyewitness testimony and credible extrabiblical evidence. No other religion can legitimately claim this kind of support from history and evidence.

Furthermore, of all the influential religious leaders of the world (Buddha, Moses, Zoroaster, Krishna, Lao Tzu, Muhammad, Baha'u'llah), only Jesus claimed to be God in human flesh (Mark 14:62), and this was not an empty boast. For through the historically verifiable fact of the resurrection, Christ vindicated His claim to deity (Romans 1:4; 1 Corinthians 15:3–8). Other religions, such as Buddhism and Islam, claim miracles in support of their faith; however, unlike Christianity, such miracles lack historical validation.

Finally, Christianity is unique in that it is a coherent belief structure. Some Christian doctrines may transcend comprehension; however, unlike the claims of other religions, they are never irrational or contradictory. Christianity is also unique in that it cogently accounts for the vast array of phenomena we encounter in everyday life: the human mind, laws of science, laws of logic, ethical norms, justice, love, meaning in life, the problem of evil and suffering, and truth. In other words, Christianity corresponds with the reality of our present condition.

We did not follow cunningly devised fables when we made known to you the power and coming of our Lord Jesus Christ, but were eyewitnesses of His majesty.

2 PETER 1:16 NKJV

For further study, see James W. Sire, *The Universe Next Door*, 3rd ed. (Downers Grove, IL: InterVarsity Press, 1997); and Lee Strobel, *The Case for Christ* (Grand Rapids: Zondervan, 1998).

What happens to a person who dies without ever hearing of Jesus?

O ne of the most frequently asked questions on the *Bible Answer Man* broadcast is "What happens to people who die without ever hearing of Jesus?" Will God condemn people to hell for not believing in someone they have never heard of?

First, people are not condemned to hell for not believing in Jesus. Rather, they are *already* condemned because of their *sin*. Thus, the real question is not how can God send someone to hell, but how can God condescend to save any one of us?

Furthermore, ignorance is not a ticket to heaven. If it were, the greatest evangelistic enterprise would not be crusade evangelism but a concerted cover-up campaign. Such a campaign would focus on ending evangelism, burning Bibles, and closing churches. Soon no one will have heard of Christ, and everyone will be on their way to heaven.

Finally, it should be emphasized that everyone has the light of both creation and conscience. God is not capricious! If we respond to the light we have, God will give us more light. In the words of the apostle Paul, "From one man he made every nation of men, that they should inhabit the whole earth; and he determined the times set for them and the exact places where they should live. God did this so that men would seek him and perhaps reach out for him and find him, though he is not far from each one of us" (Acts 17:26–27).

> *"I am the way, the truth, and the life. No one*
> *comes to the Father except through Me."*
>
> John 14:6 NKJV

For further study, see Ronald H. Nash, *Is Jesus the Only Savior?* (Grand Rapids: Zondervan, 1994); see also Hank Hanegraaf, "Is Jesus the Only Way," available at www.equip.org.

What are the characteristics of C-U-L-T-S?

I n common parlance the word *cult* connotes theological and/or sociological perversion. As such, cults run the gamut from theologically perverse Mormons to the sociologically deviant Heaven's Gate cult, which ended with the largest mass suicide in US history (thirty-nine people) in 1997. Common cultic characteristics are easily remembered using the Hankronym C-U-L-T-S.

C OUNTERFEIT. Google "counterfeit money" and one of the first hits that pops up is a US Secret Service posting titled "How to Detect Counterfeit Money." The Secret Service posting goes on to say that you and I "can help guard against the threat from counterfeiters by becoming familiar with US currency." How? "Compare the suspect note with a genuine note of the same denomination and series, paying attention to the quality of printing and paper characteristics. Look for differences, not similarities." What is true with respect to counterfeit currency is likewise true with respect to counterfeit cults. You and I must be so familiar with essential Christian doctrine that when a counterfeit looms on the horizon, we recognize it instantaneously (see "What is essential Christian D-O-C-T-R-I-N-E?" on p. 6).

U NBIBLICAL REVELATIONS. Another common cultic characteristic is unbiblical revelations. Mormonism is a classic case in point. In

1820, two celestial personages allegedly appeared to Mormon founder Joseph Smith revealing that all existing churches were wrong, all their creeds were an abomination, and all their professors were corrupt. Then they said that Smith had been chosen to restore a church that had disappeared from the face of the earth. In like fashion, the Church of Almighty God cult founder Zhao Weishan revealed that the incarnation of Jesus Christ was insufficient, thus, God had to finish the work of redemption through the incarnation and revelations of a female Christ named Deng. Such new revelations are common to cults and undermine the main and plain teachings of Scripture.

LINGUISTIC SUBVERSION. Cults are notorious for subverting biblical language by pouring their own unique meanings into key Christian words and phrases. Thus, we must prepare ourselves to scale the language barrier. Take the word *Jesus*, for example. Mormons render Jesus the spirit brother of Lucifer; Jehovah's Witnesses, the archangel Michael; and New Agers, an avatar or enlightened messenger. In biblical vernacular, Jesus is none other than the One who spoke and the limitless galaxies leapt into existence: "He is the image of the invisible God, the firstborn over all creation. For by him all things were created; things in heaven and on earth, visible and invisible, whether thrones or powers or rulers or authorities; all things were created by him and for him. He is before all things, and in him all things hold together" (Colossians 1:15–17).

THEOLOGICAL PERVERSION. From a theological perspective, cults are pseudo-Christian groups that compromise, confuse, or contradict the essentials of the historic Christian faith. Devotees become masters at taking texts out of context in order to develop pretexts for theological perversions. An apt example is Scientology. In place of resurrection they teach devotees the unbiblical notion of reincarnation. All too often such notions are buttressed by a distortion of the biblical text. For instance, John the Baptist is frequently hailed as a reincarnation of the biblical prophet Elijah despite the fact that John dismissed this absurdity with three short words. When asked by the Levites if he was indeed a reincarnation of Elijah, he replied, "I am not" (John 1:21).

SOCIOLOGICAL DEVIANCE. From a sociological perspective, a cult is a religious or semi-religious sect whose followers are controlled in virtually every dimension of their lives. As such, devotees characteristically display displaced loyalty for the guru and the group and are galvanized together through physical and/or psychological intimidation tactics. Such cults display a "we/they" siege mentality and often cut off their devotees from former associations, including their immediate families. The Almighty God cult is a prime example of a socially deviant group that is diabolically dangerous and employs socially deviant behavior including sexual manipulation, kidnapping, and even murder.

In sum, when imitations of authentic Christianity loom on the horizon, you can recognize them instantaneously by remembering the acronym C-U-L-T-S: *counterfeit*, *unbiblical revelations*, *linguistic subversion*, *theological perversion*, and *sociological deviance*.

I fear, lest somehow, as the serpent deceived Eve by his craftiness, so your minds may be corrupted from the simplicity that is in Christ. For if he who comes preaches another Jesus whom we have not preached, or if you receive a different spirit which you have not received, or a different gospel which you have not accepted—you may well put up with it!

2 Corinthians 11:3–4 NKJV

COUNTERFEIT

UNBIBLICAL REVELATIONS

LINGUISTIC SUBVERSION

THEOLOGICAL PERVERSION

SOCIOLOGICAL DEVIANCE

For further study, see Hank Hanegraaff, *Counterfeit Revival*, rev. ed. (Nashville: Word Publishing Group, 2001), part 5.

Are Jehovah's Witnesses Christian?

L ike Mormons, Jehovah's Witnesses believe that Christianity died with the last of the apostles. They believe Christianity was not resurrected until their founder, Charles Taze Russell, began organizing the Watchtower Society in the 1870s. In their view, the cross is a pagan symbol adopted by an apostate church, and salvation is impossible apart from the Watchtower. While the Witnesses on your doorstep consider themselves to be the only authentic expression of Christianity, the Society they serve compromises, confuses, and contradicts essential Christian doctrine.

First, the Watchtower Society compromises the nature of God. They teach their devotees that the Trinity is a "freakish-looking, three-headed God" invented by Satan and that Jesus is merely a god. In Watchtower theology, Jesus was created by God as the archangel Michael who, during his earthly sojourn, was merely human and who, after his crucifixion, was recreated an immaterial spirit creature. JWs also deny the physical resurrection of Jesus. According to Russell, the body that hung on a "torture stake" either "dissolved into gasses" or is "preserved somewhere as the grand memorial of God's love."

Furthermore, while Christians believe that all believers will spend eternity with Christ in "a new heaven and a new earth" (Revelation 21:1), the Watchtower teaches that only 144,000 people will make it to heaven while the rest of the faithful will live apart from Christ on earth. Thus, in Watchtower lore, there is a "little flock" of 144,000 who get to go to heaven and a "great crowd" of others who are relegated to earth. The heavenly class are born again, receive the baptism of the Holy Spirit, and partake of communion; the earthly class do not. To substantiate the notion that heaven's door was closed irrevocably in 1935, JWs point to "flashes of prophetic light" received by Joseph F. Rutherford at a JW convention in Washington, DC. Other false "flashes of prophetic light" include Watchtower predictions of end-time cataclysms that were to occur in 1914 . . . 1918 . . . 1925 . . . 1975.

Finally, under the threat of being "disfellowshipped," Jehovah's Witnesses are barred from celebrating Christmas, birthdays, or holidays such as Thanksgiving and Good Friday. Even more troubling are Watchtower regulations regarding vaccinations, organ transplants, and blood transfusions. In 1931, JWs were instructed to refuse vaccinations; by 1952, this regulation was rescinded. In 1967, organ transplants were ruled a forbidden form of cannibalism; by 1980, this edict was erased. In 1909, the Watchtower produced a prohibition against blood transfusions. No doubt this too will one day become a relic of the past. In the meantime, tens of thousands of people have not only been ravished spiritually by the Watchtower Society but have paid the ultimate physical price as well.

the NWT to their religious traditions by replacing the cross of Christ with a *torture stake*. Matthew 10:38, for example, has been altered to read, "And whoever does not accept his *torture stake* and follow after me is not worthy of me." In Watchtower lore, the cross is a pagan symbol adopted by an apostate Christianity when Satan took control of the early church. Jehovah's Witnesses view wearing a cross as a blatant act of idolatry. Conversely, Christians wear crosses as a reminder of what was simultaneously the most brutal and beautiful act in redemptive history.

Finally, the Watchtower Society claims that the Christian Scriptures have "been tampered with" in order to eliminate the name *Jehovah* from the text. In reality, it is the Translation Committee of the NWT that can rightly be accused of tampering. In well over two hundred cases, the name Jehovah has been gratuitously inserted into the New Testament text. In passages such as Romans 10:13, this is done to obscure the unique deity of Christ. In other passages, it is done under the pretext that referring to God as Lord rather than Jehovah is patently pagan. Ironically, in the Kingdom Interlinear Translation of the Greek Scriptures, Watchtower translators themselves fall into this "pagan" practice by translating the Greek word *kurios* as *Lord* even in cases where it specifically refers to the Father.

For these and a host of other reasons, Greek scholars across the board denounce the NWT. Dr. Julius Mantey, author of *A Manual Grammar of the Greek New Testament*, called the NWT a "shocking mistranslation," and Dr. William Barclay characterized the translators themselves as "intellectually dishonest."

> *I testify to everyone who hears the words of the*
> *prophecy of this book: If anyone adds to these things,*
> *God will add to him the plagues that are written in*
> *this book; and if anyone takes away from the words*
> *of the book of this prophecy, God shall take away his*
> *part from the Book of Life, from the holy city,*
> *and from the things which are written in this book.*
>
> REVELATION 22:18–19 NKJV
>
> (SEE ALSO DEUTERONOMY 4:2)

For further study, see David A. Reed, *Answering Jehovah's Witnesses: Subject by Subject* (Grand Rapids: Baker Book House, 1996).

level of the celestial kingdom and become gods of their own planets.

These and many other doctrinal perversions exclude Mormonism from rightly being called Christian.

> *"You are My witnesses," says the LORD,*
> *"And My servant whom I have chosen,*
> *That you may know and believe Me,*
> *And understand that I am He.*
> *Before Me there was no God formed,*
> *Nor shall there be after Me."*
>
> ISAIAH 43:10 NKJV

For further study, see "What separates Christian orthodoxy from the heresy of Mormonism? (M-O-R-M-O-N)" (p. 303); Richard Abanes, *One Nation Under Gods* (New York: Four Walls Eight Windows, 2003).

What separates Christian orthodoxy from the heresy of Mormonism? (M-O-R-M-O-N)

Although building ongoing relationships with Mormons can open up avenues for reaching rather than repelling, authentic Christians must never lose sight of the essential differences that separate orthodoxy from the heresy of Mormonism. To help you recall the crucial differences, I've organized them around the memorable acronym M-O-R-M-O-N. As you proceed, it is crucial to keep in mind the apostle Paul's instruction to "[speak] the truth in love" (Ephesians 4:15). We begin with the "angel" Moroni, who allegedly led Mormon founder Joseph Smith to the book that started it all.

MORONI. In sharp contrast to the crosses that adorn the steeples of Christian churches, the glittering image of an angel named Moroni is perched high atop the spires of Mormon temples. While millions have viewed his iconic image, few are aware of the significance Moroni plays in Mormon folklore. As a mortal, Moroni served as the last military commander of the Nephite nation. Upon death, Moroni was resurrected as an angel who in 1823 visited young Smith and divulged the location of golden plates inscribed in "reformed Egyptian"

O*riginal Fall.* Mormons maintain that prior to the fall, Adam and Eve were not mortal, which they redefine to mean "able to bear children." Thus, Mormons redefine the fall as "necessary and glorious," for by it the "pre-existent" progeny of Father God and Mother God could receive bodies and begin an eternal progression by which they too may become what God is. In the words of the fifth Mormon president, Lorenzo Snow, "As man is, God once was. As God is, man may become."

C*anon of Scripture.* According to the Book of Mormon, the Bible is incomplete, having lost substantial portions throughout its transmission over time. Not only so, but Joseph Smith had the unmitigated gall to delete arbitrarily the Song of Solomon, alter scores of biblical passages, and write himself into the Scriptures in his "corrected translation" of Genesis! Moreover, Mormons subscribe to "ongoing revelation" by modern-day church prophets, whose words become as binding as their Mormon quad (the Holy Bible, *Book of Mormon, Doctrine and Covenants,* and *Pearl of Great Price*). Within the maze of Mormonism, one can find living prophets contradicting dead prophets and LDS teachings once official (or quasi-official) that are no longer considered credible.

T*rinity.* Mormons worship three "separate and distinct" gods. Said Smith, "I have always declared God to be a distinct personage, Jesus Christ a separate and distinct personage from God the Father, and that the Holy Ghost was a distinct personage and a Spirit: and these three constitute three distinct personages and three Gods." Not only so, but Smith taught that God Himself was once merely human: "God himself was once as we are now, and is an exalted man, and sits enthroned in yonder heavens."

Resurrection. Mormons believe Christ's resurrection did *nothing* but guarantee that everyone, regardless of their beliefs, will be raised from the dead with the opportunity to pursue their own course of salvation. Murderers and unrepentant whoremongers attain the *telestial heaven*; lukewarm Mormons, religious people, and those who accept the Mormon gospel in the spirit world enter the *terrestrial heaven*; and temple Mormons go to the *celestial heaven*. Only those who are sealed in secret temple rituals, however, make it to the third level of the celestial kingdom and become gods of their own planets.

Incarnation. In Mormon lore Jesus was first conceived a spirit child by Heavenly Father and Heavenly Mother, and then "begotten in flesh" when Heavenly Father had sex with the Virgin Mary. Said Mormon president and prophet Ezra Taft Benson, "Jesus Christ is the Son of God in the most literal sense. The body in which He performed His mission in the flesh was sired by that same Holy Being we worship as God, our Eternal Father." Mormon apostle Bruce McConkie left no ambiguity: "Christ was begotten by an Immortal Father in the same way that mortal men are begotten by mortal fathers."

New Creation. Mormons teach that one's lot in the afterlife (post-mortality) will reflect one's obedience to the laws of Mormonism in this life. As such the Mormon road to godhood (new creation) is arduous. A Mormon must not only have faith but exhibit perfect obedience to the law, including faithful participation in LDS temple rituals (marriage, baptisms for the dead, etc.). In the words of Joseph Fielding Smith, "To enter the celestial kingdom and obtain exaltation it is necessary that the whole law be kept."

Eschatology. Mormons believe that when America's government crumbles amid social turmoil, economic instability, and religious strife, the Mormon Church will step in to restore economic security. This will ultimately lead to the return of Jesus Christ, who will set up a one-thousand-year global theocracy based in Jackson County, Missouri. Mormons will subsequently reign with Christ, and everyone will be confronted with Mormonism as the one true religion. Smith alleged God had told him the return of Christ would take place before he was eighty-five years of age.

OATHS AND TEMPLE RITUALS. Mormons once swore on oath never to reveal their secret rituals on penalty that "our throats be cut from ear to ear and our tongues torn out by their roots." After a ceremonial washing and anointing and the bestowal of a secret new name, temple Mormons receive sacred undergarments believed to repel physical and spiritual dangers. Then *comes "The Endowment,"* a false representation of mankind's fall into sin, according to which Adam ultimately accepts Mormonism. Each participant must accurately answer a series of questions to pass through a curtain and complete the ceremony. These rituals—borrowed in part from the rites of Freemasonry—are often performed on behalf of the deceased and include baptisms on behalf of the dead and, in the case of men, ordinations into the priesthood by proxy.

NEW AND EVERLASTING COVENANT OF PLURAL MARRIAGE. The "new and everlasting covenant" of plural marriage is perhaps the best example of Mormon equivocation. Under threat of exile to Mexico, the Mormon Church officially abolished polygamy in the earthly realm in 1890. However, by virtue of secret temple ceremonies, Mormon males, such as Joseph Smith, Brigham Young, and contemporary Mormon leaders, remain sealed to multiple wives in the heavenly realm. According to Smith, apart from polygamy there is no hope of attaining to godhood. Smith had at least twenty-seven wives, while Brigham Young had fifty-five wives and fifty-seven children.

In an age in which the Mormon Church is attempting to pass itself off as mainstream, it is crucial that Christians are equipped to scale the Mormon language barrier and use Mormon doctrinal deviations to communicate effectively the everlasting gospel of the historic Christian faith.

Even if we, or an angel from heaven, preach any other gospel to you than what we have preached to you, let him be accursed.

Galatians 1:8 nkjv

MORONI
ORGANIZATION
REVELATIONS
MORMON DOCTRINE

> **D**eity of Christ
> **O**riginal Fall
> **C**anon of Scripture
> **T**rinity
> **R**esurrection
> **I**ncarnation
> **N**ew Creation
> **E**schatology

OATHS & TEMPLE RITUALS
NEW & EVERLASTING COVENANT OF PLURAL MARRIAGE

For further study, see the booklet by Hank Hanegraaff, *The Mormon Mirage: Seeing through the Illusion of Mainstream Mormonism* (Charlotte: CRI, 2008); see also the pocket-sized flipchart, "Memorable Keys to the M-O-R-M-O-N Mirage," available through the Christian Research Institute at www.equip.org.

Is the Book of Mormon credible?

I n 1823, the angel Moroni allegedly visited Mormon prophet Joseph Smith and divulged the location of some golden plates containing the "fullness of the everlasting gospel." These plates—abridged by Moroni and his father, Mormon, fourteen hundred years earlier—were written in "reformed Egyptian hieroglyphics." Along with the plates, Smith found a pair of magical eyeglasses that he used to translate the cryptic writing into English. The result was a new revelation called the *Book of Mormon* and a new religion called Mormonism. How millions can take the Book of Mormon seriously is almost beyond comprehension.

First, while Smith referred to the Book of Mormon as "the most correct of any book on earth and the keystone of our religion," its flaws run the gamut from the serious to the silly. In the category of serious, the Book of Mormon contains modalistic language that militates against the biblical doctrine of the Trinity (Ether 3:14). In the category of silly, a man struggles to catch his breath after having his head cut off (Ether 15:31).

Furthermore, while archaeology is a powerful testimony to the accuracy of the Bible, the same cannot be said for the Book of Mormon. Not only is there no archaeological evidence for a language such as "reformed Egyptian hieroglyphics," there is no

Does Mormonism *really* teach that Jesus is the spirit brother of Satan?

To begin with, according to official Mormon teaching, Jesus Christ is the first spirit child conceived and begotten by Heavenly Father and one of Heavenly Father's many wives (commonly referred to as "Heavenly Mother"). Just as Heavenly Father before him progressed to godhood, so Jesus progressed through obedience to the status of a god prior to his incarnation on earth. In the words of the late Mormon apostle and general authority Bruce McConkie, Jesus Christ—through obedience and devotion—"attained that pinnacle of intelligence which ranked him as a God." As such, according to LDS authorities, Jesus is not to be worshipped or prayed to as one would worship or pray to Heavenly Father.

Furthermore, Mormons teach that Heavenly Father subsequently had other spirit children. We ourselves are thought to be spirit children of Father God and Mother God. As such, Mormons refer to Jesus as our "Elder brother." As the official LDS teacher's manual *Gospel Principles* explains, "We needed a Savior to pay for our sins and teach us how to return to our Heavenly Father. Our Father said, 'Whom shall I send?' (Abraham 3:27). Two of *our* brothers offered to help. *Our* oldest brother, Jesus Christ, who was then called Jehovah, said, 'Here am I, send me'" (emphasis added).

Finally, it stands to reason that if Jesus is the first spirit child conceived and begotten by Heavenly Father; and if Heavenly Father and Mother subsequently conceived other spirit children, including Satan, then Jesus and Satan logically are spirit brothers. While LDS spokespersons sometimes obfuscate this fundamental Mormon teaching, apostles of the Mormon Church and current official LDS publications clearly affirm it. As explained by the Mormon publication *Ensign*, "On first hearing, the doctrine that Lucifer and our Lord, Jesus Christ, are brothers may seem surprising to some—especially to those unacquainted with latter-day revelations. But both the scriptures and the prophets affirm that Jesus Christ and Lucifer are indeed offspring of our Heavenly Father and, therefore, spirit brothers."

In sharp contrast to Mormon Christology, the biblical witness is clear and convincing: Jesus Christ is the eternal Creator God (John 1; Colossians 1; Hebrews 1; Revelation 1). Paul explicitly taught that Jesus is the Creator of all, including the angelic realm to which Satan belongs (Colossians 1:15–16; cf. John 1:3). *Jesus is thus Satan's creator, not his spirit brother.*

but in the authority it signifies. Likewise, when a physician provides someone who is sick with a prescription, that person's trust is not in the paper on which it is penned, but rather the potion to which it points. So it is with baptism. The power is not in a prescribed formula but in the heavenly Physician to whom the act of baptism points. Baptism is not essential for salvation; it is, however, essential to obedience.

Furthermore, error begets error; thus, the belief that one must be baptized only in the name of Jesus has led Oneness Pentecostalism to the further error that Jesus is Himself the Father, the Son, and the Holy Spirit. They do not hold to one God revealed in three Persons who are eternally distinct, but to three manifestations of one God revealed in Jesus. Indeed, according to Oneness, the doctrine of the Trinity is pagan polytheistic philosophy.

In truth, the Trinity is neither pagan polytheism nor pagan philosophy. Rather, it is biblically based. Scripture plainly reveals personal self-distinctions within the Godhead. As such, the Father says of the Son, "Your throne, O God, will last for ever and ever" (Hebrews 1:8), and the Son says of the Father, "I am one who testifies for myself; my other witness is the Father, who sent me" (John 8:18). Moreover, the very fact that Jesus prayed to the Father demonstrates that Jesus cannot be the Father. While I am frequently told by Oneness adherents that this is explained by the notion that Jesus' human nature prays to His divine nature, this is clearly not the case. Natures can't pray; only persons can.

Finally, Oneness Pentecostalism holds to a litany of legalistic proscriptions, including the test of rebaptism by their formula with evidence of speaking in tongues. No tongues, no salvation. As one can imagine, this has placed tremendous sociopsychological pressure on adherents to conjure up the gift of tongues. Those who do not speak in tongues are thought to be lacking in faith or even to be entirely unrepentant.

In sharp distinction, the Bible relates baptism in the Spirit to empowering for service (Acts 1:5–8) rather than evidence for salvation. In the words of Jesus to His disciples, "You will receive power when the Holy Spirit comes on you; and you will be my witnesses in Jerusalem, and in all Judea and Samaria, and to the ends of the earth" (Acts 1:8). The disciples were not still awaiting salvation; rather, they awaited a special anointing of the Holy Spirit that would serve as evidence that their evangelistic message was not of men, but of God (cf. Acts 2:14–21; 1 Corinthians 14:22).

Is Kabbalah consistent
with Christianity?

K abbalah is a form of Jewish mysticism that is being packaged and popularized for Western consumption. Leading the "red string" craze are such celebrities as Madonna and Demi Moore. In the final analysis, Kabbalah is just one more dish in a smorgasbord of popular religions that distort the true meaning of Scripture and oppose the gospel of Christ.

First, Kabbalists search for mystical meanings and messages in the Torah that allegedly have power to remedy personal and social ills. Indeed, Kabbalists believe that through Kabbalah, the unfettered communion with God experienced in Eden can be regained. As such, Kabbalism has more in common with the esotericism of Gnostic cults than with orthodox Christianity.

Furthermore, Ein Sof—the dualistic and ultimately unknowable deity of Kabbalah—bears little resemblance to the God of the Bible. Unlike Ein Sof, the Everlasting Sovereign is perfect in unity and simplicity and has ultimately revealed Himself through Jesus Christ (cf. John 1; Colossians 1; Hebrews 1).

Finally, Kabbalah holds to reincarnation, which can never be reconciled with the Christian hope of resurrection. The biblical teaching of one body per person demonstrates that the gulf between reincarnation and resurrection can never be bridged. Far from the transmigration of our soul into another body, Christianity holds that Christ will transform our body like unto His resurrected body (cf. 1 Corinthians 15).

> *No one has seen God at any time. The*
> *only begotten Son, who is in the bosom of*
> *the Father, He has declared Him.*
>
> JOHN 1:18 NKJV

For further study, see Marcia Montenegro, "Kabbalah: Getting Back to the Garden," *Christian Research Journal*, 28, 2 (2005): 12–21.

being the third Person of the Triune God who inspired the text of the Bible, Islam teaches that the Holy Spirit is the archangel Gabriel who dictated the Qur'an to Muhammad over a period of twenty-three years. Ironically, while the Holy Spirit who dictated the Qur'an is said to be the archangel Gabriel, Islam identifies the Holy Spirit promised by Jesus in John 14 as Muhammad. The Bible, however, roundly rejects such corruptions and misrepresentation. Biblically, the Holy Spirit is neither an angel nor a mere mortal; rather, He is the very God who redeems us from our sins and will one day resurrect us to life eternal (Acts 5:3–4; Romans 8:11).

> *Whoever denies the Son does not have the Father either; he who acknowledges the Son has the Father also.*
> 1 JOHN 2:23 NKJV

For further study, see Timothy George, *Is the Father of Jesus the God of Muhammad?* (Grand Rapids: Zondervan, 2002).

Is the Qur'an credible?

A ccording to Islam, the Qur'an is not only credible; it is God's *only* uncorrupted revelation. Thus, according to Muslim scholars, if the Qur'an is to be compared to anything in Christianity, it is to be compared to Christ rather than the Bible. In truth, however, the Bible can be demonstrated to be divine rather than merely human in origin. The same cannot be said for the Qur'an. Moreover, unlike the Bible, the Qur'an is replete with faulty ethics and factual errors.

First, unlike the Qur'an, the Bible is replete with prophecies that could not have been fulfilled through chance, good guessing, or deliberate deceit. Surprisingly, the predictive nature of many Bible passages was once a popular argument among liberals against the reliability of the Bible. Critics argued that various passages were written later than the biblical texts indicated because they recounted events that happened sometimes hundreds of years after they supposedly were written. They concluded that subsequent to the events, literary editors went back and doctored the original nonpredictive texts. But this is simply wrong. Careful research *affirms* the predictive accuracy of the Scriptures. Since Christ is the culminating theme of the Old Testament and the Living Word of the New Testament, it should not surprise us that prophecies regarding him, but so it was made to appear to them . . . for of a surety they killed him not." In reality, however, the fatal suffering of Jesus Christ as recounted in the New Testament is one of the most well-established facts of ancient history. Even in today's modern age of scientific enlightenment, there is a virtual consensus among New Testament scholars, both conservative and liberal, that Jesus died on a Roman cross.

Archaeological discoveries not only dramatically corroborate the Bible's description of Roman crucifixion, but authenticate the biblical details surrounding the trial that led to the fatal torment of Jesus Christ—including the Pilate Stone and the burial grounds of Caiaphas, the high priest who presided over the religious trials of Christ. These discoveries have been widely acclaimed as compelling affirmation of biblical history. Not only so but the earliest Jewish response to the death and burial of Jesus Christ presupposes the reality of the empty tomb. Instead of denying that the tomb was empty, the antagonists of Christ accused His disciples of stealing the body.

One final point should be made. The Qur'anic denial of Christ's crucifixion has led to a host of other errors as well. From a Muslim perspective, Jesus was never crucified and, thus, never resurrected. Instead, in Islam, God made someone look like Jesus, and the look-alike was mistakenly crucified in His place. The notion that Judas was made to look like Jesus has recently been popularized in Muslim circles by a late-medieval invention titled *The Gospel of Barnabas.*

In short, the distance between the Muslim Qur'an and the Christian Scriptures is the distance of infinity. Not only does the prophetic prowess of the Bible elevate it far above the holy books of other religions, but as new archaeological nuggets are uncovered, the trustworthiness of Scripture as well as the unreliability of pretenders are further highlighted. Faulty ethics and factual errors demonstrate that the Qur'an is devoid of divine sanction. In sharp distinction, ethics and factual evidence demonstrate that the Bible is divine rather than human in origin.

> *Who is the liar but the one who denies that*
> *Jesus is the Christ? This is the antichrist, the*
> *one who denies the Father and the Son.*
>
> 1 JOHN 2:22 NASB

For further study, see Norman L. Geisler and Abdul Saleeb, *Answering Islam* (Grand Rapids: Baker Books, 2002).

What are the basic beliefs of Buddhism?

The year was 1893. The place was Chicago. Buddhists had arrived from the East to attend the inaugural World's Parliament of Religions. While their contingent was sizable, they were vastly outnumbered by Bible believers from the West. One hundred years later, at the centennial celebration of the original Parliament, Buddhists outnumbered Baptists, and saffron robes were more common than Christian clerical clothing. Given the growing impact of Buddhism, it is important to grasp basic Buddhist beliefs and use them as springboards for sharing the liberating truth of the gospel.

First, Buddhism, a historical offshoot of Hinduism, teaches adherents to seek refuge in the Three Jewels: *Buddha*, *Dharma*, and *Sangha*. To embrace the triple gem is to find refuge in Buddha, who became the "enlightened one" for this age during a deep state of meditation under a bodhi tree; to find refuge in the Buddha's teaching—*dharma*; and to find refuge in the community of Buddhist priests—*sangha*—who guide devotees along the path to enlightenment.

Furthermore, the essence of Buddhism is summed up in the Four Noble Truths: (1) all life is suffering (*dukkha*); (2) the source of suffering is desire and attachment because all is impermanent; (3) liberation from suffering is found in the elimination of desire; and (4) desire is eliminated by following the eightfold path.

Finally, the eightfold path consists of right understanding, right thought, right speech, right action, right livelihood, right effort, right awareness, and right meditation. By following this path through many reincarnations, Buddhists hope to erase karmic debt and achieve the *nirvanic* realization of "no self," thus attaining liberation from suffering and escaping the endless cycle of life, death, and rebirth (*samsara*).

In sharp contrast to the Buddhist teaching that we must eliminate desire, the Bible teaches that we must exercise disciplines in order to transform our desires (Romans 6:17–19). Ultimately, suffering is not overcome through stamping out the self, but through the selfless sacrifice of a sinless Savior.

Having been justified by faith, we have peace with God through our Lord Jesus Christ, through whom also we have access by faith into this grace in which we stand, and rejoice in hope of the glory of God. And not only that, but we also glory in tribulations, knowing that tribulation produces perseverance; and perseverance, character; and character, hope. Now hope does not disappoint,

In sharp distinction to Zen, biblical meditation calls for centering one's self on the personal Creator of the universe through a singular focus on Scripture. Far from emptying our minds, Christians seek to be filled with the Holy Spirit and transformed by the renewing of our minds.

> *Do not be conformed to this world, but be*
> *transformed by the renewing of your mind,*
> *that you may prove what is that good and*
> *acceptable and perfect will of God.*
> ROMANS 12:2 NKJV

The basics of Zen Buddhism are:

ZAZEN—**"sitting in meditation" to achieve emptiness**

ENLIGHTENMENT—**inner perception that all reality is one**

NONSENSICAL RIDDLES—**for rejecting reason and dismantling the mind**

For further study, see J. Isamu Yamamoto, "Zest for Zen: North Americans Embrace a Contemplative School of Buddhism," *Christian Research Journal* 17, 3 (1995): 8–15, available through the Christian Research Institute at www.equip.org.

What sets Christianity apart from an Eastern worldview?

lthough many people have tried to merge Eastern spirituality with biblical Christianity, the chasm that separates these worldviews is an unbridgeable gulf.

First, in an Eastern worldview, God is an impersonal force or principle. In sharp distinction, the God of Christianity is a personal Being who manifests such communicable attributes as spirituality, rationality, and morality (John 4:24; Colossians 3:10; Ephesians 4:24).

Furthermore, in an Eastern worldview, humanity's goal is to become one with nature because nature is God. In this sense, the Eastern worldview is pantheistic: God is all and all is God. Conversely, Christianity teaches that man is created in the image and likeness of his Creator and, as such, is distinct from both nature and God (Genesis 1:26–27).

Finally, in an Eastern worldview, truth is realized through intuition rather than through the cognitive thinking process. In contrast, Christianity teaches that truth is realized through revelation (Hebrews 1:1–2), which is apprehended by the intellect (Luke 1:1–4) and then embraced by the heart (Mark 12:29–31).

While the Hindu scriptures tout the hell of reincarnation, the Holy Scriptures teach the hope of resurrection. The solution to the fear of karmic reincarnation is faith in our Kinsman Redeemer.

> *Thus says the LORD, your Redeemer,*
> *And He who formed you from the womb:*
> *"I am the LORD, who makes all things,*
> *Who stretches out the heavens all alone,*
> *Who spreads abroad the earth by Myself;*
> *Who frustrates the signs of the babblers,*
> *And drives diviners mad;*
> *Who turns wise men backward,*
> *And makes their knowledge foolishness.*
> ISAIAH 44:24–25 NKJV

For further study, see "Can reincarnation and resurrection be reconciled?" (p. 348); and Dean Halverson, *The Illustrated Guide to World Religions* (Minneapolis: Bethany House Publishers, 2003).

HANK HANEGRAAFF

What is Y-O-G-A?

S ince Swami Vivekananda first introduced yoga to the West more than a hundred years ago, yoga has become as American as apple pie. According to the *Columbia Journalism Review*, "If you've been awake and breathing air in the twenty-first century, you already know that this Hindu practice of health and spirituality has long ago moved on from the toe-ring set. Yoga is American; it has graced the cover of *Time* twice, acquired the approval of A-list celebrities like Madonna, Sting, and Jennifer Aniston, and is still the go-to trend story for editors and reporters, who produce an average of eight yoga stories a day in the English-speaking world." Because of its rock-star status, I've developed the acronym Y-O-G-A to give you an easy-to-remember overview on what this practice entails.

Y OGA. The word *yoga* comes from the Sanskrit word *yogah*, which means "to yoke or to unite." As such, the goal of yoga is to uncouple oneself from the material world and to unite oneself with the God of Hinduism, commonly understood to be *Brahman*, the impersonal cosmic consciousness of the universe. Put another way, yoga is the means by which the user's mind is merged into the universal mind.

O M. The Hindu mantra *Om* is a sacred Sanskrit syllable cherished by Hindu yogis as the spoken quintessence of the universe. Repeating the mantra *Om* over and over is a principal means by which traditional

Does the Bible *really* teach reincarnation?

Reincarnation—literally "rebirth in another body"—has long been considered a universal law of life in the Eastern world. Tragically, today in the West, many people believe it to be backed by the Bible. The words of Jeremiah, John, and Jesus are typically cited as irrefutable evidence. A quick look at these Scripture passages within their context, however, reveals that they have nothing whatsoever to do with reincarnation.

First, in Jeremiah, God allegedly told His prophet that He knew him as the result of a prior incarnation: "Before I formed you in the womb I knew you, before you were born I set you apart; I appointed you as a prophet to the nations" (Jeremiah 1:5). In reality, far from suggesting that His prophet had existed in a prior incarnation, Jeremiah underscored the reality that the One who exists from all eternity preordained Jeremiah as "a prophet to the nations."

Furthermore, in John's gospel, the disciples allegedly wonder whether a man born blind is paying off karmic debt for himself or for his parents (cf. John 9:1–2). The gospel of John dispels this notion by overtly stating that the man's blindness had nothing to do with either his sin or that of his parents (John 9:3). If indeed the man were suffering karmic payback for past indiscretions, Jesus would have violated the law of karma by healing him.

Finally, Jesus Himself is cited as suggesting that Elijah was reincarnated as John the Baptist (cf. Matthew 11:14). This tired tale is explicitly dismissed by Scripture itself. When the priests and the Levites asked John if he was Elijah, he replied, "I am not" (John 1:21). In context, Elijah and John are not said to be two incarnations of the same *person*, but rather two separate people who function in a strikingly similar *prophetic* role. Or as Luke put it, John came "in the spirit and power of Elijah" (1:17).

One thing is certain! Reincarnation is completely foreign to the teachings of Scripture.

> *"Do not marvel at this; for the hour is coming
> in which all who are in the graves will hear His
> voice and come forth—those who have done good,
> to the resurrection of life, and those who have
> done evil, to the resurrection of condemnation."*
>
> JOHN 5:28–29 NKJV

For further study, see "Can reincarnation and resurrection be reconciled?" (p. 348).

What is the New Age movement?

Not everyone who wears a cross is a Christian. Likewise, not everyone who owns a crystal is a New Ager. To accurately identify New Agers, we must move beyond superficial symbols such as crystals, unicorns, and rainbows to identify their beliefs and practices.

First, New Agers hold to pantheistic monism: in their view, God is all, all is God, and all is one. Additionally, they believe that the universe operates under the law of karma and its corollary, the doctrine of reincarnation.

Furthermore, the goal of New Agers is to spiritually evolve and tap into their human potential through the help of "ascended masters" or spirit guides. To attain such enlightenment, New Agers engage in occult practices such as astrology, magic, psychic healing, out-of-body experiences, and meditation. In New Age meditation, the goal is to stamp out the self and to become one with the impersonal cosmic consciousness of the universe. In sharp contrast, biblical meditation calls for centering one's self on the personal Creator of the universe through a singular focus on Scripture (Joshua 1:8).

Finally, New Agers share the vision of a coming "age of Aquarius" that will be marked by global peace, prosperity, and planetary transformation. Their ultimate goal is encapsulated in such catchphrases as *global village* and *planetary consciousness*. Far from being a monolith, however, the New Age movement is a multifaceted amorphous network of organizations such as Planetary Initiative for the World, Divine Light Mission, and Self-Realization Fellowship, loosely linked yet autonomous.

> *When you come into the land which the LORD your God is giving you, you shall not learn to follow the abominations of those nations. There shall not be found among you anyone who makes his son or his daughter pass through the fire, or one who practices witchcraft, or a soothsayer, or one who interprets omens, or a sorcerer, or one who conjures spells, or a medium, or a spiritist, or one who calls up the dead. For all who do these things are an abomination to the LORD, and because of these abominations the LORD your God drives them out from before you. You shall be blameless before the LORD your God.*
>
> DEUTERONOMY 18:9–13 NKJV

For further study, see Douglas R. Groothuis, *Unmasking the New Age* (Downers Grove, IL: InterVarsity Press, 1986); for a comprehensive work, see Elliot Miller, *A Crash Course on The New Age Movement* (Grand Rapids: Baker Book House, 1989).

Let now the astrologers, the stargazers,
And the monthly prognosticators
Stand up and save you
From what shall come upon you.
Behold, they shall be as stubble,
The fire shall burn them;
They shall not deliver themselves
From the power of the flame. . . .
They shall wander each one to his quarter.
No one shall save you.

ISAIAH 47:13–15 NKJV

For further study, see Charles R. Strohmer, *America's Fascination with Astrology: Is it Healthy?* (Greenville, SC: Emerald House, 1998).

What is Scientology? (T-E-A-R-S)

The Church of Scientology was founded in the 1950s by science fiction author L. Ron Hubbard. Since its inception, Scientology has emerged as one of the most socially influential, financially powerful, and decidedly controversial religions of the twenty-first century. Devotees range from liberal Hollywood personalities such as Tom Cruise to Fox News icon Greta Van Susteren. Yet behind the glitz and glamor, Scientology has left a veritable trail of T-E-A-R-S that, ironically, provides a helpful way of remembering its tenets.

THETANS. Scientology teaches that humans are immortal thetans trapped in a physical universe of their own mental construction. As such, humans are not sinners in need of a Savior, but immortal beings who must overcome enslaving engrams.

ENGRAMS. In the pseudoscience of Scientology, all human failings are traceable to engrams—subconscious memories of past negative experiences lurking in our "reactive minds." In *Dianetics: The Modern Science of Mental Health*, Hubbard described engrams as the cause of unhappiness, sickness, depression, and other psychological and physical maladies.

What is the occult?

While the word *occult* (from the Latin *occultus*) literally means "hidden" or "secret," the world of the occult is clearly out of the closet. It has been glamorized as New Age, but its genesis is as old age as the hiss of the serpent: "Your eyes will be opened, and you will be like God, knowing good and evil" (Genesis 3:5). The objective of occultism is self-deification through sorcery, spiritism, and soothsaying.

First, through sorcery (magick), occultists seek to harness paranormal powers for private purposes. Using ritualistic formulas, spells, and incantations, occultists seek to harness what they perceive to be the natural and spiritual powers of the universe in order to satisfy their own desires. God warned the ancient Israelites that these very practices would inevitably lead to their downfall (Deuteronomy 18:9–14; cf. 2 Kings 17:16–18). Likewise, He rebuked the ancient Babylonians for supposing that they could bypass His power through their "many sorceries" and "potent spells" (Isaiah 47:8–15).

Furthermore, occultists employ spiritualistic practices (mediumship) in order to contact nonphysical entities, including the souls of the dead. These spirits are believed to be capable of providing cosmic insights into this world and the next. As such, spiritists employ Ouija boards, crystal balls, and the belongings of the dead to conjure up the departed. God's warning against those who practice spiritism could not be more ominous or direct: "I will set my face against the person who turns to mediums and spiritists to prostitute himself by following them, and I will cut him off from his people" (Leviticus 20:6; cf. 19:31; 1 Chronicles 10:13–14; Isaiah 8:19).

Finally, occultists seek to access secret or hidden information about the future through soothsaying (divination). Among the most common tools of the soothsayer are Tarot cards, astrological charts, horoscopes, and tea leaves. The Lord's command is emphatic and explicit: "Do not practice divination" (Leviticus 19:26). Indeed, a tremendous insult to the power and providence of the Almighty is to seek guidance through the occult. Thus, when the Israelites were about to enter the land of promise, the Lord warned them not to imitate the detestable ways of the nations there: "Let no one be found among you who sacrifices his son or daughter in the fire, who practices divination or sorcery, interprets omens, engages in witchcraft, or casts spells, or who is a medium or spiritist or who consults the dead. Anyone who does these things is detestable to the LORD" (Deuteronomy 18:10–12; cf. Acts 13:6–11; 16:16–18; Galatians 5:19–21).

What is wrong with Wicca?

Wicca is a neopagan, earth-centered religion that has its modern origins in the teaching and practice of the original English Wiccan, Gerald Gardner (1884–1964). Over the past few decades, Wicca has experienced dramatic growth as teens reject what they perceive as Christian paternalism, homophobia, and insensitivity to the environment. While stereotypes of Wiccans as Satanists or sinister spell-casters are spurious, the worldviews of Christianity and Wicca are nonetheless worlds apart.

First, Wicca—also known as "The Craft" or "The Old Religion"—holds that all reality is divine. Thus, Wiccans revere the natural world as a living, breathing organism, and they revere people as "gods" and "goddesses." Since Wicca is a distinctively feminist form of neopaganism, however, Wiccans often consider the supreme manifestation of deity to be a nature goddess (such as the Triple Goddess of the Moon). In sharp contrast to the Christian worldview, Wiccans worship creation rather than the Creator (cf. Romans 1:25). While the Bible does teach that people should care for the environment (Genesis 2:15; Deuteronomy 20:19–20; Psalm 115:16) and appreciate its magnificence (Psalm 19; Matthew 6:28–30), our worship belongs only to the Creator whose glory is reflected in creation (Job 38–41; Psalm 148; Romans 1).

Furthermore, the supreme ethical rule of Wicca is the Wiccan Rede: "If it harms none, do as ye Will." Despite this proscription against harming others, Wiccans hold that moral and religious truths are ultimately relative. Thus, while the Wiccan Rede sets the Craft apart from the malevolent activities of Satanists, the Wiccan worldview stands in direct opposition to the biblical notions of absolute moral truth and exclusive salvation through Jesus Christ who alone is "the way and the truth and the life" (John 14:6).

Finally, Wiccans practice magick (spelled with a *k* to differentiate it from conjuring for entertainment) in an attempt to manipulate the natural world and alter mental and material conditions. As such, Wicca is an esoteric occult practice designed to manipulate reality in concert with the Wiccan's will. Tools of the Craft include swords and spell books, as well as chalices, censers, cords, and crystals. Regardless of whether the motivation is benevolent or malevolent, Scripture unequivocally condemns all occult practices as detestable to the Lord (Deuteronomy 18:10–12; Acts 13:6–11; 16:16–18; Galatians 5:19–21).

Spirit's descent on Pentecost Sunday. Additionally, while Ellen White (1827–1915) claimed divine authority for her prophecies, she was obviously wrong when she prophesied that she would be alive at the second coming of Christ.

> *There remains therefore a rest for the people of God. For he who has entered His rest has himself also ceased from his works as God did from His.*
>
> HEBREWS 4:9–10 NKJV

For further study, "Why do Christians worship on Sunday rather than on the Sabbath day?" (p. 404); "Is soul sleep biblical?" (p. 544); and "Is there evidence for life after death?" (p. 75).

What's the difference between Orthodoxy and Catholicism?

F or the first millennium of church history, there was essentially one orthodox New Testament faith rooted in seven ancient ecumenical councils. This may well have remained so had it not been for the Bishop of Rome assuming dominance and, apart from an ecumenical council, altering the universal creed of the church. Since the Great Schism (1054), Catholicism has deviated from Orthodoxy in at least three significant ways.

First, Roman Catholicism forwards the notion that in the intermediate state after death, there are certain sins that can be atoned for by way of temporal punishment in purgatory. Orthodoxy considers the notion of purgation—defined by the Council of Florence (fifteenth century) and defended by the Council of Trent (sixteenth century)—to be a late innovation lacking precedence in both Scripture and the teachings of the Fathers. In distinction to the Catholic idea of purgatory, the Orthodox community views the intermediate state as a foretaste of either eternal reward or eternal punishment, both of which are ultimately fixed on the Day of Judgment.

Furthermore, Catholicism and Orthodoxy are divided on the

Should Christians judge the teachings of their leaders?

Not only is judging permissible, it is our responsibility. Nobody's teachings are above sound judgment—especially those of influential leaders! Biblically, authority and accountability go hand in hand (cf. Luke 12:48). The greater the responsibility one holds, the greater the accountability (cf. James 3:1).

First, the precedent for making right judgments comes from Scripture itself. In the Old Testament, the Israelites were commanded to practice sound judgment by thoroughly testing the teachings of their leaders (Deuteronomy 13). Similarly, in the New Testament, the apostle Paul commanded the Thessalonians to test all things and to hold fast to that which is good (1 Thessalonians 5:21–22). Moreover, Paul lauded the Bereans for testing his teachings (Acts 17:11).

Furthermore, while our Lord cautioned followers not to judge self-righteously (Matthew 7:1–5), He also counseled them to make judgments based on right standards (John 7:24). In the context of His oft-misquoted command "Judge not, or you too will be judged" (Matthew 7:1), Jesus exhorted us to judge false prophets, whose teachings and behavior lead people astray (vv. 15–20). Thus, while we are commanded not to judge hypocritically, we are nevertheless called to judge.

Finally, common sense should be sufficient to alert us to the importance of making public as well as private judgments regarding false doctrine. During the infamous Tylenol scare in 1982, public warnings were issued by the media and the medical community regarding the physical danger of ingesting Tylenol capsules that someone had laced with cyanide. In similar fashion, when spiritual cyanide is dispensed within the Christian community, we are duty-bound to warn the public. As such, Paul publicly rebuked Hymenaeus and Philetus, whose teachings "spread like gangrene" (2 Timothy 2:17–18; cf. Galatians 2:11–14).

> *"Do not judge according to appearance,*
> *but judge with righteous judgment."*
>
> JOHN 7:24 NKJV

For further study, see Hank Hanegraaff, "The Untouchables: Are 'God's Anointed' Beyond Criticism?" and Bob and Gretchen Passantino, "Christians Criticizing Christians: Can It Be Biblical?" both available through the Christian Research Institute at www.equip.org.

robe." Hagee is so committed to presenting a Jesus who wears a Rolex that he is willing to do whatever it takes to sell this myth to parishioners. "What's the good news to the poor?" asks Hagee. "The curse of poverty has been broken at the cross. If you have the anointing, you don't have the curse of poverty. If you will practice the principles of prosperity in the Word of God, God will make you the head, not the tail." If Hagee and company are right, if prosperity is indeed a promise and poverty a curse, the apostle Paul would have been among the most cursed of all men. Yet far from being cursed, Paul was content: "I have learned the secret of being content in any and every situation, whether well fed or hungry, whether living in plenty or in want" (Philippians 4:12).

SICKNESS AND SUFFERING. Kenneth Hagin, the father of the Word of Faith movement, may have boasted that he had not had a headache, the flu, or even "one sick day" in nearly sixty years, yet he suffered at least four cardiovascular crises, including one full-scale heart stoppage. In the end, he experienced the reality that the death rate is one per person. Absent the descent of our Savior, we are all going to physically die. Some time ago I received a letter from a woman whose brother-in-law had enrolled in Kenneth Hagin's Rhema Bible Training Center. While there, his wife contracted ovarian cancer. Rather than seeking medical attention, the couple denied the symptoms of cancer. Predictably, she died. Tragically, her Faith friends resorted to regurgitating the standard line of the health and wealth gospel: the woman had not been healed due to her lack of faith. Who knows what untold tragedies testify to the devastation that follows in the wake of the Word of Faith crowd.

In part adapted from *Christianity in Crisis: 21st Century*

> *"These things I have spoken to you, that*
> *in Me you may have peace. In the world*
> *you will have tribulation; but be of good*
> *cheer, I have overcome the world."*

John 16:33 NKJV

FAITH FORCE
LITTLE GOD
ATONEMENT ATROCITIES
WEALTH AND WANT
SICKNESS AND SUFFERING

For further study, see Hank Hanegraaff, *Christianity in Crisis: 21st Century* (Nashville: Thomas Nelson, 2009).

Is being slain in the Spirit consistent with a biblical worldview?

oday thousands of people are routinely being slain in the Spirit as a fashionable and palpable demonstration of Holy Ghost power. Practitioners claim ample validation for this phenomenon in Scripture, church history, and experience. However, the phenomenon not only is conspicuous by its absence in the ministry of Jesus and the apostles, but it is also generally inconsistent with a biblical worldview.

First, as aptly noted by pro-Pentecostal sources such as *The Dictionary of Pentecostal and Charismatic Movements* (*DPCM*), "An entire battalion of Scripture proof texts is enlisted to support the legitimacy of the phenomenon, although Scripture plainly offers no support for the phenomenon as something to be expected in the normal Christian life."

Furthermore, the experience of being slain in the Spirit can be attributed to mere human manipulation. According to the *DPCM*, "in addition to God, the source of the experience can be a purely human response to autosuggestion, group 'peer pressure,' or simply a desire to experience the phenomenon." Cynics may write off the use of altered states of consciousness, peer pressure, expectations, and suggestive powers as mere sociopsychological manipulation, but Christians must perceive an even more significant threat: these techniques are fertile soil for satanic and spiritual deception.

Finally, the slain-in-the-spirit phenomenon has more in common with occultism than with a biblical worldview. As popular slain-in-the-spirit practitioner Francis MacNutt candidly confesses in his book *Overcome by the Spirit*, the phenomenon is externally similar to "manifestations of voodoo and other magic rites" and is "found today among different sects in the Orient as well as among primitive tribes of Africa and Latin America." In sharp contrast, Scripture makes it clear that as Christians we must be "self-controlled and alert" (1 Peter 5:8) rather than being in an altered state of consciousness or slain in the Spirit.

Adapted from *Counterfeit Revival*

Be sober, be vigilant; because your adversary the devil walks about like a roaring lion, seeking whom he may devour. Resist him, steadfast in the faith.
1 PETER 5:8–9 NKJV

For further study, see Hank Hanegraaff, *Counterfeit Revival: Looking for God in All the Wrong Places*, rev. ed. (Nashville: Word Publishing, 2001).

Ghost, in reality it has much more in common with Hindu gurus and hucksters who employ sociopsychological manipulation tactics in order to dupe devotees. The *Dictionary of Pentecostals and Charismatic Movements* candidly notes that "an entire battalion of Scripture proof texts is enlisted to support the legitimacy of the phenomenon, although Scripture plainly offers no support for the phenomenon as something to be expected in the normal Christian life." Despite the pious attribution of this phenomenon to the Holy Spirit as well as the pragmatic addition of "catchers," multitudes continue to suffer spiritual, emotional, and physical damage from this practice. Some have even died. While the counterfeit revival is fixated on sensational manifestations, genuine revival is focused on salvation and sanctification in the Spirit.

HYPNOTISM. What was once relegated to the ashrams of cults is now replicated at the altars of churches. Whether they are referred to as Hindu gurus or Holy Ghost bartenders, the methods they employ have much in common. They work subjects into altered states of consciousness, use peer pressure to conform them to predictable patterns, depend heavily on arousing people's expectations, and, by the power of suggestion, make subjects willing to accept virtually anything that enters their minds. Cynics may write off the use of altered states of consciousness, peer pressure, expectations, and suggestive powers as mere sociopsychological manipulation, but Christians must perceive an even more significant threat—these techniques are fertile soil for satanic and spiritual deception. While leaders of the Counterfeit Revival enslave devotees through hypnotic schemes, leaders of genuine revival enlighten disciples through Holy Scripture.

While multitudes clamor for a massive *revival*, what the body of Christ desperately needs is a mighty *reformation*. Only as the church is reformed will the culture be revived. The real experience is not found in the works of the F-L-E-S-H; rather, it is found in the fundamentals of the faith.

> *Be on guard for yourselves and for all the flock, among*
> *which the Holy Spirit has made you overseers, to*
> *shepherd the church of God which He purchased with*
> *His own blood. I know that after my departure savage*
> *wolves will come in among you, not sparing the*
> *flock; and from among your own selves men will arise,*
> *speaking perverse things, to draw away the disciples*
> *after them. Therefore be on the alert, remembering*
> *that night and day for a period of three years I*
> *did not cease to admonish each one with tears.*
>
> ACTS 20:28–31 NASB

FABRICATIONS, FANTASIES, AND FRAUDS
LYING SIGNS AND WONDERS
END-TIME RESTORATIONISM
SLAIN IN THE SPIRIT
HYPNOTISM

For further study, see Hank Hanegraaff, *Counterfeit Revival*, rev. ed. (Nashville: Word Publishing Group, 2001).

Are Bible codes credible?

A significant number of Christian leaders today hail Bible codes as important evidence for the inspiration of Scripture. While they claim post-prophecies such as Israeli prime minister Yitzhak Rabin's assassination in 1995 are encoded in the biblical text, Bible codes, in reality, are little more than a fringe variety of Jewish mysticism repackaged for Christian consumption.

First, like its older permutation Bible numerics, Bible codes are at best a pseudoscience. Codes are "discovered" by searching for equidistant letter sequences (ELS) that can be compiled into intelligible messages pertaining to past events. One can search left to right, right to left, top to bottom, bottom to top, or in diagonal directions. Although sequencing can vary from word to word, none of the prophecies can be known *beforehand*. Like Monday-morning quarterbacking, hindsight is always perfect.

Furthermore, Bible codes are a rigged game complete with after-the-fact prophecies and self-validating messages. While ELS practitioners contend such historical events as the assassination of Rabin are encoded in the Torah, nothing could be further from the truth. Because Old Testament Hebrew does not contain vowels, an alleged code such as "Rabin Bang Bang" could just as easily refer to Christopher Robin's shooting his pop gun at the balloons Winnie the Pooh was holding when he floated over the Hundred Acre Wood ("Robin Bang Bang"). For that matter, the self-validating message could refer to the tire blowout that Batman's sidekick Robin experienced while riding in the Batmobile. It could even refer to a Mafia hitman named Robino who had two successful kills—bang, bang.

Finally, although the message of the *autographa* (the original texts of the Bible) is unquestionably clear in the best available manuscript copies, minor differences in spelling and style make it impossible to validate the supposed divine inspiration of equidistant letter sequencing. Such minor inconsistencies leave the meaning unaltered but completely undermine all attempts to find equidistant letter sequences. Moreover, the coincidences of equidistant letter sequences that do occur in the Torah are not unique. They occur in every other work of literature from Homer to Hobbes and from Tolkien to Tolstoy.

Bible codes shift the focus of biblical apologetics from the essential core of the gospel to esoteric speculations. Those who deny the incontrovertible evidence that Jesus rose from the dead are not likely to be persuaded by the pseudo-apologetic of Bible codes.

to mastering genuine apologetic arguments. Every Christian should be equipped to communicate the evidence that God created the universe, that Jesus Christ demonstrated that He was God through the immutable fact of His resurrection, and that the Bible is divine rather than merely human in origin.

> *God said, "Let there be lights in the firmament of*
> *the heavens to divide the day from the night; and let*
> *them be for signs and seasons, and for days and years;*
> *and let them be for lights in the firmament of the*
> *heavens to give light on the earth"; and it was so.*
>
> GENESIS 1:14–15 NKJV

For further study, see "What is wrong with astrology" (p. 352); see also Charles Strohmer, "Is There a Christian Zodiac, a Gospel in the Stars?" *Christian Research Journal* 22, 4 (2000), available through the Christian Research Institute at www.equip.org.

Did Darwin have a deathbed conversion?

I n order to demonstrate the falsity of evolution, Bible-believing Christians for more than a century have passed on the story of Charles Darwin's deathbed conversion. Evolutionists have attempted to counter them by loudly protesting that Darwin died believing that Christianity was a fraud and that chance was the Creator.

In response, it should first be noted that whether Darwin did or did not renounce evolution does *not* speak to the issue of whether or not evolution is true or false. Maybe Darwin renounced evolution because he was senile or he had taken a mind-altering drug. He may have even just hedged his bets with some "eternal fire insurance."

Furthermore, as followers of the One who proclaimed Himself not only "the way" and "the life" but also "the truth" (John 14:6), we must set the standard for the evolutionist, *not* vice versa. James Fegan, an acquaintance of Darwin, was correct in calling the Darwin legend "an illustration of the recklessness with which the Protestant Controversialists seek to support any cause they are advocating."

Finally, in *The Darwin Legend*, James Moore painstakingly

Should Christians celebrate Christmas?

Every year around Christmas time, serious concerns are voiced regarding the validity of celebrating Christmas. Some people note that the origins of Christmas are pagan, others point out that the Bible overtly denounces Christmas trees as idolatrous, and still others suggest that Santa Claus is a dangerous fairy tale.

First, let me acknowledge that when Christmas was originally instituted, December 25 was indeed a pagan festival commemorating the birthday of a false god. This is historical fact, but what is frequently overlooked is that the church's choice of December 25 was intentional. Instead of Christianizing a pagan festival, the church established a rival celebration. While the world has all but forgotten the Greco-Roman gods of antiquity, they are annually reminded that two thousand years ago Christ invaded time and space.

Furthermore, the Bible nowhere condemns Christmas trees as idolatrous. The oft-cited passage in Jeremiah 10:2–4 might at first glance appear compelling support for this idea, but context precludes the pretext. Jeremiah's description of a tree chopped down in a forest, adorned with silver and gold, and fastened with a hammer and nails so that it would not totter is a reference to wooden idols, not Christmas trees. In fact, Christmas trees originated in

Christian Germany two thousand years after Jeremiah's condemnation of man-made idols. They evolved over time from two Christian traditions. One was a "Paradise tree" hung with apples as a reminder of the tree of life in the garden of Eden. The other was a triangular shelf holding Christmas figurines decorated by a star. In the sixteenth century, these two symbols merged into the present Christmas tree tradition. Next Christmas you might well consider using the Christmas tree in an unbeliever's home as a springboard or opportunity to explain the reason for the season, from the fall in Paradise to redemption in Christ.

Finally, believe it or not, Santa can be saved! Far from merely being a dangerous fairy tale, *Santa Claus* is, in reality, an Anglicized form of the Dutch name *Sinter Klaas*, which in turn is a reference to the real-life Saint Nicholas. According to tradition, Saint Nick not only lavished gifts on needy children but also valiantly supported the doctrine of the Trinity at the Council of Nicea in AD 325. Thus, Christians may legitimately look to Saint Nick as a genuine hero of the faith.

This December 25 as you celebrate the coming of Christ with a Christmas tree surrounded by presents, may the selflessness of Saint Nick be a reminder of the Savior who gave the greatest gift of all: "Greater love has no one than this, that one lay down his life for his friends" (John 15:13 NASB).

*Now there were in the same country shepherds living
out in the fields, keeping watch over their flock
by night. And behold, an angel of the Lord stood
before them, and the glory of the Lord shone around
them, and they were greatly afraid. Then the angel
said to them, "Do not be afraid, for behold, I bring
you good tidings of great joy which will be to all
people. For there is born to you this day in the city
of David a Savior, who is Christ the Lord. And
this will be the sign to you: You will find a Babe
wrapped in swaddling cloths, lying in a manger."*

*And suddenly there was with the angel a multitude
of the heavenly host praising God and saying:*

*"Glory to God in the highest,
And on earth peace, goodwill toward men!"*

Luke 2:8–14 nkjv

For further study, see Paul Maier, *The First Christmas* (Grand Rapids: Kregel Publications, 2001).

What about Easter celebrations?

While Christmas is commonly regarded as the high-light of the Christian calendar, it is Easter that deserves our utmost consideration. Without the resurrection of Jesus, there is little point in discussing His birth. "If Christ has not been raised," said Paul, "our preaching is useless and so is your faith" (1 Corinthians 15:14). Thus, the body of Christ annually initiates its resurrection celebration on Clean Monday (in the East) or Ash Wednesday (in the West). Thereafter Christians engage in the forty days of Lent, culminating in Holy Week.

The first day of the Great Lent initiates a spirit of repentance and forgiveness. As the Orthodox sing, "The springtime of the Fast has dawned; the flower of repentance has begun to open." Western Christians in turn inaugurate the day of ashes by marking their foreheads with the sign of the cross. As Daniel did, they turn to the Lord God, pleading with Him "in prayer and petition, in fasting, and in sackcloth and ashes" (Daniel 9:3).

Furthermore, during Easter, Christians celebrate the Great Lent itself. This is forty days (not including the Lord's Day on which His glorious resurrection is remembered) during which there is a rekindled devotion to the principles of the kingdom—including prayer, fasting, and almsgiving; repentance leading to forgiveness; and recommitment to loving the Lord our God with all our heart and mind and loving our neighbor as ourself. All of this together is but preparation for the feast of Christ's resurrection, which in turn is emblematic of our being raised with Him in newness of life on the day of His second appearing.

Finally, Easter is the commemoration of Holy Week beginning with Palm Sunday, which memorializes Jesus' triumphal entry into Jerusalem. On Maundy Thursday (*Mandatum novum do vobis*, "a new commandment I give you"), Christians pray, partake of communion, and even wash one another's feet in humble obedience to the command of Christ: "As I have loved you, so you must love one another" (John 13:34). Good Friday is a time of somber reflection on Christ's death and burial—a remembrance that our Lord suffered on the cross more than any human, more than the cumulative sufferings of all humanity, so that we might experience life "to the full" (John 10:10). On Saturday evening or early Sunday morning, Christians worldwide gather in glorious certainty that as the sun dawns in the east, so the Son of glory has risen from the dead.

Easter traditionally culminates with a congregational feast in joyous expectation of the wedding supper of the Lamb. There is no wedding without a bridegroom, no redemption apart from the risen Redeemer, and no renewal of cosmos and creature apart from resurrection. And "blessed are those who are invited to the wedding supper of the Lamb!" (Revelation 19:9).

> *If there is no resurrection of the dead, then Christ is not risen. And if Christ is not risen, then our preaching is empty and your faith is also empty. Yes, and we are found false witnesses of God, because we have testified of God that He raised up Christ, whom He did not raise up—if in fact the dead do not rise. For if the dead do not rise, then Christ is not risen. And if Christ is not risen, your faith is futile; you are still in your sins! Then also those who have fallen asleep in Christ have perished. If in this life only we have hope in Christ, we are of all men the most pitiable.*
>
> *But now Christ is risen from the dead, and has become the firstfruits of those who have fallen asleep.*
>
> 1 CORINTHIANS 15:13–20 NKJV

For further study, see "Resurrection: What are memorable keys to the greatest F-E-A-T in history?" (pp. 251–254).

Why do Christians worship on Sunday rather than on the Sabbath day?

A lthough some Christian traditions denounce Sunday worship as the end time "mark of the Beast," there are good reasons why millions of Christians gather on the first day of the week for worship.

First, in remembrance of the resurrection, the early Christian church changed the day of worship from Saturday to Sunday. Within weeks, thousands of Jews willingly gave up a theological tradition that had given them their national identity. God Himself had provided the early church a new pattern of worship with Christ's resurrection on the first day of the week as well as with the Holy Spirit's descent on Pentecost Sunday.

Furthermore, Scripture provides us with the reasons behind the symbol of the Sabbath. In Genesis, the Sabbath was a celebration of God's completed work in creation (Genesis 2:2–3; Exodus 20:11). After the Exodus, the Sabbath expanded to a celebration of God's deliverance from oppression in Egypt (Deuteronomy 5:15). As a result of Jesus' resurrection, the Sabbath's emphasis shifted once again. It became a celebration of the rest we have through Christ who delivers us from sin and the grave (Hebrews 4:1–11). For the emerging Christian church, the most dangerous snare was a failure to recognize that Jesus was the substance that fulfilled the symbol of the Sabbath.

Finally, if you insist on being slavishly bound to Old Testament laws, you should also be forewarned that failing to keep the letter of the law might be hazardous to your health. According to the Mosaic law, anyone who does any work on the Sabbath "must be put to death" (Exodus 35:2). As the apostle Paul explained, however, "Christ redeemed us from the curse of the law by becoming a curse for us, for it is written: 'Cursed is everyone who is hung on a tree'" (Galatians 3:13). The Sabbath was "a shadow of the things that were to come; the reality, however, is found in Christ" (Colossians 2:17). In the end, religious rites must inevitably bow to redemptive realities.

> *Let no one judge you in food or in drink,*
> *or regarding a festival or a new moon or*
> *sabbaths, which are a shadow of things to*
> *come, but the substance is of Christ.*
> Colossians 2:16–17 NKJV

For further study, see D. A. Carson, ed., *From Sabbath to Lord's Day: A Biblical, Historical, and Theological Investigation* (Eugene, OR: Wipf and Stock Publishers, 1999, originally published by Zondervan, 1982).

Is it ever morally permissible to lie?

In the interest of truth, I should first disclose the fact that Christian theologians are divided on this subject. Some—like Saint Augustine—believe that it is never permissible to lie. Others—like Dietrich Bonhoeffer, who had ample time to contemplate this issue from the perspective of a Nazi prison cell—hold that under certain circumstances lying is not only morally permissible but morally mandated. Thus, Bonhoeffer advocated deceiving the enemy in circumstances of war, and he had no compunction about lying in order to facilitate escape for Jews facing extermination.

Furthermore, while the Bible never condones lying *qua* lying (lying for the sake of lying), it does condone lying in order to preserve a higher moral imperative. For example, Rahab purposed to deceive (the lesser moral law) in order to preserve the lives of two Jewish spies (the higher moral law). Likewise, a Christian father today should not hesitate to lie in order to protect his wife and daughters from the imminent threat of rape or murder.

Finally, there is a difference between *lying* and *not telling the truth*. This is not merely a matter of semantics; it is a matter of substance. By way of analogy, there is a difference between unjustified and justified homicide. Murder is unjustified homicide and is always wrong. Not every instance of killing a person, however, is murder. Capital punishment and self-defense occasion justified homicide. Similarly, in the case of a lie (Ananias and Sapphira, Acts 5) there is an unjustified discrepancy between what you believe and what you say, so *lying* is always wrong. But *not telling the truth* in order to preserve a higher moral law (Rahab, Joshua 2) may well be the right thing to do and thus is not actually a lie.

> *The king of Jericho sent to Rahab, saying, "Bring out the men who have come to you, who have entered your house, for they have come to search out all the country."*
>
> *Then the woman took the two men and hid them. So she said, "Yes, the men came to me, but I did not know where they were from. And it happened as the gate was being shut, when it was dark, that the men went out. Where the men went I do not know; pursue them quickly, for you may overtake them." (But she had brought them up to the roof and hidden them with the stalks of flax, which she had laid in order on the roof.)*
>
> JOSHUA 2:3–6 NKJV

For further study, see Norman L. Geisler, *Christian Ethics: Options and Issues* (Grand Rapids: Baker Book House, 1989), chapter 7.

Is capital punishment biblical?

Christians who believe in capital punishment and those who do not both use the Bible to buttress their beliefs. So what does the Bible really teach regarding capital punishment?

To begin with, it should be noted that in the very first book of the Bible, God clearly communicates His position on capital punishment: "Whoever sheds the blood of man, by man shall his blood be shed; for in the image of God has God made man" (Genesis 9:6). It is instructive to note that this passage not only predates the Mosaic law, but it demands universal adherence to the sanctity of life.

Furthermore, in Exodus 21 and Deuteronomy 19, the Bible reaffirms God's perspective on capital punishment by underscoring the principle of life for life. To murder a person who is made in the image of God is not only to show contempt for the apex of God's creation but also to show contempt for the Creator Himself. Thus, while capital punishment may be reprehensible from a secular perspective, it is basic to a biblical worldview.

Finally, capital punishment is implicitly validated in the New Testament. Jesus acknowledged the legitimacy of capital punishment before Pilate (John 19:11), as did the apostle Paul before the Roman governor Festus (Acts 25:11). Not only so, but one of the thieves crucified with Christ had the candor to confess, "We are punished justly, for we are getting what our deeds deserve" (Luke 23:41). Moreover, Romans 13 implies that the failure of the governing authorities to apply the "sword"—the Roman symbol for capital punishment—exalts evil and eradicates equity.

In short, God instituted capital punishment in the earliest stages of human civilization before the Mosaic law, and capital punishment is never abrogated by Jesus or the apostles. Thus, capital punishment appears to be an enduring moral principle undergirding the sanctity of life.

> *Surely for your lifeblood I will demand a reckoning; from the hand of every beast I will require it, and from the hand of man. From the hand of every man's brother I will require the life of man.*
>
> *"Whoever sheds man's blood,*
> *By man his blood shall be shed;*
> *For in the image of God*
> *He made man."*
>
> GENESIS 9:5–6 NKJV

For further study, see Hank Hanegraaff, "Karla Faye Tucker and Capital Punishment," available from the Christian Research Institute at www.equip.org; see also J. Daryl Charles, "Sentiments as Social Justice: The Ethics of Capital Punishment," *Christian Research Journal*, Spring/Summer 1994.

Is euthanasia ever permissible?

Organizations such as the Hemlock Society are aggressively seeking to legalize euthanasia (Greek: *eu* = good; *thanatos* = death). In their view, "mercy murders" for the diseased, disabled, and dying are a step into the light. From a Christian perspective it is a step into the dark.

First, in Christian theology the timing and terms of death are the province of God alone (Deuteronomy 32:39). As such, a doctor is never permitted to usurp the prerogative of Deity. Hastening death based on subjective judgments concerning one's quality of life is a direct violation of Scripture (cf. Genesis 9:6; Exodus 20:13). While passive euthanasia is morally permissible in that it allows the process of dying to run its natural course, active euthanasia is morally prohibited because it directly involves the taking of human life.

Furthermore, from a biblical perspective, suffering "produces perseverance; perseverance, character; and character, hope" (Romans 5:3–4). Like suffering for our faith, physical suffering has redemptive value. It may be likened unto a furnace that rids us of the dross and fashions us more and more like unto our Lord. In the words of Charles Haddon Spurgeon, "I am certain that I never grew in grace one half as much anywhere as I have on the bed of pain." Or, as C. S. Lewis put it, "God whispers to us in our pleasures, speaks in our conscience, but shouts in our pains: it is his megaphone to rouse a deaf world." This, of course, is not to say that there is virtue in needless suffering. To mitigate suffering through the modern medical miracle of pain management is consistent with both the Hippocratic Oath and biblical morality.

Finally, permitting voluntary active euthanasia opens the door to the greater evil of non-voluntary euthanasia. It is not difficult to imagine financial pressures coercing the diseased, disabled, and dying to surrender to doctor-assisted suicide so as not to burden their families. Worse still, doctors and nursing-home directors may take it upon themselves to euthanize patients without their consent and without the family's knowledge (*crypthanasia* = "hidden death"). There is ample evidence that this is already occurring at an alarming rate in places like the Netherlands where euthanasia has slid down the slippery slope into crypthanasia.

Cultural thanatologists may urge us to accept death as a friend, but Christian theology sees death as the enemy. We are not called to come to peaceful terms with death; we are called to overcome death through resurrection. As my father told me in the final stages of his life, "Hank, though painful, every moment is precious."

problem resurrecting the cremated, cremation does not point to the resurrection of God.

Adapted from *Resurrection*

> *We were buried with Him through baptism*
> *into death, that just as Christ was raised from*
> *the dead by the glory of the Father, even so*
> *we also should walk in newness of life.*
>
> ROMANS 6:4 NKJV

For further study, see Hank Hanegraaff, *Resurrection* (Nashville: Word Publishing, 2000), chapter 15; and Norman L. Geisler and Douglas E. Potter, "From Ashes to Ashes: Is Burial the Only Christian Option?" available from the Christian Reserach Institute at www.equip.org.

Should Christians be tolerant?

oday *tolerance* is being redefined to mean that all views are equally valid and all lifestyles equally appropriate. As such, the notion that Jesus is the only way to God is vilified as the epitome of intolerance. Rather than capitulating to culture, Christians must be equipped to expose the flaws of today's tolerance, while simultaneously exemplifying true tolerance.

First, to say that all views are equally valid sounds tolerant, but in reality it is a contradiction in terms. If indeed all views are equally valid, then the Christian view must be valid. The Christian view, however, holds that not all views are equally valid. Thus, the redefinition of tolerance in our culture is a self-refuting proposition. Moreover, we do not tolerate people with whom we agree; we tolerate people with whom we disagree. If all views were equally valid, there would be no need for tolerance.

Furthermore, today's redefinition of tolerance leaves no room for objective moral judgments. A modern terrorist could be deemed as virtuous as Mother Teresa. With no enduring reference point, societal norms are being reduced to mere matters of preference. As such, the moral basis for resolving international disputes and condemning such practices as genocide, if a same-sex attraction develops, celibacy and singleness—as opposed to homosexual licentiousness—is the proper response (cf. 1 Corinthians 7:8). Indeed, anyone suffering from gender confusion should not pursue marriage until the confusion has been biblically resolved. Though this may seem harsh, it is no different from the requirement placed on all believers to die to sin and live for righteousness through the power of Christ and the help of the Holy Spirit (Romans 6).

Finally, it is crucial to recognize that all disorders, diseases, deformities, decay, and death ultimately result from the fall. While sin, suffering, and sickness are present realities, we have the certain promise that "in all things God works for the good of those who love him, who have been called according to his purpose" (Romans 8:28).

> *Now as Jesus passed by, He saw a man who was blind from birth. And His disciples asked Him, saying, "Rabbi, who sinned, this man or his parents, that he was born blind?"*
>
> *Jesus answered, "Neither this man nor his parents sinned, but that the works of God should be revealed in him."*
>
> JOHN 9:1–3 NKJV

For further study, see Scott B. Rae, *Moral Choices*, 3rd ed. (Grand Rapids: Zondervan, 2009).

What's the problem with pornography?

Sexually explicit images are as near as the click of a mouse. Consequently, pornography has become pandemic. As Joe Dallas has aptly noted, pornography is not only an enslaving addiction and a violation of marriage vows but a precursor to increasingly dangerous and degrading sexual practices.

First, pornography is an addictive behavior that enslaves the mind and conditions users to view others as mere objects of self-gratification. As such, our Lord warns us to guard our gaze: "The eye is the lamp of the body. If your eyes are good, your whole body will be full of light. But if your eyes are bad, your whole body will be full of darkness. If then the light within you is darkness, how great is that darkness!" (Matthew 6:22–23).

Furthermore, pornography breaks the sacred bond of marriage and, as such, tears apart the very fabric of society. Moreover, when pornographic images are used to satisfy sexual desire, a marriage partner is betrayed. In the Sermon on the Mount, Jesus rendered lustful visual encounters the moral equivalent of extramarital sexual relations (Matthew 5:28).

Finally, just as marijuana is a precursor to experimenting with even more dangerous substances, so pornography often leads to increasingly degrading sexual behaviors. Said James, "Each one regarding homosexuality and temporary civil and ceremonial laws relegated to a particular historical context.

Furthermore, we would do well to recognize that the God of the Bible does not condemn homosexuality in an arbitrary and capricious fashion. Rather, He carefully defines the borders of human sexuality so that our joy may be complete. It does not require an advanced degree in physiology to appreciate the fact that the human body is not designed for homosexual relationships. Spurious slogans and sound bites do not change the scientific reality that homosexual relationships can be devastating not only from a psychological but also from a physiological perspective.

Finally, far from being irrelevant and antiquated, the Bible's warnings regarding homosexuality are eerily relevant and up-to-date. The book of Romans aptly describes both the perversion and the penalty: "Their women exchanged natural relations for unnatural ones. In the same way the men also abandoned natural relations with women and were inflamed with lust for one another. Men committed indecent acts with other men, and *received in themselves the due penalty for their perversion*" (1:26–27). It would be difficult to miss the relationship between Paul's words and the current health-care holocaust. More people already have died worldwide from AIDS than the United States of America has lost in all its wars combined. This is but the tip of an insidious iceberg. The homosexual lifestyle causes a host of complications including hemorrhoids, prostate damage, and infectious fissures. And even that merely scratches the surface. Nonviral infections transmitted through homosexual activity include gonorrhea, chlamydia, and syphilis. Viral infections involve condylomata, herpes, and hepatitis A and B.

While there are attendant moral and medical problems with sexual promiscuity in general, it would be homophobic in the extreme to obscure the scientific realities concerning homosexuality. Attempting to keep a whole segment of the population in the dark concerning such issues is a hate crime of unparalleled proportions. Thus, far from demonstrating that the Bible is out of step with the times, its warnings regarding homosexuality demonstrate that it is as relevant today as it was in the beginning.

Even their women exchanged the natural use for what is against nature. Likewise also the men, leaving the natural use of the woman, burned in their lust for one another, men with men committing what is shameful, and receiving in themselves the penalty of their error which was due.

ROMANS 1:26–27 NKJV

For further study, see Joe Dallas, *A Strong Delusion: Confronting the "Gay Christian" Movement* (Eugene, OR: Harvest House Publishers, 1996); see also Hank Hanegraaff, "President Bartlett's Fallacious Diatribe," available at www.equip.org.

fags" mentality is more conducive to repelling than reaching a culture steeped in sin and confusion. As Joe Dallas has rightly said, "We can preach the right things in all the wrong ways, either too aggressively or too meekly. When either conviction or compassion is being compromised, a revision is in order." Tolerance when it comes to personal relationships is a virtue, but tolerance when it comes to untruth is a travesty.

YIELD NOT! We must never yield our consciences to the subtle lure of political correctness. Rather, with Luther we ought to say, "My conscience is captive to the Word of God, . . . [and] to go against conscience is neither right nor safe." The temptation to yield to cultural norms will continue to be pressed upon us with increasing ferocity. Yet to yield is to abandon the very call that God has placed upon our collective lives. This is no trifling matter. It is a matter of natural law. As Dr. Jay Richards has well said, to deny natural law is to strike "a mortal blow to the foundation of a free society."

> *We should no longer be children, tossed to and fro*
> *and carried about with every wind of doctrine, by the*
> *trickery of men, in the cunning craftiness of deceitful*
> *plotting, but, speaking the truth in love, may grow*
> *up in all things into Him who is the head—Christ.*
>
> Ephesians 4:14–15 NKJV

GOD HAS SPOKEN!
ADJUST YOUR ATTITUDE.
YIELD NOT!

For further study, see "Does its condemnation of homosexuality demonstrate that the Bible is antiquated?" (p. 423); and Joe Dallas, "Now What? Same-Sex Marriage and Today's Church," *Christian Research Journal* 37, 1 (2014), available through the Christian Reserach Institute at www.equip.org.

In the end, the US Supreme Court's redefinition of marriage has not only undermined the foundation of human civilization but has opened Pandora's grizzly box. Given the court's reasoning, it's hard to imagine how polyamory, polygamy, polyandry, even pedophilia will not likewise be blessed by the court. If there is no special virtue in opposite-sex marriage, is there any magic in the number two? And why arbitrarily assign eighteen as the magical age of consent? Once we abandon the biblical definition of marriage, there is no limit on where our unsanctified passions may lead us.

> *So God created man in His own image; in the*
> *image of God He created him; male and female*
> *He created them. . . . Therefore a man shall*
> *leave his father and mother and be joined to*
> *his wife, and they shall become one flesh.*
>
> GENESIS 1:27; 2:24

ANTHROPOLOGICAL REALITY
BIOLOGICAL REALITY
CIVIL REALITY

For further study, see also "How should Christians respond to the LGBTQ community? (G-A-Y)" (p. 426); and Jay W. Richards, "To Defend Marriage, We Should Learn a Lesson from Apologetics," *Christian Research Journal* 35, 04 (2012), available at www.equip.org.

Should Christians use birth control?

In light of recent advances in biotechnology, it is crucial to consider the issue of birth control through the lens of a biblical worldview.

First, while there is much debate among Christians on the question of whether birth control is appropriate in any form, there is no question that birth control methods designed to destroy or prevent the implantation of a fertilized egg (i.e., embryo) should be avoided at all costs. From the moment of conception, an embryo is a living, growing person made in the image in God (Genesis 1:26–27; 9:6; Exodus 20:13). Thus, the abortion pill (RU486) and the "morning-after pill" must never be used! I should note as well that oral contraceptives (i.e., the birth control pill) not only prevent fertilization but may also prevent uterine implantation if fertilization should occur.

Furthermore, the necessary openness to children that accompanies the sexual union serves to protect against the abuse of sex for mere self-gratification. When birth-control methods are employed out of a selfish unwillingness to have children, sex can quickly degenerate into nothing more than what Oxford's Oliver O'Donovan has aptly described as "a profound form of play."

Finally, it is imperative that children be viewed as a blessing from above rather than a burden or blight. While birth control may be used for reasons of health or financial stewardship, birth control should never be employed out of purely selfish motives. If we consider a Cadillac more valuable than a child, our priorities are seriously skewed. Such an attitude toward the miracle of life and the blessings of parenthood pains our Father in heaven.

> *Little children were brought to [Jesus] that He might put His hands on them and pray, but the disciples rebuked them. But Jesus said, "Let the little children come to Me, and do not forbid them; for of such is the kingdom of heaven."*
> MATTHEW 19:13–14 NKJV

For further study, see Randy Alcorn, *Does the Birth Control Pill Cause Abortion?* 7th ed. (Gresham, OR: Eternal Perspective Ministries, 1997).

Should Christians use in vitro fertilization?

I n vitro—literally "in glass"—fertilization (IVF) is an increasingly popular form of reproductive technology that should raise significant moral concerns in the hearts and minds of believers.

First, there are major moral concerns associated with using biotechnology in place of the natural means of procreation. The fertilization of an egg in a glass dish can lead to viewing children as products to be made (and disposed of) rather than gifts from God. Indeed, IVF is already being used in the production and genetic selection of "designer babies." It is imperative that we guard against subtle shifts in thinking that ultimately lead to the erosion of our Christian worldview.

Furthermore, the introduction of a third party through sperm or egg donation or through surrogate motherhood is inconsistent with the biblical pattern of continuity between procreation and parenthood (Genesis 1:28; 2:24). Accordingly, if IVF is used at all, the sperm and the egg must come from the husband and wife committed to raising the child. The potentially disastrous consequences of third-party involvement are clearly demonstrated in the lives of Abram, Sarai, and Hagar (Genesis 16).

Finally, because it is an established scientific fact that human life begins at conception (an embryo has a distinct human genetic code and exhibits metabolism, development, the ability to react to stimuli, and cell reproduction), discarding embryos or destroying them through experimentation is the moral equivalent of killing innocent human beings. Freezing embryos is likewise morally objectionable. Thus, if IVF is used, no more eggs should be fertilized than the couple is willing to give a reasonable chance at full-term life.

> *You formed my inward parts;*
> *You covered me in my mother's womb.*
> *I will praise You, for I am fearfully and wonderfully*
>   *made;*
> *Marvelous are Your works,*
> *And that my soul knows very well.*
>   PSALM 139:13–14 NKJV

For further study, see Joni Eareckson Tada and Nigel M. de S. Cameron, *How to Be a Christian in a Brave New World* (Grand Rapids: Zondervan, 2006).

What is abortion?

People who continue to fight legislation restricting abortion are in reality *not* "pro-choice;" rather, they are clearly "pro-murder." While rhetoric has served to camouflage the carnage of abortion, the act remains the *painful killing of an innocent human being*.

First, abortion is *painful* in that the methods employed to kill a preborn child involve burning, smothering, dismembering, and crushing. And such procedures are executed on live babies who have not been specifically anesthetized.

Furthermore, abortion involves *killing*. The zygote—that fulfills the criteria needed to establish the existence of biological life (metabolism, development, the ability to react to stimuli, and cell reproduction)—is indeed terminated. In *Woman and the New Race*, Planned Parenthood founder Margaret Sanger tacitly acknowledged this point when she wrote, "The most merciful thing a large family can do for one of its infant members is to kill it."

Finally, abortion kills innocent *human beings*. The child who is terminated is the product of human parents and has a totally distinct human genetic code. Although the emerging embryo does not have a fully developed personality, it does have complete personhood from the moment of conception. Thus, far from deserving capital punishment, these innocent humans deserve care and protection.

Thankfully, in God's economy there is hope for those who have experienced the ravages of abortion. Not only can they receive God's forgiveness in the here and now, but they can yet look forward to the ecstasy of reuniting with their unborn loved ones in eternity.

Adapted from *The Face That Demonstrates the Farce of Evolution*

> *You formed my inward parts;*
> *You covered me in my mother's womb.*
> *I will praise You, for I am fearfully and wonderfully*
>   *made;*
> *Marvelous are Your works,*
> *And that my soul knows very well.*
> *My frame was not hidden from You,*
> *When I was made in secret,*
> *And skillfully wrought in the lowest parts of the earth.*
> *Your eyes saw my substance, being yet unformed.*
> *And in Your book they all were written,*
> *The days fashioned for me,*
> *When as yet there were none of them.*
>
> PSALM 139:13–16 NKJV

For further study, see "How do we annihilate A-B-O-R-T-I-O-N arguments?" (p. 439); and Francis J. Beckwith, *Politically Correct Death: Answering the Arguments for Abortion Rights* (Grand Rapids: Baker Books, 1993).

How do we annihilate
A-B-O-R-T-I-O-N arguments?

Abortion is the painful killing of an innocent human being. *Painful* for the child because the methods employed involve burning, smothering, dismembering, and crushing. *Killing* in that, from the beginning, that which is terminated fulfills the criteria necessary for establishing the existence of biological life, including metabolism, development, the ability to react to stimuli, and cell reproduction. *Innocent* in that a preborn child deserves protection rather than capital punishment. A *human being* in that the child who is killed is the offspring of human parents and has a totally distinct genetic code. Since abortion is nothing short of terminating the life of a person created in the image of God, I've developed the acronym A-B-O-R-T-I-O-N as a memorable tool by which to annihilate pro-abortion arguments.

ADOPTION. Whoopi Goldberg et al. employed the adoption argument in suggesting that abortion rights advocates would take pro-lifers more seriously if they were willing to adopt babies slated for abortion. The fallacy becomes obvious when it's put in different words: "If you won't adopt my babies, don't tell me I can't kill them!"

BIBLICAL PRETEXTS. Pro-abortionists routinely use biblical pretexts to retain some semblance of religiosity while at the same time that oral contraceptives [i.e., the birth control pill] not only prevent fertilization but may also prevent uterine implantation if fertilization should occur.)

NONPERSONHOOD. Nonpersonhood is perhaps the subtlest of all contemporary pro-abortion arguments. While conceding that science has demonstrated that human life begins at conception, some pro-abortionists—like the aforementioned Sagan—argue that the fetus is a nonperson until the second or third trimester of gestation. Only then does the creature become a child. In reality, we are distinctly human in each stage of our development. Moreover, we are conceived not only with all the earmarks of biological life but with eternity etched in our hearts. Put another way, both the physical and nonphysical aspects of our humanity are present at the moment of conception.

Sad but true, ethics and morality are frequently a function of the size and strength of the latest lobby group rather than being firmly rooted in scientific and spiritual standards. With no enduring reference point, societal norms have been reduced to mere matters of choice. As a result, year by year multiplied millions of preborn children are sacrificed on the altar of abortion. To be silent or uninformed in an age of scientific enlightenment is to be complicit in the carnage. Thankfully, however, those who have participated in abortion may receive God's forgiveness in the present, and they can also look forward to the ecstasy of reuniting with unborn loved ones in eternity.

Behold, children are a heritage from the LORD,
The fruit of the womb is a reward.

ADOPTION
BIBLICAL PRETEXTS
OPIUM EFFECT
RAPE AND INCEST
TOLERANCE
INEQUALITY
ORAL ABORTIFACIENTS
NONPERSONHOOD

For further study, see "What is abortion?" (p. 437) and "Should abortion be permitted in the case of rape or incest?" (p. 444).

Should Christians support a ban on embryonic stem cell research?

I n 2004, the cash-strapped state of California passed Proposition 71, allocating $3 billion to finance the cloning of human embryos and their subsequent destruction through embryonic stem cell research. Support for this proposition was largely influenced by celebrities such as Brad Pitt, Nancy Reagan, and the late Christopher Reeve who reiterated the biotech industry's promises that embryonic stem cell research will lead to cures for debilitating diseases and spinal cord injuries. Other celebrities such as Mel Gibson and Joni Eareckson Tada, herself a quadriplegic, rightly responded that all who are concerned about the sanctity of human life must support a complete ban on the use of this technology.

First, while an embryo does not have a fully developed personality, it does have full personhood from the moment of conception. You did not *come* from an adolescent; you once *were* an adolescent. Likewise, you did not *come* from an embryo; you once *were* an embryo. All human beings are created in the image of God and endowed with the right to life, regardless of size, location (in or out of the womb), or level of dependency. Make no mistake about it, extracting stem cells from an embryo kills the embryo.

Furthermore, while we should sympathize with those who suffer from debilitating diseases and injuries, cures and therapies must be sought within appropriate moral boundaries. Killing human embryos in the search for cures is tantamount to subjecting one class of people to harmful experimentation for the sake of another. To do so violates the biblical injunction against murdering humans made in the image of God (Genesis 1:26–27; 9:5–6), as well as the Nuremberg Code compiled by the tribunal responsible for judging the Nazis after World War II.

Finally, in light of the promising results of adult stem cell research, state funding for the destruction of embryos is not only morally repugnant but fiscally irresponsible. Stem cells extracted from non-embryonic sources such as bone marrow, blood, brain cells, and baby teeth are similar to embryonic stem cells in their ability to grow into multiple types of tissues. While embryonic stem cells used in research have demonstrated a tendency to grow into tumors, adult stem cells have already shown success in human trials for treatment of multiple sclerosis, sickle cell anemia, stroke, Parkinson's disease, and more. The frightening conclusion is that the fervor over embryonic stem cell research is more a pretext for human cloning than a context for responsible medical progress.

Finally, it should be noted that cloning has serious implications regarding what constitutes a family. While children are the result of spousal reproduction, clones are essentially the result of scientific replication. And that raises the question "Who owns the clone?" It is terrifying to think that the first human clone might well be owned and operated by the very scientists who conduct such ghastly experiments.

> *The Spirit of God has made me,*
> *And the breath of the Almighty gives me life.*
> JOB 33:4 NKJV

For further study, see Hank Hanegraaff, *The Face That Demonstrates the Farce of Evolution* (Nashville: Word Publishing, 1998), Appendix E "Human Cloning" and also Appendix D "Annihilating Abortion Arguments"; see also The Center for Bioethics and Human Dignity, 2065 Half Day Road, Bannockburn, IL 60015, www.cbhd.org.

How should Christians think about global warming?

Global warming is hot . . . hot . . . hot! This morning I opened *USA Today* and encountered a full-page ad that begins as follows: "Rising temperatures. Disastrous droughts. Melting glaciers and polar ice sheets. Polar bears headed to extinction. The climate crisis isn't on the way. It's here." CNN founder Ted Turner is similarly pessimistic: "We will be eight degrees hotter in 30 to 40 years and basically none of the crops will grow." As a result, says Turner, "most of the people will have died and the rest of us will be cannibals." Former vice president Al Gore is equally emphatic. In his view, global warming is the single greatest threat facing our planet. Ellen Goodman of the *Boston Globe* puts global warming deniers on par with holocaust deniers. And prominent Baptist pastor Oliver "Buzz" Thomas has gone so far as to castigate spiritual leaders for failing to urge followers to have smaller families in light of this global catastrophe. Says Thomas, "We must stop having so many children. Clergy should consider voicing the difficult truth that having more than two children during such a time is selfish. Dare we say sinful?" As global warming rhetoric continues to boil over, what is a Christian to do?

tens of trillions of dollars. By comparison, providing clean water for areas of the world that currently have contaminated water could be accomplished for around $200 billion. It is a genuine tragedy that while Christian leaders were hyping Y2K in America, millions of God's children were dying from malaria in Africa. And malaria is but one of the prevailing planetary problems. A whole range of issues from toxic waste to the war on terrorism could be addressed for a fraction of the cost. The point is: we dare not be wrong this time around!

Finally, what *is* incontrovertible is that Christians are called to be caretakers or stewards of God's creation. As such, not only are we called to carry out the Great Commission, but we are commissioned to carry out the cultural mandate. In the words of cultural apologist Nancy Pearcey, we are to "develop the social world: build families, churches, schools, cities, governments, laws" as well as "plant crops, build bridges, design computers, compose music." In other words, as crowning jewels of God's creation, we are to care for the created order. The tragedy is that those who approach catastrophic human-induced global warming with a healthy dose of skepticism are routinely castigated as environmental enemies. Moral judgments are meted out with breathless abandon on everything from the size of one's family to the size of one's family car. The aforementioned Baptist preacher Buzz Thomas goes so far as to judge those who have more than two children as "selfish" and "sinful." In like fashion, leaders of the Evangelical Environmental Network have taken it upon themselves to posit that Jesus wouldn't drive an SUV. They seem blithely unaware that their idiosyncratic fundamentalism often flies in the face of the facts.

As should be obvious, there are myriad factors to be considered with respect to family size. Whether one has two or twelve children is less important than whether those children grow up to be selfless producers as opposed to merely selfish consumers. Likewise, fuel savings do not necessarily dwarf such factors as family size or family safety. As Richards has well said, "Fuel economy doesn't trump the other factors, especially since some cars (such as hybrids) have better than average fuel economy, but require more energy both to construct and to recycle than do other, less fuel efficient cars. So an outside observer is in no position to make a moral judgment just by observing that you drive an SUV."

In an age when Christians are all too often characterized as "poor, undereducated, and easily led," we should avoid lending credence to the stereotype. Instead we should commit ourselves to care for Christ's creation with tender hearts as well as with tenacious minds.

aspects of our humanity. To fail to do so is to sin against the very One who created us in the *imago Dei*.

> *Do not be drunk with wine, in which is*
> *dissipation; but be filled with the Spirit.*

EPHESIANS 5:18 NKJV

Psychophysical Problems
Occult Dangers
THC Liabilities

For further study, see Elliot Miller, "What Should Christians Do as America Goes to Pot?" and Richard Poupard, "Medical Marijuana: Miracle Drug or Spiritual Poison?" in *Christian Research Journal* 37, 5 (2014), available through the Christian Research Institute at www.equip.org.

PETA or just P-E-T?

People for the Ethical Treatment of Animals (PETA) embrace a worldview that elevates animals to equivalency with humans. From their perspective, that is precisely what animals are: fellow beings on a level playing field with humanity. Some, such as bioethics professor Peter Singer, have gone even further. From his perspective, a disabled newborn has less value than a chimpanzee. As an animal lover, I embrace the ethical treatment of animals but hardly the ethics of Singer or the PETA organization. Instead, in the tradition of William Wilberforce, who fought against the tyranny of slavery and founded the Royal Society of the Prevention of Cruelty to Animals (RSPCA), I am deeply committed to the humane treatment of pets and to the sanctified preservation of wildlife. As such, allow me to forward the acronym P-E-T (*pecking order, exceptionalism, treatment tenets*) in place of PETA.

PECKING ORDER. A primary precept of biblical theology is that there is a hierarchical structure in God's good creation. Within that construction animals are to serve human beings in order that human beings might rightly serve the King of creation. As the Belgic Confession aptly puts it, "All creation is intended to serve man, so that man may in turn serve God. In the wisdom of God, His creation,

MONEY

What does the Bible teach about debt?

Not only has America become a debtor nation, but most Americans are drowning in debt. Our day-to-day dependence on debt begs the question: "What does the Bible say about debt?"

First, the Bible warns that "the borrower is servant to the lender" (Proverbs 22:7). As such, we are warned against the folly of being excessively indebted to those who may be unforgiving in their demands for repayment. We ought to take seriously the wisdom of the proverb, "Do not be a man who strikes hands in pledge or puts up security for debts; if you lack the means to pay, your very bed will be snatched from under you" (Proverbs 22:26–27).

Furthermore, Scripture condemns the failure to repay our debts as wickedness. In the words of the psalmist, "the wicked borrow and do not repay, but the righteous give generously" (Psalm 37:21). Likewise, the apostle Paul urged believers to diligently repay their debts (Romans 13:8).

Finally, whether in the theocracy of ancient Israel or the democracy of modern America, God's people are called to be good stewards of the resources He has entrusted to them. If we lend, we should do so with kindness, and if we borrow, we should do so with prudence.

Owe no one anything except to love one another,
for he who loves another has fulfilled the law.

ROMANS 13:8 NKJV

For further study, see "Is the tithe for today?" (p. 468) and "What is the biblical view of wealth?" (p. 466).

What is the biblical view of wealth?

I am persuaded that the Bible teaches a form of Christian capitalism: responsibility associated with wealth. God's Word does not promote the possession of money for the sake of possessing money, but instead encourages us to use money for the sake of the kingdom. In short, a biblical view of wealth involves an eternal perspective.

First, it is crucial to realize that "the earth is the LORD's, and everything in it, the world, and all who live in it" (Psalm 24:1). God is the Landlord; we are just tenants. We did not arrive with anything, and we will not take anything with us when we leave. Just remembering this fact of life will save us from a world of hurt.

Furthermore, poverty does not equal piety, nor do riches equal righteousness. God prospers some, and He puts others in more humble circumstances. If there were a one-to-one ratio between godliness and wealth, the godliest people in the world would be the wealthiest. A quick check of the Forbes 500 will quickly dash such an illusion.

Finally, it is important to view wealth with eternity in mind. In other words, lead your life here below as a responsible steward—whether you have a little or a lot—so that one day, at the judgment, God Himself will richly reward you (Matthew

25:21). It is your bank statement in *heaven* that counts (Matthew 6:19–21); if you fix your hope on the one you have down here, you are bankrupt no matter how many digits you count next to your name.

Adapted from Christianity in Crisis

> *"No one can serve two masters; for either he will hate the one and love the other, or else he will be loyal to the one and despise the other. You cannot serve God and mammon."*
> MATTHEW 6:24 NKJV

For further study, see "Is the tithe for today?" (p. 468); see also John Piper, *Desiring God: Meditations of a Christian Hedonist* (Sisters, OR: Multnomah Publishers, 1986), chapter 7; and Hank Hanegraaff, *Christianity in Crisis 21st Century* (Nashville: Thomas Nelson, 2009), part 5.

Is the tithe for today?

O f all the questions I am asked to answer, this is beyond a doubt the most difficult. Not only because the subject of tithing is hotly debated, but because I must confess that I personally have not always been faithful in giving a tenth or more to the work of the Lord. And I am not alone. Research demonstrates that not only do the vast majority of Christians not tithe regularly, but many give little or nothing at all. Thus, addressing this question is not only incredibly convicting, but it also is increasingly crucial.

First, as Randy Alcorn has well said, tithing may well be regarded as the training wheels of giving. As such, tithing is as important today as it has ever been. We all need to learn what it is to stride free and unfettered down the path of Christian stewardship. For in learning to give, we also are learning to lean more heavily upon our heavenly Father and less heavily upon ourselves. Those who have traveled the Calvary road for any length of time surely can testify to the truth that God is ever faithful. Not only so, but as we weekly set aside our tithes and offerings, we are reminded that all we are—or ever hope to be—is a gift from God.

Furthermore, as Moses communicated to the children of Israel, we tithe "so that [we] may learn to revere the LORD [our]

God always" (Deuteronomy 14:23). As we all know, learning to reverence the name of God is a timeless principle—as crucial today as in the days of Moses. Long *before* Moses, the Bible records Jacob's promise to God: "Of all that you give me I will give you a tenth" (Genesis 28:22). Long *after* Moses, Jesus reaffirmed the practice of tithing (Matthew 23:23) not for outward appearances, but as an outward expression of an inward reality. Additionally, in the fourth century, the great church father Jerome echoed the words of Malachi who intimated that failing to pay tithes and offerings was tantamount to robbing God—a prescription for financial ruin (Malachi 3:8).

Finally, it should be noted that tithing in the Old Testament not only prepared God's people to become hilarious givers but also produced a temple of unparalleled splendor. Tithing transformed the Israelites, who pined for the pleasures and protection of pagan Egypt more than for the One who had miraculously parted the Red Sea, into joyful givers. The Bible chronicles the prayer of David as he thanked God for the very privilege of being able to give to the work of the Lord: "But who am I, and who are my people, that we should be able to give as generously as this? Everything comes from you, and we have given you only what comes from your hand. . . . And now I have seen with joy how willingly your people who are here have given to you" (1 Chronicles 29:14, 17). What began as a spiritual discipline had evolved into sheer delight.

Can Christians be demonized?

O ver the years, I have read a wide variety of stories that convey the notion that Christians can be demonized. In the end, they all have one thing in common: they greatly overestimate the power and province of Satan. Some deliverance ministers make a more valiant attempt than others to provide a biblical basis for the contention that a Christian can be inhabited by a demon. Inevitably, however, Scripture itself undermines their stories.

First, Christ Himself precluded the possibility that a Christian could be inhabited by demons. Using the illustration of a house, Jesus asked, "How can anyone enter a strong man's house and carry off his possessions unless he first ties up the strong man?" (Matthew 12:29). In the case of a demon-possessed person, the strong man is obviously the devil. In a Spirit-indwelt believer, however, the strong man is God. The force of Christ's argument leads inexorably to the conclusion that, in order for demons to possess believers, they would first have to bind the One who occupies them—namely God Himself!

Furthermore, I discovered an equally airtight argument against Christian demonization in the gospel of John. The Jews once again were accusing Jesus of being demon-possessed.

Rather than circumvent their accusations, Jesus condescended to reach out to His accusers with reason. The essence of His argument is "I am not possessed by a demon" because "I honor my Father" (John 8:49). The point is impossible to miss: being demon-possessed and honoring God are mutually exclusive. The two cannot be true at the same time.

Finally, Scripture does not contain a single credible example of a demonized believer. Instead, the consistent teaching of the Bible is that Christians cannot be controlled against their wills by demonic inhabitation. The principle is foolproof. If you are a follower of Christ, the King Himself indwells you. And you can rest assured that "the one who is in you is greater than the one who is in the world" (1 John 4:4).

Adapted from *The Covering*

*You are of God, little children, and have
overcome them, because He who is in you
is greater than he who is in the world.*

1 JOHN 4:4 NKJV

For further study, see Hank Hanegraaff, *The Covering*: *God's Plan to Protect You from Evil* (Nashville: W Publishing, 2002).

Is the binding and loosing
of demons biblical?

A common expression in certain Christian circles is "I bind you, Satan, in the name of Jesus." Biblically, however, the phrase *binding and loosing* has nothing whatsoever to do with demons.

First, when Jesus told the disciples, "Whatever you bind on earth will be bound in heaven, and whatever you loose on earth will be loosed in heaven" (Matthew 16:19), He was not talking about demons, but discipline. In other words, in the context of church discipline, those who repent are to be "loosed" (i.e., restored to fellowship). Those who persist in sin are to be "bound" (i.e., removed from fellowship). Demons are totally foreign to the context.

Furthermore, humans are not authorized anywhere in Scripture to bind or loose Satan. Even the archangel Michael did not tackle Satan on his own. Despite his wisdom and power, he called on God to rebuke Satan. Christians should never suppose that they are smart enough to engage Satan on their own. Rather they, like Michael, should pray, "The Lord rebuke you" (Jude v. 9).

Finally, while it makes sense to ask the Lord to "bind" the power of demons in the sense of thwarting their plans to undo us, to "loose" Satan and his minions makes no sense at all.

Thus, common sense alone should be enough to convince us that biblically binding and loosing has nothing whatsoever to do with demons.

> "Moreover if your brother sins against you, go and tell him his fault between you and him alone. If he hears you, you have gained your brother. But if he will not hear, take with you one or two more, that 'by the mouth of two or three witnesses every word may be established.' And if he refuses to hear them, tell it to the church. But if he refuses even to hear the church, let him be to you like a heathen and a tax collector.
>
> "Assuredly, I say to you, whatever you bind on earth will be bound in heaven, and whatever you loose on earth will be loosed in heaven.
>
> "Again I say to you that if two of you agree on earth concerning anything that they ask, it will be done for them by My Father in heaven. For where two or three are gathered together in My name, I am there in the midst of them."
>
> MATTHEW 18:15–20 NKJV

For further study on biblical spiritual warfare, see Hank Hanegraaff, *The Covering: God's Plan to Protect You from Evil* (Nashville: W Publishing, 2002).

Does Satan have access to our minds?

e would greatly overestimate Satan's power by supposing that he can interact directly with us in a physical sense, but an equal and opposite error would be to suppose that he does *not* have access to our minds.

First, Satan cannot read our minds, but he can influence our thoughts. Thus, the Bible instructs us to "put on the full armor of God so that you can take your stand against the devil's schemes" (Ephesians 6:11). Without the armor, you are a guaranteed casualty in the invisible war; with it, you are invincible. Spiritual warfare is waged against invisible beings that personify the extremities of evil. And their weapons are spiritual, not physical. While they cannot bite us physically, violate us sexually, or cause us to levitate, they can tempt us to cheat, steal, and lie.

Furthermore, it is crucial to note that if we open the door to Satan by failing to put on the full armor of God, he does—as it were—sit on our shoulders and whisper into our ears. The whisper cannot be discerned with the physical ear; it can, however, penetrate the ear of the mind. We cannot explain how such communication takes place any more than we can explain how our immaterial minds can cause the physical synapses of the brain to fire. But that such mind-to-mind communication takes place is indisputable. If it were not so, the devil could not have tempted Judas to betray his Master, seduced Ananias and Sapphira to deceive Peter, or incited David to take a census.

Finally, while fallen angels are not material beings and thus cannot interact with us directly in the physical sense, they are as real as the very flesh upon our bones. No doubt much to the devil's delight, we often depict him as either a cartoonish clown with an elongated tail, red tights, and a pitchfork—or as a cultural caricature. Far from silly or stupid, however, Satan appears as a cosmopolitan angel of enlightenment. He knows full well that without our spiritual armor we are but pawns in a devil's game.

In the final analysis, the whole of Scripture informs us that spiritual warfare is the battle for the mind.

Adapted from *The Covering*

For further study, see Hank Hanegraaff, *The Covering: God's Plan to Protect You from Evil* (Nashville: W Publishing Group, 2002); and C. S. Lewis, *The Screwtape Letters* (New York: Macmillan, 1982).

Did demons have sexual relations with women in Genesis 6:4?

Genesis 6:4 is one of the most controversial verses in the Bible. As with any difficult section of Scripture, it is open to a wide variety of interpretations. It is my conviction, however, that those who hold consistently to a biblical worldview must reject the notion that women and demons can engage in sexual relations. I reject this interjection of pagan superstition into the Scriptures for the following reasons.

First and foremost, the notion that demons can "produce" real bodies and have real sex with real women would invalidate Jesus' argument for the authenticity of His resurrection. Jesus assured His disciples that "a spirit does not have flesh and bones as you see I have" (Luke 24:39 NKJV). If indeed a demon could produce flesh and bones, Jesus' argument would be not only flawed but also misleading. In fact, then it might be logically argued that the disciples did not actually see post-resurrection appearances of Christ but rather a demon masquerading as the resurrected Christ.

Furthermore, demons are nonsexual, nonphysical beings and, as such, are incapable of having sexual relations and producing physical offspring. To say that demons can create bodies with DNA and fertile sperm is to say that demons have creative power—which is an exclusively divine prerogative. If demons could have sex with women in ancient times, we would have no assurance they could not do so in modern times. Nor would we have any guarantee that the people we encounter every day are fully human. While a biblical worldview does allow for fallen angels to possess unsaved human beings, it does not support the notion that a demon-possessed person can produce offspring that are part-demon, part-human. Genesis 1 makes it clear that all of God's living creations are designed to reproduce "according to their own kinds" (v. 25).

Finally, the mutant theory raises serious questions pertaining to the spiritual accountability of hypothetical demon-humans and their relation to humanity's redemption. Angels rebelled individually, are judged individually, and are offered no plan of redemption in Scripture. On the other hand, humans fell corporately in Adam, are judged corporately in Adam, and are redeemed corporately through Jesus Christ. We have no biblical way of determining what category the demon-humans would fit into—whether they would be judged as angels or as men or, more significantly, whether they would even be among those for whom Christ died.

I believe the better interpretation is that "sons of God" simply refers to the godly descendants of Seth and "daughters of is Satan "who leads the whole world astray" (Revelation 12:9).

Finally, Satan is the *de facto* ruler of all who willingly subject themselves to his masterful deceit (2 Corinthians 4:4; 11:3). If we do not belong to the God of the ages, then we are of Satan, the god of this age.

> *"Thus says the LORD, the King of Israel,*
> *And his Redeemer, the LORD of hosts:*
> *'I am the First and I am the Last;*
> *Besides Me there is no God.'"*
>
> ISAIAH 44:6 NKJV

For further study, see Hank Hanegraaff, *The Covering: God's Plan to Protect You from Evil* (Nashville: W Publishing, 2002).

Are generational curses biblical?

Based on texts taken out of context and used as pretexts, it has become increasingly common for Christians to suppose that they are victims of generational curses. As such, they suppose they have inherited demons ranging from anger to alcoholism, from laziness to lust. Closer examination, however, reveals this notion to be seriously flawed.

First, Scripture clearly communicates that consequences—not curses—are passed on through the generations. In this sense, the Bible says that children are punished for the sins of their fathers "to the third and fourth generation" (Exodus 20:5). The children of alcoholic fathers frequently suffer neglect and abuse as a direct consequence of their father's sinful behavior. Moreover, the descendants of those who hate God are likely to follow in the footsteps of their forefathers.

Furthermore, Scripture explicitly tells us that "the son will not share the guilt of the father, nor will the father share the guilt of the son" (Ezekiel 18:20). Indeed, when ancient Israel quoted the proverb, "The fathers eat sour grapes, and the children's teeth are set on edge" (Ezekiel 18:2), God responded in no uncertain terms: "As surely as I live, declares the Sovereign LORD, you will no longer quote this proverb in Israel. . . . The soul who sins is the one who will die" (vv. 3–4).

Have the land promises God made to Abraham been fulfilled?

Christian Zionists are convinced that the land promises God made to Abraham, Isaac, and Jacob are as yet unfulfilled. They are convinced that Israel must gain control of a land mass roughly thirty times its present size. Here is how John Hagee explains it in the book *Should Christians Support Israel?*: "The Royal Land Grant that God, the original owner, gave to Abraham, Isaac, and Jacob and their seed forever, includes the following territory which is presently occupied by Israel, the West Bank, all of Lebanon, one half of Syria, two-thirds of Jordan, all of Iraq, and the northern portion of Saudi Arabia." But is this really true?

First, the land promises that God made to Israel were fulfilled in the fore future when Joshua led the descendants of Abraham into Palestine. As the book of Joshua records, "The LORD gave Israel all the land he had sworn to give their forefathers, and they took possession of it and settled there" (21:43). Even as the life ebbed from his body, Joshua reminded the children of Israel that the Lord had been faithful to His promises: "You know with all your heart and soul that *not one* of all the good promises the LORD your God gave you has failed. Every promise has been fulfilled; *not one has failed*" (23:14). Solomon, during whose reign the glorious temple was constructed, was equally unambiguous: "Not one word has failed of all the good promises [the LORD] gave through his servant Moses" (1 Kings 8:56). In fact, at the height of the Solomonic kingdom, "the people of Judah and Israel were *as numerous as the sand on the seashore*; they ate, they drank and they were happy. And Solomon ruled over all the kingdoms from the River [Euphrates] to the land of the Philistines, as far as the border of Egypt" (4:20–21).

Furthermore, the land promises were fulfilled in the far future through Jesus who provides true Israel with permanent rest from their wanderings in sin. The writer of Hebrews made clear that the rest the descendants of Abraham experienced when they entered the land is but a type of the rest we experience when we enter an eternal relationship with the Lord. The land provided temporal rest for the *physical* descendants of Abraham, but the Lord provides eternal rest for his *spiritual* descendants. The land was never the focus of our Lord; instead, our Lord is forever the locus of the land.

The quintessential point of understanding for the disciples began to dawn at the time of Christ's post-resurrection appearances. Previously, they had been under the same misconceptions as modern-day Christian Zionists. They had expected Jesus to establish Jerusalem as the capital of a sovereign Jewish empire. The notion was so ingrained in their psyches that, even as Jesus was about to ascend into heaven, they asked, "Lord, are you at

Does the Bible make a distinction between Israel and the church?

At the heart of a currently popular end-times theology is the belief that God has two distinct people, and one group must be raptured before God can continue His plan with the other. Rather than teaching that God has two categories of people, however, Scripture reveals only one chosen people who form one covenant community, beautifully symbolized as one cultivated olive tree.

First, far from communicating a distinction between Israel and the church, the Scriptures from beginning to end reveal that God has only ever had *one chosen people* purchased "from every tribe and language and people and nation" (Revelation 5:9). As Paul explained, the "mystery is that through the gospel the Gentiles are heirs together with Israel, members together of *one* body, and sharers together in the promise in Christ Jesus" (Ephesians 3:6). Indeed, the precise terminology used to describe the children of Israel in the Old Testament is ascribed to the church in the New Testament. Peter called them "a chosen people, a royal priesthood, a holy nation, a people belonging to God" (1 Peter 2:9). Ultimately, they are the one chosen people of God, not by virtue of their genealogical relationship to

Abraham, but by virtue of their genuine relationship to "the living Stone—rejected by men but chosen by God" (1 Peter 2:4).

Furthermore, just as the Old and New Testaments reveal only one chosen people, so, too, they reveal only *one covenant community*. While that one covenant community is physically rooted in the offspring of Abraham—whose number would be like that of "the stars" of heaven (Genesis 15:5) or "the dust of the earth" (Genesis 13:16)—it is spiritually grounded in one singular Seed. Paul made this explicit in his letter to the Galatians: "The promises were spoken to Abraham and to his seed. The Scripture does not say "and to seeds," meaning many people, but "to your seed," meaning one person, who is Christ" (3:16). As Paul went on to explain: "If you belong to Christ, then you are Abraham's seed, and heirs according to the promise" (v. 29). The faithful remnant of Old Testament Israel and the New Testament Christian believers are, together, the one genuine seed of Abraham and thus heirs according to the promise. This remnant is chosen not on the basis of religion or race but rather on the basis of relationship to the resurrected Redeemer.

Finally, the one chosen people, who form one covenant community, are beautifully symbolized in the book of Romans as *one cultivated olive tree* (11:11–24). The tree symbolizes Israel; its branches symbolize those who believe; and its root symbolizes Jesus, "the Root and the Offspring of David" (Revelation 22:16). Natural branches broken off represent Jews who reject Jesus.

Finally, the use of the term *replacement* is highly *ironic*. Why? Because the very people who wield the term as an insult believe the mistaken notion that Israel will *replace* a soon-to-be-raptured church during seven horrific years of tribulation. Ironically, those who suffer the rebuke are repulsed by the very rhetoric of replacement. Also ironic is the fact that those who are now claiming that replacement theologians are guilty of spreading "the message of anti-Semitism" are themselves in the process of herding Jews into the Holy Land. They firmly believe that these Jews will soon be slaughtered in a blood bath that exceeds even that of Hitler's Holocaust.

In part adapted from *The Apocalypse Code*

Then Peter began to speak: "I now realize how true it is that God does not show favoritism but accepts men from every nation who fear him and do what is right."

ACTS 10:34–35

For further study, see "Does the Bible make a distinction between Israel and the church?" (p. 492) and "Is the pre-tribulational rapture theory biblical?" (p. 497). See also Hank Hanegraaff, *The Apocalypse Code: Find Out What the Bible* Really *Says About the End Times . . . and Why It Matters Today* (Nashville: W Publishing Group, 2007).

Is the pre-tribulational
rapture theory biblical?

The pre-tribulational rapture theory, popularized by John Nelson Darby in the nineteenth century, contends that God has two distinct people and two distinct plans for their two distinct destinies. The *church* will be raptured seven years prior to the second coming of Christ, and *Jews* will suffer tribulation. Beginning with Darby, rapture theorists held that, due to the murder of Messiah, Jews were in for a time of unprecedented suffering referred to as the "Great Tribulation." Dr. Tim LaHaye, author of the *Left Behind* series, describes the coming Jewish holocaust as "Antichrist's 'final solution' to the 'Jewish problem.'" According to LaHaye, "the mind-boggling terror and turmoil of the Tribulation" will be a nightmarish reality far exceeding "even the Holocaust of Adolf Hitler in the twentieth century." Concurrent with the carnage, a "soul harvest" will emerge due to the proselytizing prowess of 144,000 Jewish virgins. Multiplied millions today hold firmly to this belief. But is it biblical?

First, it is significant to note that *the pre-tribulational rapture theory is without a biblical basis.* There is not a single passage in Scripture that speaks of Jesus coming to rapture the church seven years prior to His second appearing. Our Lord's own words negate the notion: "A time is coming when *all* who are in their graves will hear his voice and come out—those who have done good will rise to live, and those who have done evil will rise to be condemned" (John 5:28–29). The plain and literal sense of our Lord's words suggests a moment in the future when both the righteous and the unrighteous will be resurrected and judged *together*. The notion that *some* believers will come out of their graves at the rapture and others 1,007 years later is clearly an imposition on the text.

Furthermore, there is no biblical basis for *a coming seven-year tribulation during which a vast majority of Jews will die*. That, of course, is not to suggest that Jews have not faced such tribulation in the past. Who can forget the terrible seven-year tribulation suffered by Jews during the beastly reign of Antiochus IV Epiphanes? He plundered the temple treasury, dedicated the sanctuary to the Olympian god Zeus, and sacrificed a pig on the altar. The annual Hanukkah celebration ensures that the world will always remember the *seven-year tribulation* during the reign of the abominable Old Testament antichrist. Had God not supernaturally intervened through Judas Maccabaeus, the epicenter of Jewish spiritual and sociological identity would not just have been desecrated but destroyed.

Two centuries later, the Jewish Jesus looked back to "the abomination that causes desolation spoken of by the prophet

Daniel" (Matthew 24:15) to warn His followers that another tribulation was in store. From the great fire of Rome to the fiery destruction of the great temple in Jerusalem, the Roman Beast unleashed its fury against a fledgling Christian church. In the end, Peter and Paul themselves were persecuted and put to death at the hands of the Beast. On August 30, AD 70, seven years after the beginnings of tribulation, the second temple was set ablaze. By September 26, all Jerusalem was in flames. This time the blood that desolated the sacred altar flowed not from the carcasses of unclean pigs but from the corpses of unbelieving Pharisees. This time the Holy of Holies was not merely desecrated by the defiling statue of a pagan god but manifestly destroyed by the pathetic greed of despoiling soldiers. This time no Judas Maccabaeus intervened. Within a generation, the temple was not just desecrated; it was destroyed. Jesus emphatically placed the time of "Jewish Tribulation" in the first century (Matthew 24:34). His words must never be used as a pretext for a Jewish holocaust in the twenty-first.

In short, there simply is no biblical warrant for a fatalistic preoccupation with a future seven-year Tribulation. Nor is there warrant for a rebuilt temple and reinstituted temple sacrifices. Scripture forbids Christians to take part in or encourage the building of a third temple, which would occasion the trampling of the holy Son of God underfoot by counting the blood of the covenant a common thing through the offering of unholy animal sacrifices (Hebrews 10:29). Indeed, the shekinah glory of God will never again descend upon a temple constructed of lifeless stones; it forever dwells within "the living Stone—rejected by men but chosen by God" (1 Peter 2:4). As the apostle Peter went on to explain, "You also, like living stones, are being built into a *spiritual house* to be a holy priesthood, offering *spiritual sacrifices* acceptable to God through Jesus Christ" (v. 5).

Finally, just as there is no biblical warrant for a pre-tribulational rapture or a future seven-year Tribulation, so, too, there is no biblical basis for believing in a *second chance for salvation after the second coming of Christ.* Christ is clear: all given to Him by the Father will be raised up on the last day (John 6:37–40). Likewise, Paul pointed out that the liberation of creation goes hand in hand with the redemption of our bodies (Romans 8:18–25). Thus, we can be certain that no one will be saved following the second coming of Christ. The notion that our bodies are redeemed at the rapture and the earth is liberated from its bondage to decay approximately 1,007 years later is without biblical basis. At the second appearing, the bride of Christ—the church universal—is complete. No one else can be saved.

While the notion that twenty-first-century Christians are destined for seven years of bliss and Jews are in for a holocaust of unparalleled proportions is being trumpeted in current Christianily with great bravado, it is simply not great Bible.

In part adapted from *The Apocalypse Code* and *Has God Spoken?*

The Lord Himself will descend from heaven with a shout, with the voice of an archangel, and with the trumpet of God. And the dead in Christ will rise first. Then we who are alive and remain shall be caught up together with them in the clouds to meet the Lord in the air. And thus we shall always be with the Lord. Therefore comfort one another with these words.

1 THESSALONIANS 4:16–18 NKJV

For further study, see Hank Hanegraaff, *AfterLife: What You Need to Know About Heaven, the Hereafter, and Near-Death Experiences* (Brentwood, TN: Worthy, 2013); and *The Apocalypse Code: Find Out What the Bible Really Says About the End Times . . . and Why It Matters Today* (Nashville: W Publishing Group, 2007).

Is "coming on clouds" a reference to Christ's second coming?

Many modern skeptics, who follow scholars such as Bertrand Russell and Albert Schweitzer, have believed Jesus to be a false prophet because He predicted His "coming on clouds" within the lifetime of His disciples. Did Jesus have the Second Coming in mind, or does "coming on clouds" have a different meaning?

First, when Jesus told Caiaphas and the court that condemned Him to death that He was the Son of Man who would come "on the clouds of heaven," He was not speaking of His second coming but of the coming judgment of Jerusalem (Matthew 26:63–64). As Caiaphas and the court well knew, clouds were a common Old Testament symbol pointing to God as the sovereign Judge of the nations. In the words of Isaiah, "See, the Lord rides on a swift *cloud* and is *coming* to Egypt. The idols of Egypt tremble before him, and the hearts of the Egyptians melt within them" (Isaiah 19:1). Like the Old Testament prophets, Jesus employed the symbolism of clouds to warn His hearers that just as judgment fell on Egypt, so would judgment soon befall Jerusalem.

Furthermore, the "coming on clouds" judgment metaphor was clearly intended for Caiaphas and the first-century crowd who condemned Christ to death. In the words of our Lord, "I say to all of *you*: In the future *you* will *see* the Son of Man sitting at the right hand of the Mighty One and coming on the clouds of heaven" (Matthew 26:64). The generation that crucified Christ would *see* the day that He was exalted and enthroned at "the right hand of the Mighty One."

Finally, Jesus' "coming on clouds" to judge Jerusalem in the first century points forward to the end of time when He will appear again to "judge the living and the dead" (2 Timothy 4:1; cf. 1 Peter 4:5). Indeed, as Jesus promised, a day is coming when "all who are in their graves will hear his voice and come out—those who have done good will rise to live, and those who have done evil will rise to be condemned" (John 5:28–29). Or, as the writer of Hebrews put it, Jesus "will appear a second time, not to bear sin, but to bring salvation to those who are waiting for him" (9:28).

> *Behold, He is coming with clouds, and every*
> *eye will see Him, even they who pierced*
> *Him. And all the tribes of the earth will*
> *mourn because of Him. Even so, Amen.*
>
> REVELATION 1:7 NKJV

For further study, see Hank Hanegraaff, *The Apocalypse Code: Find Out What the Bible Really Says About the End Times . . . and Why It Matters Today* (Nashville: W Publishing Group, 2007).

were weighed out into my hands, I would not lift my hand against the king's son" (2 Samuel 18:12). A thousand more examples (figuratively speaking) could easily be added to the list.

Finally, the 144,000 represent true Israel as it was intended to be—in perfect symmetry and providentially sealed. Who can help but think back to Ezekiel's epic depiction of a man clothed in linen and etching a mark on the foreheads of those who grieved and lamented over all the detestable things done in Jerusalem prior to its destruction by the Babylonians six centuries before Christ (Ezekiel 9:4)? Or fail to realize that those who were marked were the earnest of the 144,000 sealed prior to Jerusalem's destruction in AD 70? She is the purified bride from every nation, tribe, people, and language that will step over Jordan into the New Jerusalem prepared for her from the very foundations of the world.

Indeed, the 144,000 is the limitless great multitude of all whose names are written in the Book of Life and who will inhabit the courts of God for all eternity.

> *These are the ones who come out of the great*
> *tribulation, and washed their robes and made*
> *them white in the blood of the Lamb.*
> REVELATION 7:14 NKJV

For further study, see Hank Hanegraaff, *The Apocalypse Code: Find Out What the Bible Really Says About the End Times . . . and Why It Matters Today* (Nashville: W Publishing, 2007).

Who are the two witnesses
of Revelation?

The book of Revelation describes an apocalypse. Not just in the sense of recording an unveiling but also in terms of its composition in what might best be described as a language system or matrix deeply embedded in the Old Testament. As such, if we are to rightly identify the two witnesses of Revelation 11, it is crucial to have the background music of the Old Testament coursing through our minds. But we must neither attempt to draw exact parallels between the apocalyptic imagery and their Old Testament referents nor attempt to press the language system of Revelation into a literalistic labyrinth such that the two witnesses actually turn their mouths into blowtorches.

First, the two witnesses are a metaphorical reference to Moses and Elijah. Old Testament jurisprudence mandated at least two witnesses to convict someone of a crime (Deuteronomy 19:15), and in this case the two witnesses accuse Israel of apostasy. The imagery also harkens back to a familiar Old Testament passage in which Zechariah sees two olive trees on the right and the left of a lampstand, trees that symbolize "the two who are anointed to serve the Lord of all the earth" (Zechariah 4:14). The two witnesses in Zechariah were identified as Zerubbabel, the governor of Judah who returned to Jerusalem to lay the foundation

Who is the Antichrist?

For centuries Christians have speculated about the identity of Antichrist. Likely candidates have included princes and popes of the past as well as potentates and presidents in the present. Rather than joining the sensationalistic game of pin-the-tail-on-the-Antichrist, Christians need only go to Scripture to find the answer.

First, the apostle John exposed the identity of Antichrist when he wrote, "Who is the liar? It is the man who denies that Jesus is the Christ. Such a man is the antichrist—he denies the Father and the Son. No one who denies the Son has the Father; whoever acknowledges the Son has the Father also" (1 John 2:22–23). In his second epistle, John gave a similar warning: "Many deceivers, who do not acknowledge Jesus Christ as coming in the flesh, have gone out into the world. Any such person is the deceiver and the antichrist" (v. 7).

Furthermore, John taught that all who deny the incarnation, messianic role, and deity of Jesus are instances of antichrist. As such, the term *antichrist* refers not only to the apostasy of individuals but to the apostasy of institutions and ideologies as well. In this sense, institutions such as modern-day cults and world religions as well as ideologies such as evolutionism and communism can rightly be considered antichrist.

Finally, in the book of Revelation, John identified both an

HANK HANEGRAAFF

individual and an institution that represent the ultimate manifestation of evil—the archetypal antichrist. John referred to this archetypal antichrist as a beast who "deceived the inhabitants of the earth" (Revelation 13:14). Drawing on Daniel's apocalyptic depiction of evil world powers (Revelation 13; cf. Daniel 7–8), John described an emperor in his own epoch of time who arrogantly set himself and his empire against God (13:5–6), violently persecuting the saints (13:7) and grossly violating the commandments through a long litany of disgusting demonstrations of depravity, not the least of which was his demand to be worshipped as Lord and God (13:8, 15).

> *Little children, it is the last hour; and as you have heard that the Antichrist is coming, even now many antichrists have come, by which we know that it is the last hour. They went out from us, but they were not of us; for if they had been of us, they would have continued with us; but they went out that they might be made manifest, that none of them were of us.*
>
> 1 JOHN 2:18–19 NKJV

For further study, see "What is the meaning of 666?" (p. 514) and Hank Hanegraaff, *The Apocalypse Code: Find Out What the Bible Really Says About the End Times . . . and Why It Matters Today* (Nashville: W Publishing Group, 2007).

Here is wisdom. Let him who has understanding
calculate the number of the beast, for it is the
number of a man: His number is 666.

REVELATION 13:18 NKJV

For further study, see "Who is the Antichrist?" (p. 512) and "Is the mark of the Beast
a microchip?" (p. 518). See also Hank Hanegraaff, *The Apocalypse Code: Find
Out What the Bible Really Says About the End Times . . . and Why It Matters Today*
(Nashville, W Publishing Group, 2007).

HANK HANEGRAAFF

Nero Caesar in Greek (Νέρων Καῖσαρ) transliterated into Hebrew (ברון קסד) adds up to 666 = (נ = 50) + (ר = 200) + (ו = 6) + (ן = 50) + (ק = 100) + (ם = 60) + (ר = 200).

Nero Caesar in Latin (Nero Caesar) transliterated into Hebrew (ברו קסר) adds up to 616 = (נ = 50) + (ר= 200) + (ו = 6) + (ק =100) + (ם =60) + (ר = 200).

Nero in Greek (Νέρων) adds up to 1,005 = (N=50) + (έ=5) + (ρ=100) + (ω=800) + (ν=50); *murdered his own mother* in Greek (ἰδίαν μητέρα ἀπέκτεινε) also adds up to 1,005.

α	=	1	=	א	ν	=	50	= ן or ן
β	=	2	=	ב	ξ	=	60	= ס
γ	=	3	=	ג	o	=	70	= ע
δ	=	4	=	ד	π	=	80	= פ
ε	=	5	=	ה	Ϙ	=	90	= צ
ς	=	6	=	ו	ρ	=	100	= ק
ζ	=	7	=	ז	σ	=	200	= ר
η	=	8	=	ח	τ	=	300	= ש
θ	=	9	=	ט	υ	=	400	= ת
ι	=	10	=	י	φ	=	500	= חק
κ	=	20	=	כ	χ	=	600	
λ	=	30	=	ל	ψ	=	700	
μ	=	40	=	מ	ω	=	800	

Who or what is the great prostitute of Revelation 17?

W hat has puzzled me over the years is not the identity of "the great prostitute," but how so many people could mistake her historical identity. On the one hand, hundreds of prophecy experts misidentify the great prostitute as the contemporary Roman Catholic Church. On the other hand, hundreds of commentators identify the great harlot as ancient (or revived) imperial Rome. The application of the historical principle of biblical interpretation, however, demonstrates that both are a clear case of mistaken identity.

First, in biblical history only one nation is inextricably linked to the moniker "harlot"—*and that nation is Israel!* Anyone who has read the Bible even once has flashbacks to the graphic images of apostate Israel when they first encounter the great prostitute of Revelation. From the Pentateuch to the Prophets, the image is repeated endlessly. Verse by verse, the painful picture of a people who prostitute themselves with pagan deities emerges (e.g., Jeremiah 2:20–24; 3:2–3; Ezekiel 23:9–20). The prostituted bride had little interest in seeking intimacy with God in His temple. Instead, she craved intimacy with foreign gods on the threshing floors of perverse temples (Hosea 9:1).

Furthermore, the fact that Revelation is a virtual recapitulation of Ezekiel and adds credibility to the notion that apostate Israel is the great prostitute depicted in Revelation 17. Nowhere are the parallels more poignant than in Ezekiel 16 and Revelation 17—sequentially linked and memorable. In both Ezekiel and Revelation, the prostitute commits adultery with the kings of the earth; is dressed in splendor; glitters with gold and precious jewels; and is intoxicated with the blood of the righteous. And that is but a glimpse of her unveiling. In Ezekiel, the prostitution of Jerusalem made that of her sisters—Samaria and Sodom—look insignificant by comparison. And in Revelation she is in bed with imperial Rome. In the end, the great prostitute aligns herself with Caesar in piercing Christ and persecuting Christians. The golden cup in her hand is filled with "the blood of prophets and of the saints, and of all who have been killed on the earth" (Revelation 18:24). Shrouded in mystery, she was glorious, like "the most beautiful of jewels" (Ezekiel 16:7). Unveiled as apostate Israel, she is grotesque.

Finally, when we consider the fact that the key to Revelation is a contrast between the purified bride and a prostituted bride, the identity of apostate Israel as the great prostitute becomes unmistakable. While the prostituted bride bears the mark, "MYSTERY, BABYLON THE GREAT, THE MOTHER OF PROSTITUTES AND OF THE ABOMINATIONS OF THE EARTH" (17:5), the purified bride bears the moniker of the Lord and the Lamb on her forehead. Unlike "synagogue of Satan" (2:9)—those who claim to be Jews though they are would return to a restored universe in which there is "no more death or mourning or crying or pain, *for the old order of things has passed away*" (Revelation 21:4). As the apostle John made plain, "Nothing impure will ever enter [the New Jerusalem], nor will anyone who does what is shameful or deceitful, but only those whose names are written in the Lamb's book of life" (21:27).

Finally, the number 1,000 is invariably used figuratively. God increased the number of the Israelites a thousand times (Deuteronomy 1:11); God is "keeping his covenant of love to a thousand generations" (7:9); God owns "the cattle on a thousand hills" (Psalm 50:10); "better is one day in [God's] courts than a thousand elsewhere" (84:10); "the least of [Zion] will become a thousand, the smallest a mighty nation" (Isaiah 60:22); God "[shows] love to a thousand generations" (Exodus 20:6); and a thousand more examples could easily be added to the list.

In context of the seven-year tribulation of Revelation (mirroring the seven-year tribulation under the Old Testament antichrist, Antiochus), the apostle John wanted his hearers to have an eternal perspective. Satan will be bound forever—a thousand years—and those who have not taken his mark will rule forever—a thousand years. As such, Satan's defeat is complete, just as the victory and vindication of Jesus' followers is complete.

In part adapted from *AfterLife*

Who wrote Revelation?

In the same way that buildings contain clues that unveil the identity of their architects, so, too, books contain clues that unveil the identity of their authors. In the case of Revelation, three possibilities have been put forward, but only one fits the design.

First is a notion that can be dismissed rather rapidly, namely, the idea that Revelation was written pseudonymously. Pseudonymity (writing under a false name) was largely practiced by writers who lacked authority. Thus, they borrowed the names of authentic eyewitnesses to the life and times of Christ to create an air of credibility. In sharp contrast, the book of Revelation provides ample internal evidence that it was written by a Jew intimately acquainted with the historical events and locations he wrote about. Only a handful of extremists today even countenance the possibility that Revelation could have been written pseudonymously.

Furthermore, it is commonly argued that Revelation was written by a shadowy figure named John the Elder. Like pseudonymity, this contention has its feet firmly planted in midair. It would be better grounded if there were even a shred of historical certainty that John the Elder existed in the first place. (According to eminent New Testament scholar R. C.

Was Revelation written before or after the destruction of the temple in AD 70?

Just as it is common to describe Patmos as a barren Alcatraz, misidentify the great prostitute as the Roman Catholic Church, or identify the 144,000 as exclusively Jewish male virgins, so, too, it is common to contend that Revelation was written long after the destruction of the temple in AD 70. Thus, according to modern-day prophecy pundits, Revelation describes events that will likely take place in the twenty-first century rather than the first century.

First, if the apostle John were indeed writing in AD 95—long after the destruction of the temple—it seems incredible that he would make no mention whatsoever of the most apocalyptic event in Jewish history: the demolition of Jerusalem and the destruction of the temple at the hands of Titus. Imagine writing a history of New York City today and making no mention of the destruction of the Twin Towers of the World Trade Center at the hands of terrorists on September 11, 2001. Or, more directly, imagine writing a thesis on the future of terrorism in America and failing to mention the Manhattan Massacre. Consider another parallel: Imagine that you are reading a history concerning Jewish struggles in Nazi Germany and find no mention whatsoever of the Holocaust. Would it not be reasonable to suppose that this history was written prior to the outbreak of World War II? The answer is self-evident. Just as it stretches credulity to suggest that a history of the Jews in Germany would be written in the aftermath of World War II and yet make no mention of the Holocaust, so, too, it is unreasonable to think that Revelation was written twenty-five years after the destruction of Jerusalem and yet makes no mention of the most apocalyptic event in Jewish history.

Furthermore, those who hold that the book of Revelation was written long after the destruction of the temple in AD 70 face an even more formidable obstacle. Consider one of the most amazing prophecies in all of Scripture. Jesus was leaving the temple when His disciples called His attention to its buildings. As they gazed upon its massive stones and magnificent buildings, Jesus uttered the unthinkable: "I tell you the truth, not one stone here will be left on another; everyone will be thrown down" (Matthew 24:2; Mark 13:2; Luke 21:6). One generation later, this prophecy—no doubt still emblazoned on the tablet of their consciousness—became a vivid and horrifying reality. As noted by Josephus, the temple was doomed on August 30, AD 70, "the very day on which the former temple had been destroyed by the king of Babylon." As incredible as Christ's prophecy and its fulfillment one generation later are, it is equally incredible to suppose that the apostle John would make no mention of it if he were indeed writing after the temple was destroyed. As the student of Scripture well knows, New Testament writers were quick to highlight fulfilled prophecy. The phrase "This was to fulfill what was spoken of by the prophet" permeates the pages of Scripture. Thus, it is inconceivable that Jesus would make an apocalyptic prophecy concerning the destruction of Jerusalem and the Jewish temple and that John would fail to mention that the prophecy was fulfilled one generation later exactly as Jesus had predicted it.

Finally, let me highlight an additional piece of internal evidence that should give pause to those who are overly dogmatic about the late-dating of Revelation. In Revelation 11, John said, "I was given a reed like a measuring rod and was told, 'Go and measure the temple of God and the altar, and count the worshipers there. But exclude the outer court; do not measure it, because it has been given to the Gentiles. They will trample on the holy city for 42 months'" (vv. 1–2). In context, Jesus had sent His angel "to show his servants what must soon take place" (Revelation 1:1) Thus, the prophecy concerns a future event, not one that took place twenty-five years earlier.

While some fundamentalists on both left and right dogmatically dispute such realities, liberal scholars like John A. T. Robinson, author of *Redating the New Testament*, have been compelled by evidence to rethink late-dating paradigms. Indeed Robinson's research led him to contend that all of sacred

Scripture was completed prior to the fall of Jerusalem. Says Robinson, "One of the oddest facts about the New Testament is that what on any showing would appear to be the single most datable and climactic event of the period—the fall of Jerusalem in AD 70, and with it the collapse of institutional Judaism based on the temple—is never once mentioned as a past fact."

Robinson's redating is not just a dogmatic assertion, but it is a defensible argument. If vast portions of the New Testament are late-dated, as per fundamentalists, it seems incredible that there would be no mention of the most apocalyptic event in Jewish history—the demolition of Jerusalem and the destruction of the temple at the hands of Titus.

In summary, among the reasons we can be certain that the book of Revelation was not written twenty-five years after the destruction of Jerusalem, three tower above the rest. First, just as it is unreasonable to suppose that someone writing a history of the World Trade Center in the aftermath of September 11, 2001, would fail to mention the destruction of the Twin Towers, so, too, it stretches credulity to suggest that Revelation was written in the aftermath of the devastation of Jerusalem and the Jewish temple yet makes no mention of this apocalypse. Additionally, if John had been writing in AD 95, it is incredible to suppose he would not mention the fulfillment of Christ's most improbable and apocalyptic vision: the destruction of Jerusalem and the temple. Finally, New Testament documents—including the book of Revelation—speak of Jerusalem and the Jewish temple being intact at the time they were written. If Revelation was written *before* AD 70, it is reasonable to assume that the vision given to John was meant to reveal the apocalyptic events surrounding the destruction of Jerusalem—events that were still in John's future but are in our past. This, of course, does not presuppose that *all* the prophecies in Revelation have already been fulfilled. Just as thoughtful Christians should distance themselves from the fully futurist fallacy, they should disavow a predominantly preterist (i.e., past) perspective as well.

The Revelation of Jesus Christ, which God gave Him to show His servants—things which must shortly take place. And He sent and signified it by His angel to His servant John, who bore witness to the word of God, and to the testimony of Jesus Christ, to all things that he saw. Blessed is he who reads and those who hear the words of this prophecy, and keep those things which are written in it; for the time is near.

REVELATION 1:1–3 NKJV

For further study, see Hank Hanegraaff, *The Apocalypse Code: Find Out What the Bible Really Says About the End Times . . . and Why It Matters Today* (Nashville: Thomas Nelson, 2007).

RESURRECTION
AND AFTERLIFE

of those who have fallen asleep" (1 Corinthians 15:20). In the end, "perfect love drives out fear" (1 John 4:18).

In part adapted from *AfterLife*

Whoever confesses that Jesus is the Son of God, God abides in him, and he in God. We have come to know and have believed the love which God has for us. God is love, and the one who abides in love abides in God, and God abides in him. By this, love is perfected with us, so that we may have confidence in the day of judgment; because as He is, so also are we in this world. There is no fear in love; but perfect love casts out fear, because fear involves punishment, and the one who fears is not perfected in love. We love, because He first loved us.

1 JOHN 4:15–19 NASB

For further study, see Hank Hanegraaff, *AfterLife: What You Need to Know About Heaven, the Hereafter, and Near-Death Experiences* (Brentwood, TN: Worthy, 2013).

What is a near-death experience?

The moniker *near-death experience* (NDE) was coined in 1975 by the occult parapsychologist and philosopher Raymond Moody in the runaway bestseller *Life After Life*. Since then, stories of near-death experiences have produced a virtual cottage industry.

First, NDEs typically involve an *autoscopic* episode during which those who are believed to be clinically dead view the physical world from outside their bodies. After viewing various aspects of the physical world from this out-of-body perspective, roughly a third of NDErs promptly return to their bodies.

Furthermore, there is what is referred to as the *transcendental* experience. NDErs allegedly enter what is described as a dark tunnel, are pulled inexorably toward a distant light, enter a luminous environment, and encounter previously deceased loved ones as well as extraordinary beings of light variously identified as Abraham, Jesus, or Buddha. In some cases, NDErs move seamlessly from the autoscopic to the transcendental phase of the out-of-body experience. In other cases they skip the autoscopic phase altogether.

Finally, in addition to heavenly encounters, a number of NDErs report hellish episodes. In *Beyond Death's Door*, cardiologist Maurice Rawlings recounts the tale of a clinically dead

Is soul sleep biblical?

S eventh-day Adventists are among the most well-known sects currently promoting the idea of soul sleep. From their perspective, the soul of a man is indistinguishable from the whole of a man. Thus, the soul cannot continue to exist consciously apart from the body.

First, as the Bible makes clear, the soul is not the whole of a human being. The New Testament unambiguously communicates that the soul continues to have awareness after the body has died. In Luke 16, for instance, Jesus told the parable of a rich man and a beggar who die physically yet experience conscious awareness in the intermediate state—a fact difficult to deny in that the rich man's brothers are living and final judgment has not yet occurred.

Furthermore, sleep is a common biblical metaphor for the death of the body. John 11 provides the clearest of examples. Jesus told His disciples, "'Our friend Lazarus has fallen asleep; but I am going there to wake him up.' His disciples replied, 'Lord, if he sleeps, he will get better.' Jesus had been speaking of his death, but his disciples thought he meant natural sleep. So then he told them plainly, 'Lazarus is dead'" (vv. 11–14). Here, as in myriad other examples, the Bible speaks of the body asleep in death (e.g., 1 Kings 2:10; Daniel

12:2; Ephesians 5:14). Conversely, the Bible never speaks of the soul asleep in death.

Finally, if the soul did not continue in conscious awareness after the death of the body, it would be incongruent for the apostle Paul to desire to be away from the body in order to be at home with the Lord. Said Paul, "For to me, to live is Christ and to die is gain. If I am to go on living in the body, this will mean fruitful labor for me. Yet what shall I choose? I do not know! I am torn between the two: I desire to depart and be with Christ, which is better by far; but it is more necessary for you that I remain in the body" (Philippians 1:21–24; cf. 2 Corinthians 5:6–9). How could death be "better by far" than further fruitful ministry if it entails soul sleep? The point here, as elsewhere in the biblical text, is that far from soul sleep, to be with Christ is soul satisfaction (see Hebrews 12:23; Luke 23:42–43; especially Luke 23:46; cf. 24:37–39 and Acts 7:59; cf. 2 Corinthians 12:2–4).

In short, soul sleep has nothing to commend it biblically. As the Bible makes clear, the soul continues to have conscious existence apart from the body that dies.

In part adapted from *AfterLife*

For further study, see Hank Hanegraaff, *AfterLife: What You Need to Know About Heaven, the Hereafter, and Near-Death Experiences* (Brentwood, TN: Worthy, 2013).

Will we be able to sin in heaven?

To assert that we are not capable of sinning in heaven would seem to suggest that we will not have free will in heaven. Yet to claim that we *could* start sinning again in heaven raises the possibility of another fall—this time in paradise restored. How, then, can we be certain that the problem of sin is resolved in eternity?

First, we can be absolutely certain that we will not sin in heaven because that is what the Scriptures teach. In this life our *position* in Christ is one of righteousness. In the life to come, we will be righteous in *practice* as well. Christ's ultimate purpose for His bride is "to present her to himself as a radiant church, without stain or wrinkle or any other blemish, but holy and blameless" (Ephesians 5:27).

Furthermore, where there is no temptation, there likewise will be no sin. While in the present we are bombarded by the temptations of the world, the flesh, and the devil, in paradise restored the problem of sin and Satan is forever resolved.

Finally, in heaven we will be actualized in righteousness, free to be what God made us to be. Far from robbing us of freedom, such actualization is the quintessence of freedom. We freely give up the freedom *to* sin in exchange for freedom *from* sin.

In His infinite wisdom, the Holy Spirit inspired the human

authors of Scripture to illustrate this unwaveringly faithful relationship between the Lord Jesus and the church with the analogy of marriage. Jesus is the church's singularly sinless and freely faithful bridegroom. Likewise, in heaven the church will be His "holy and blameless" bride. A bride freed forever from enslavement to sin. Freed to enjoy paradise restored.

In part adapted from *AfterLife*

There shall by no means enter it anything that defiles, or causes an abomination or a lie, but only those who are written in the Lamb's Book of Life.
REVELATION 21:27 NKJV

For further study, see Hank Hanegraaff, *AfterLife: What You Need to Know About Heaven, the Hereafter, and Near-Death Experiences* (Brentwood, TN: Worthy, 2013).

Will there be animals in heaven?

Scripture does not conclusively tell us whether our pets will make it to heaven. However, the Bible does provide us with some significant clues regarding whether or not animals will inhabit the new heaven and the new earth.

First, animals populated the garden of Eden. Thus, there is a reason for believing that animals will populate Eden Restored as well. Animals are among God's most creative creations. Thus, it would seem incredible that He would banish such wonders from heaven.

Furthermore, while we cannot say for certain that the pets we enjoy today will be "resurrected" in eternity, I am not willing to preclude the possibility. Some of the keenest thinkers from C. S. Lewis to Peter Kreeft are not only convinced that animals in general but that pets in particular will be restored in the resurrection. If God resurrected our pets, it would be in total keeping with His overwhelming grace and goodness.

Finally, the Scriptures from first to last suggest that animals have souls. Both Moses in Genesis and John in Revelation communicate that the Creator endowed animals with souls. In the original languages of Genesis 1:20 and Revelation 8:9, *nephesh* and *psyche,* respectively, refer to the essence of life or soul. Not until Descartes and Hobbes and the Enlightenment did people think otherwise about animals. However, because the soul of an animal is qualitatively different from the soul of a human, there is reasonable doubt that it can survive the death of its body. One thing is certain: Scripture provides us with sufficient precedence for believing that animals will inhabit the new heaven and new earth. In the words of Isaiah: "The wolf will live with the lamb, the leopard will lie down with the goat, the calf and the lion and the yearling together; and a little child will lead them" (Isaiah 11:6).

Adapted from *Resurrection*

Your kingdom is an everlasting kingdom,
and your dominion endures through all generations.
The LORD is faithful to all his promises
and loving toward all he has made.

PSALM 145:13

For further study, see Hank Hanegraaff, *Resurrection* (Nashville: Word Publishing, 2000), chapter 13.

So will there be sex in the resurrection? Again, yes and no. Yes, there will be *sexuality* in heaven in that we will be in heaven, and *we* by our very nature are sexual beings. And no, there is no warrant for believing that sex in terms of the physical act will be in heaven.

Adapted from Resurrection

> *God created man in His own image;*
> *in the image of God He created him;*
> *male and female He created them.*
> GENESIS 1:27 NKJV

For further study, see Hank Hanegraaff, *Resurrection* (Nashville: Word Publishing), chapter 17. See also Peter J. Kreeft, *Everything You Ever Wanted to Know About Heaven, But Never Dreamed of Asking* (San Francisco: Ignatius Press, 1990).

If heaven is perfect, won't it be perfectly boring?

An all-too-prevalent perception in Christianity and the culture is that heaven is going to be one big bore. That, however, is far from true. Rather, heaven will be a place of continuous learning, growth, and development. By nature, humans are finite, and that is how it always will be. While we will have an incredible capacity to learn, we will never come to the end of learning.

To begin with, we will never exhaust exploring our Creator. God by nature is infinite, and we are limited. Thus, what we now merely apprehend about the Creator we will spend an eternity seeking to comprehend. Imagine finally beginning to get a handle on how God is one in nature and three in Person. Imagine exploring the depths of God's love, wisdom, and holiness. Imagine forever growing in our capacities to fathom His immensity, immutability, and incomprehensibility. And the more we come to know Him, the more there will be to know.

Furthermore, we will never come to the end of exploring fellow Christians. Our ability to appreciate one another will be enhanced exponentially. Imagine being able to love another human being without even a hint of selfishness. Imagine

Moreover, Jesus made essentially the same point in His parables. In the parable of the talents (Matthew 25:14–30), for instance, Jesus told the story of a man who entrusted his property to his servants before going on a long journey. Each servant received an amount commensurate with his abilities. To one the master gave five talents; to another, two talents; and to a third, he gave one. The servant who received five talents doubled his money, as did the servant who had received two. The last servant, however, showed gross negligence and buried his master's money in the ground. When the master returned, he rewarded the faithful servants with the words, "Well done, good and faithful servant! You have been faithful with a few things; I will put you in charge of many things. Come and share your master's happiness!" (v. 23). The unfaithful servant not only forfeited his reward but was thrown into outer darkness "where there will be weeping and gnashing of teeth" (v. 30).

Furthermore, the canon of Scripture communicates about degrees of reward given in the resurrection. The basis of our salvation is the finished work of Christ, but Christians can erect a building of rewards upon that foundation. As Paul put it, "No one can lay any foundation other than the one already laid, which is Jesus Christ. If any man builds on this foundation using gold, silver, costly stones, wood, hay or straw, his work will be shown for what it is, because the Day will bring it to light. It will be revealed with fire, and the fire will test the quality of each man's work. If what he has built survives, he will receive his reward. If it is burned up, he will suffer loss; he himself will be saved, but only as one escaping through the flames" (1 Corinthians 3:11–15).

Paul here illustrated the sober reality that some Christians will be resurrected with precious little to show for the time they spent on earth: they "will be saved, but only as one escaping through the flames." These words conjure up images of people escaping burning buildings with little more than the charred clothes upon their backs. This will be the lot of even the most visible Christian leaders whose motives were selfish rather than selfless. Conversely, those who build selflessly upon the foundation of Christ using "gold, silver, [and] costly stones" will receive enduring rewards. Indeed, a selfless Christian layman who labors in virtual obscurity will hear the words he has longed for throughout his life: "Well done, good and faithful servant! You have been faithful with a few things; I will put you in charge of many things. Come and share your master's happiness!" (Matthew 25:21). While deeds are our duty, not even the smallest act of kindness will go without its reward.

Finally, degrees of reward in eternity involve both enlarged responsibilities as well as enhanced spiritual capacities. An experience I had several years ago aptly underscores this biblical reality. I received an invitation to play Cypress Point, arguably the most spectacular golf course on planet Earth. While the

Are there degrees of punishment in hell?

On the basis of what the Bible teaches, we may safely conclude that not all existence in hell is equal.

First, the unified testimony of Scripture is that God is perfectly just and will reward and punish each person in accordance with what he or she has done (Psalm 62:12; Proverbs 24:12; Jeremiah 17:10; Ezekiel 18:20, 30; Romans 2:5–16; 1 Corinthians 3:8, 11–15; 2 Corinthians 5:10; Colossians 3:23–25; 1 Peter 1:17; Revelation 20:12).

Furthermore, the Bible is clear that with greater revelation and responsibility comes stricter judgment (cf. James 3:1). Jesus warned the Pharisees that they would "be punished most severely" for their willful hypocrisy (Luke 20:47). In denouncing the cities where most of His miracles had been performed, Jesus said, "Woe to you, Korazin! Woe to you, Bethsaida! If the miracles that were performed in you had been performed in Tyre and Sidon, they would have repented long ago in sackcloth and ashes" (Matthew 11:21). Thus, said Jesus, "It will be more bearable for Tyre and Sidon on the day of judgment than for you" (v. 22). Moreover, Jesus used the metaphor of physical torture to warn His hearers that those who knowingly disobey God's commands will experience greater torment in hell than those who disobey in ignorance (Luke 12:47–48).

HANK HANEGRAAFF

Finally, the canon of Scripture ratifies the common-sense notion that not all sins are created equal (cf. John 19:11). To think a murderous thought is sin; to carry that thought to its logical conclusion is far graver sin. Every sin is an act of rebellion against a holy God, but some sins carry far more serious consequences than others and thus receive severer punishment in this life and the next. Indeed, according to Scripture, the torment of Hitler's hell will greatly exceed that of the less wicked.

> *I saw the dead, small and great, standing before*
> *God, and books were opened. And another book*
> *was opened, which is the Book of Life. And the*
> *dead were judged according to their works, by*
> *the things which were written in the books.*
> REVELATION 20:12 NKJV

For further study, see "Why should I believe in hell?" (p. 562) and "Is annihilationism biblical?" (p. 564). See also Hank Hanegraaff, *AfterLife: What You Need to Know About Heaven, the Hereafter, and Near-Death Experiences* (Brentwood, TN: Worthy, 2013).

Why should I believe in hell?

The horrors of hell are such that they cause us to instinctively recoil in disbelief and doubt, yet there are compelling reasons that should cause us to erase such doubt from our minds.

First, Christ, the Creator of the cosmos, clearly communicated hell's irrevocable reality. In the Sermon on the Mount (Matthew 5–7), Jesus explicitly warned His followers about the dangers of hell a half dozen times. In the Olivet Discourse (Matthew 24–25), Christ repeatedly warned His followers of the judgment that is to come. And in His famous story of the rich man and Lazarus (Luke 16), Christ graphically portrayed the finality of eternal torment in hell.

Furthermore, the concept of choice demands that we believe in hell. Without hell, there is no choice. And without choice, heaven would not be heaven; heaven would be hell. The righteous would inherit a counterfeit heaven, and the unrighteous would be incarcerated in heaven against their wills, which would be a torture worse than hell. Imagine spending a lifetime voluntarily distancing yourself from God only to find yourself involuntarily dragged into His loving presence for all eternity; the alternative to hell is worse than hell itself in that humans made in the image of God would be stripped of freedom and forced to worship God against their will.

Finally, common sense dictates that there must be a hell. Without hell, the wrongs of Hitler's Holocaust will never be righted. Justice would be impugned if, after slaughtering six million Jews, Hitler merely died in the arms of his mistress with no eternal consequences. The ancients knew better than to think such a thing. David knew that for a time it might seem as though the wicked prosper in spite of their deeds, but in the end God's justice will be served.

Common sense also dictates that without a hell there is no need for a Savior. Little needs to be said about the absurdity of suggesting that the Creator should suffer more than the cumulative sufferings of all of mankind if there were no hell to save us from. Without hell, there is no need for salvation. Without salvation, there is no need for a sacrifice. And without sacrifice, there is no need for a Savior. As much as we may wish to think that all will be saved, common sense precludes the possibility.

Adapted from *Resurrection*

For further study, see Hank Hanegraaff, *AfterLife: What You Need to Know About Heaven, the Hereafter, and Near-Death Experiences* (Brentwood, TN: Worthy, 2013).

Is annihilationism biblical?

Just as universalism is the rage in liberal Christianity, so, too, annihilationism is gaining momentum in conservative Christian circles. The question, of course, is whether or not annihilationism is biblical.

First, common sense dictates that a God of love and justice does not arbitrarily annihilate the crowning jewels of His creation. Far from rubbing us out, He graciously provides us the freedom to choose between redemption and rebellion. It would be a horrific evil to think that God would create people with freedom of choice and then annihilate them because of their choices.

Furthermore, common sense leads to the conclusion that nonexistence is not better than existence since nonexistence is nothing at all. Moreover, not all existence in hell is equal. We may safely conclude that the torment of Hitler's hell will greatly exceed the torment experienced by a garden-variety pagan.

God is perfectly just, and each person who spurns His grace will suffer exactly what he or she deserves (Luke 12:47–48; Matthew 16:27; Colossians 3:25; Revelation 20:11–15; Proverbs 24:12).

Finally, humans are fashioned in the very image of God; therefore, to eliminate them would do violence to His nature.

The alternative to annihilation is quarantine. And that is precisely what hell is.

Adapted from *Resurrection*

> *If anyone worships the beast and his image, and*
> *receives a mark on his forehead or on his hand, he*
> *also will drink of the wine of the wrath of God, which*
> *is mixed in full strength in the cup of His anger;*
> *and he will be tormented with fire and brimstone*
> *in the presence of the holy angels and in the presence*
> *of the Lamb. And the smoke of their torment goes*
> *up forever and ever; they have no rest day and*
> *night, those who worship the beast and his image,*
> *and whoever receives the mark of his name.*
> REVELATION 14:9–11 NASB

For further study, see Robert A. Peterson, *Hell on Trial: The Case for Eternal Punishment* (Phillipsburg, NJ: Presbyterian and Reformed Press, 1995); and Hank Hanegraaff, *AfterLife: What You Need to Know About Heaven, the Hereafter, and Near-Death Experiences* (Brentwood, TN: Worthy, 2013).

What about purgatory?

Roman Catholicism teaches that believers incur debts that must inevitably be satisfied in purgatory "before the gates of heaven can be opened." While purgatory is not equivalent to a second chance for unbelievers, it is nonetheless decidedly unbiblical.

First, the doctrine of purgatory undermines the sufficiency of Christ's atonement on the cross. Scripture declares that Christ, through "one sacrifice . . . has made perfect forever those who are being made holy" (Hebrews 10:14; see also Hebrews 1:3). Thus, we can rest assured that Christ received in His own body all the punishment we deserved, absolutely satisfying the justice of God on our behalf (Romans 3:25–26; 2 Corinthians 5:19, 21; 1 Peter 3:18; 1 John 2:2). When Jesus cried out from the cross, "It is finished!" (John 19:30), He was in effect saying, "The debt has been paid in full."

Furthermore, Roman Catholicism clearly undermines the seriousness of sin by forwarding the notion that there are venial sins that can be atoned for through temporal punishment in purgatory. In reality, as the Bible makes clear, all our transgressions and iniquities are sins against a holy, eternal God (Psalm 51:4). And as such, they rightly incur an eternal rather than a temporal debt (Ezekiel 18:4; Matthew 5–7; Romans 6:23; James 2:10).

Finally, while purgatory was officially defined by the Council of Florence (1439) and officially defended by the Council of Trent in the late sixteenth century, nowhere is purgatory officially depicted in the canon of Scripture. As *The New Catholic Encyclopedia* readily acknowledges, "The doctrine of Purgatory is not explicitly stated in the Bible." Thus, Catholicism is forced to appeal to the traditions of the fathers rather than the testimony of the Father—who through His Word has graciously provided salvation by grace alone, though faith alone, on account of Christ alone (Romans 4:2–8, 11:6; Ephesians 2:8–9).

> *By one offering [Jesus] has perfected forever*
> *those who are being sanctified.*
> HEBREWS 10:14 NKJV

For further study, see Norman L. Geisler and Ralph E. MacKenzie, *Roman Catholics and Evangelicals: Agreements and Differences* (Grand Rapids: Baker Books, 1995).

How can I develop an
eternal perspective?

I f we are looking for the personification of an eternal perspective, we need look no further than our Lord and Savior Jesus Christ. He immersed Himself in Scripture, sacrificed Himself for the needs of others, and treasured fellowship with His heavenly Father. Like the Master, we are called to elevate our gaze from earthly vanities to eternal verities.

First, we develop an eternal perspective by saturating ourselves with Scripture. Jesus modeled daily devotion to the Word of God. In the ultimate spiritual battle, Jesus took up the sword of the Spirit, which is the Word of God. He had mined, memorized, and meditated on Scripture. Thus, when the slanderer sought to tempt the Savior to turn stones into bread, Jesus was prepared. "It is written:" He said, "'Man does not live on bread alone, but on every word that comes from the mouth of God'" (Matthew 4:4).

Furthermore, we begin to view this world with an eye toward eternity by focusing on the needs of others. As our Master sacrificed Himself for the sins of the world, we must learn to live selflessly rather than selfishly. At the Judgment those who fed the hungry, gave drink to the thirsty, clothed the naked, cared for the sick, and visited those in prison will be rewarded as if they had done these things for the Lord Himself (Matthew 25:31–40).

Finally, we develop an eternal perspective by withdrawing from the invasive sounds of this world so that we can hear the sounds of another place and another voice. Dr. Luke told us that "Jesus often withdrew to lonely places and prayed" (Luke 5:16). Unlike the religious leaders of His day, Jesus did not pray to be seen by men. He prayed because He treasured fellowship with His Father. If you wish to develop the kind of perspective that leads to abundant living both now and for all eternity, "go into your room, close the door and pray to your Father, who is unseen. Then your Father, who sees what is done in secret, will reward you" (Matthew 6:6).

> *"Do not lay up for yourselves treasures on earth,*
> *where moth and rust destroy and where thieves break*
> *in and steal; but lay up for yourselves treasures in*
> *heaven, where neither moth nor rust destroys and*
> *where thieves do not break in and steal. For where*
> *your treasure is, there your heart will be also."*
>
> MATTHEW 6:19–21 NKJV

For further study, see Dallas Willard, *The Divine Conspiracy* (San Francisco: Harper San Francisco, 1998); see also Hank Hanegraaff, *The Prayer of Jesus* (Nashville: Word Publishing, 2001) and *Resurrection* (Nashville: Word Publishing, 2000).

How can a person find
more Bible answers?

his revised and updated edition of *The Complete Bible Answer Book* addresses some of the most significant questions I've been asked during twenty-five years of hosting the *Bible Answer Man* radio broadcast. In well over three thousand *live* broadcasts, I've answered thousands more. I invite you to ask me *your* questions live on the *Bible Answer Man* broadcast by dialing toll-free 888.ASK.HANK, Monday through Friday, 5:50 p.m. to 7:00 p.m., Eastern Time, or access additional answers online at www.equip.org.

Furthermore, it is your responsibility to search the Scriptures daily. My opinion is no better than anyone else's opinion unless it squares with Scripture. The apostle Paul commended the Berean believers "for they received the message with great eagerness *and examined the Scriptures every day to see if what Paul said was true*" (Acts 17:11).

Finally, it is crucial that you get into the Word of God and get the Word of God into you. If you fail to eat well-balanced meals on a regular basis, you eventually will suffer the physical consequences. Likewise, if you do not regularly feed on the Word of God, you will suffer spiritual consequences. Jesus said, "Man does not live on bread alone, but on every word that comes from the mouth of God" (Matthew 4:4). Great physical meals are one thing; great spiritual meals are quite another. Begin your journey forward by reading the next entry "What are the main ingredients for spiritually nourishing M-E-A-L-S?"

Whatever things are true, whatever things are noble, whatever things are just, whatever things are pure, whatever things are lovely, whatever things are of good report, if there is any virtue and if there is anything praiseworthy—meditate on these things.

PHILIPPIANS 4:8 NKJV

What are the main ingredients for spiritually nourishing M-E-A-L-S?

Nothing should take precedence over getting into the Word and getting the Word into us. If we fail to eat well-balanced meals on a regular basis, we will eventually suffer the physical consequences. Likewise, if we do not regularly feed on the Word of God, we will suffer the spiritual consequences. Physical *meals* are one thing; spiritual *meals* are quite another. The acronym M-E-A-L-S will serve to remind you that the Spirit will illumine your heart and mind as you **m**emorize, **e**xamine, **a**pply, **l**isten, and **s**tudy the Bible for all it's worth. The Word of God is the sword of the Spirit. When we grasp it, His illuminating power will flood our being.

MEMORIZE. One of the best things that happened to me as a young believer was being told that all Christians memorize Scripture. By the time I found out that not all of them did, I was already hooked. Now, as I look back, I can say truthfully that nothing compares to the excitement of memorizing Scripture. God has called us to write His Word on the tablet of our hearts (Proverbs 7:1–3; cf. Deuteronomy 6:6), and with the call He has provided the ability. Your mind is like a muscle. If you exercise it, you will increase its capacity to remember and recall. If you don't, like a muscle, it will atrophy.

EXAMINE. In Acts 17:11, we read that the Bereans "*examined* the Scriptures" daily to see if what Paul was teaching was true. For that, they were commended as being noble in character. Examining the Scriptures may take discipline and dedication, but the dividends are dramatic. The Bereans examined the Bible daily, and so should we. Examination requires the use of our minds, and the Bible exhorts believers to use their minds to honor God. Paul urged Christians to test all things (1 Thessalonians 5:21) and to be transformed by the renewing of their minds in order to discern the will of God (Romans 12:2).

APPLY. As wonderful and worthwhile as it is to memorize and examine Scripture, it's simply not enough. We must take the knowledge we have gleaned from the Word of God and *apply* it to every aspect of our daily lives. Wisdom is the *application* of knowledge, and wisdom is precisely what Jesus emphasized in concluding His majestic Sermon on the Mount:

> *Everyone who hears these words of mine and puts them into practice is like a wise man who built his house on the rock. The rain came down, the streams rose, and the winds blew and beat against that house; yet it did not fall, because it had its foundation on the rock. But everyone who hears these words of mine and does not put them into practice is like a foolish man who built his house on sand. The rain came down, the streams rose, and the winds blew and beat against that house, and it fell with a great crash.* (Matthew 7:24–27)

LISTEN. In order to apply God's directions to our everyday lives, we must learn to *listen* carefully as God speaks to us through the majesty of His Word. Like Samuel, we should say, "Speak, [Lord,] for your servant is *listening*" (1 Samuel 3:10). As Jesus so wonderfully put it, "My sheep *listen* to my voice; I know them, and they follow me" (John 10:27). One of the most amazing aspects of Scripture is that it is alive and active, not dead and dull. In other words, God continues to speak through His Word. The Spirit illumines our minds so that "we may know the things freely given to us by God" (1 Corinthians 2:12 NASB).

STUDY. Scripture exhorts us to study to show ourselves approved by God, to show ourselves as workmen who do not need to blush with embarrassment but who instead "correctly [handle] the word of truth" (2 Timothy 2:15). In *examining* Scripture, it is typically best to start with one good translation and stick with it. In *studying*, however, it is best to use a number of good Bible translations. To aid in your study of Scripture, there are many wonderful resources including *study Bibles*, *commentaries*, and *Bible dictionaries*.

Jesus said, "I am the bread of life. He who comes to Me shall never hunger, and he who believes in Me shall never thirst" (John 6:35 NKJV). May the acronym M-E-A-L-S daily remind you to nourish yourself with the Bread of Life.

My son, keep my words
And treasure my commandments within you.
Keep my commandments and live,
And my teaching as the apple of your eye.
Bind them on your fingers;
Write them on the tablet of your heart.

PROVERBS 7:1–3 NASB

MEMORIZE

EXAMINE

APPLY

LISTEN

STUDY

For further study, see Hank Hanegraaff, *Truth Matters, Life Matters More* (Brentwood, TN: Worthy, 2016).

What is the L-E-G-A-C-Y Reading Plan?

Make no mistake. Reading through the Bible—particularly in a year's time—is a daunting proposition. Thus, the *Legacy Reading Plan* is strategically designed to empower you to "eat the elephant" one book at a time. The format is specifically formulated to make your time in the Bible the best it can be. There's no time like the present to engage. Consideration of the principles identified in the acronym L-E-G-A-C-Y provide a memorable framework around which reading the Bible may well become an addictive and intoxicating habit.

LOCATION. Do you have a secret place, a location where you can shut out the noise of the world and hear the voice of your heavenly Father as He speaks to you through the majesty of His Word? For some, that place may be the sauna; for others, a study. The point is we all desperately need a place away from the invasive sounds of the world so we can hear the sounds of another place, the sound of another Voice. So begin your Legacy Reading Plan by locating *your* secret place.

ESSENCE. The Legacy Reading Plan is unique in that it requires you to process books of the Bible rather than piecing together bits of books. The goal is to comprehend the essence of what God is communicating by reading each book as a whole. The exceptions are

Psalms and Proverbs. Psalms constituted a hymnbook or devotional guide for ancient Israel and can do so for you as well. And because Proverbs is replete with principles for successful daily living, you may find it helpful to read a chapter of Proverbs each day, progressing through the entire book once a month. You may also wish to add the Apocrypha to your reading plan. Its historical details are exhilarating. For example, the Maccabean revolt chronicled in Maccabees, and celebrated by Jews during Hanukkah, is a powerful testimony to God's fulfillment of Daniel's prophecies.

GENRE. To understand Scripture in the sense in which it is intended, it is important to pay special attention to the *genre* we are reading. In other words, to interpret the Bible as literature, it is crucial to consider the *kind* of literature we are reading. Just as a legal brief differs from a prophetic oracle, there is a difference in genre between Leviticus and Revelation. Genre is particularly significant when considering writings that are difficult to categorize, such as Genesis, which is largely a historical narrative interlaced with symbolism and repetitive poetic structure.

AUTHOR. Just as it is essential to read through books rather than bits of the Bible, so it is helpful to read biblical authors sequentially. As such, the Legacy Reading Plan is grouped by author. This is helpful because even though biblical authors wrote "as they were carried along by the Holy Spirit" (2 Peter 1:21), their personalities and proclivities are clearly evident in their writings. For example, only John identifies Jesus as the Word, or Logos (John 1:1; Revelation 19:13). Likewise, John alone identifies Jesus as the true witness

(John 5; Revelation 2), and it is John who most exploits the Mosaic requirement of two witnesses (John 8:17–18; Revelation 2).

CONTEXT. Context has an impact on how you think of one set of biblical books in relation to another. For this reason, the Epistles are read prior to the Synoptic Gospels in the Legacy Reading Plan. The didactic (teaching) principles of the Epistles provide a theological context that will help you better understand the gospel narratives. Moreover, because the book of Revelation draws heavily upon the imagery of the Hebrew prophets, the reading of Revelation is placed in close proximity to the Old Testament prophets. And because the Gospels recount the birth and ministry of Christ, the Synoptics and the book of Acts are assigned to the final month of the reading plan.

YEAR. The overarching objective of the Legacy Reading Plan is to read through the Bible once a year, every year, for the rest of your life. The reading calendar is naturally segmented into seasons and those seasons, into months. The sample layout has you starting in January, but whatever time of year you start, your focus will first be on the Pentateuch and poetry (249 chapters); second, the historical books (249 chapters); next, the prophets (250 chapters); and, finally, the New Testament (260 chapters). Each of these seasons is further broken down into months. The goal of the first month is to read through Genesis and Exodus and in the last month, the Synoptic Gospels and Acts. At times you will find yourself naturally reading ten chapters at a time and at other times, one or two. More importantly you will read the Bible just as you read other literature, not just a paragraph here or a half a chapter there.

For the word of God is living and powerful,
and sharper than any two-edged sword,
piercing even to the division of soul and spirit,
and of joints and marrow, and is a discerner
of the thoughts and intents of the heart.

HEBREWS 4:12 NKJV

LOCATION

ESSENCE

GENRE

AUTHOR

CONTEXT

YEAR

The *Legacy*

Winter (249 chapters) Psalms—3 per week Proverbs—1 chapter per day	***Hebrew*** **January** Genesis Exodus
Spring (249 chapters) Psalms—3 per week Proverbs—1 chapter per day	**April** Joshua Judges Ruth 1 and 2 Samuel
Summer (250 chapters) Psalms—3 per week Proverbs—1 chapter per day	**July** Isaiah Jeremiah Lamentations
Fall (260 chapters) Psalms—3 per week Proverbs—1 chapter per day	**October** John 1, 2, 3 John Revelation

HANK HANEGRAAFF

Reading Plan

Pentateuch and Hebrew Poetry

February	March
Leviticus Numbers Deuteronomy	Job Ecclesiastes Song of Solomon

Hebrew History

May	June
1 and 2 Kings 1 and 2 Chronicles	Ezra Nehemiah Esther

Hebrew Prophets

August	September	
Ezekiel Daniel	Hosea Joel Amos Obediah Jonah Micah	Nahum Habakkuk Zephaniah Haggai Zechariah Malachi

New Testament

November		December
Romans 1 and 2 Corinthians Galatians Ephesians Philppians 1 and 2 Thessalonians	1 and 2 Timothy Titus Philemon Hebrews James 1 and 2 Peter Jude	Matthew Mark Luke John Acts

Additional Resources

Richard Abanes, *One Nation Under Gods* (New York: Four Walls Eight Windows, 2003).

Randy Alcorn, *Does the Birth Control Pill Cause Abortion?* 7th ed. (Gresham, OR: Eternal Perspective Ministries, 1997).

Randy Alcorn, *Money, Possessions, and Eternity*, rev. ed. (Wheaton, IL: Tyndale House Publishers, 2003).

Gleason L. Archer, *New International Encyclopedia of Bible Difficulties* (Grand Rapids: Zondervan, 1982).

Francis J. Beckwith, "Baha'i-Christian Dialogue: Some Key Issues Considered," *Christian Research Journal* 11, 3 (1989), available through the Christian Research Institute at www.equip.org.

Francis J. Beckwith, "Intelligent Design in the Schools: Is it Constitutional?" *Christian Research Journal* 25, 4 (2003), available through the Christian Research Institute at www.equip.org.

Francis J. Beckwith, *Politically Correct Death: Answering the Arguments for Abortion Rights* (Grand Rapids: Baker Books, 1993).

Craig L. Blomberg, *Jesus and the Gospels* (Nashville: Broadman and Holman Publishers, 1997).

Gregory A. Boyd, *Oneness, Pentecostals, and the Trinity* (Grand Rapids: Baker Books, 1992).

Gary M. Burge, *Whose Land? Whose Promise?* (Cleveland, OH: The Pilgrim Press, 2003).

D. A. Carson, ed., *From Sabbath to Lord's Day: A Biblical, Historical, and Theological Investigation* (Eugene, OR: Wipf and Stock Publishers, 1999, originally published by Zondervan, 1982).

The Center for Bioethics and Human Dignity, www.cbhd.org.

J. Daryl Charles, "Sentiments as Social Justice: The Ethics of Capital Punishment," *Christian Research Journal*, Spring/Summer (1994).

David Chilton, *The Days of Vengeance: An Exposition of the Book of Revelation* (Ft. Worth, TX: Dominion Press, 1987).

Charles W. Colson and Nigel M. de S. Cameron, *Human Dignity in the Biotech Century: A Christian Vision for Public Policy* (Downers Grove, IL: InterVarsity Press, 2004).

Paul Copan and William Lane Craig, *Creation Out of Nothing: A Biblical, Philosophical, and Scientific Exploration* (Grand Rapids: Baker Academic, 2004).

Paul Copan, *That's Just Your Interpretation: Responding to Skeptics Who Challenge Your Faith* (Grand Rapids: Baker Books, 2001), 171–78.

Paul Copan, *"True for You, but Not for Me": Deflating the Slogans That Leave Christians Speechless* (Minneapolis: Bethany House Publishers, 1998).

William Lane Craig, *Reasonable Faith* 3rd ed. (Wheaton, IL: Crossway Books, 2008).

William Lane Craig, *On Guard: Defending Your Faith with Reason and Precision* (Colorado Springs: David C. Cook, 2010).

Joe Dallas, "Darkening Our Minds: The Problem of Pornography Among Christians," *Christian Research Journal* 27, 3 (2004), available through the Christian Research Institute at www.equip.org.

Joe Dallas, *Desires in Conflict*, updated ed. (Eugene, OR: Harvest House Publishers, 2003).

Joe Dallas, *A Strong Delusion: Confronting the "Gay Christian" Movement* (Eugene, OR: Harvest House Publishers, 1996).

Joe Dallas, *The Game Plan: The Men's 30-Day Strategy for Attaining Sexual Integrity* (Nashville: Thomas Nelson, 2005).

William Dembski, *The Design Revolution* (Grand Rapids: IVP, 2004).

Millard J. Erickson, *What Does God Know and When Does He Know It?* (Grand Rapids: Zondervan, 2003).

Millard J. Erickson, *The Word Became Flesh: A Contemporary Incarnational Christology* (Grand Rapids: Baker Book House, 1996).

Gordon Fee and Douglas Stewart, *How to Read the Bible for All Its Worth*, 3rd ed. (Grand Rapids: Zondervan, 2003).

Norman L. Geisler and Abdul Saleeb, *Answering Islam* (Grand Rapids: Baker Books, 2002).

Norman L. Geisler, *Baker Encyclopedia of Christian Apologetics* (Grand Rapids: Baker Books, 1999), 553–54; see also 283–88.

Norman L. Geisler, *Christian Ethics: Options and Issues* (Grand Rapids: Baker Book House, 1989), chapter 7.

Norman L. Geisler and Douglas E. Potter, "From Ashes to Ashes: Is Burial the Only Christian Option?" *Christian Research Journal*, Summer 1998, available at www.equip.org/free/dc765.htm.

Norman L. Geisler and Ralph E. MacKenzie, *Roman Catholics and Evangelicals: Agreements and Differences* (Grand Rapids: Baker Books, 1995).

R. Douglas Geivett and Gary R. Habermas, eds., *In Defense of Miracles: A Comprehensive Case for God's Action in History* (Downers Grove, IL: InterVarsity Press, 1997).

Timothy George, *Is the Father of Jesus the God of Muhammad?* (Grand Rapids: Zondervan, 2002).

Douglas R. Groothuis, *Unmasking the New Age* (Downers Grove, IL: InterVarsity Press, 1986).

Os Guinness, *Time for Truth* (Grand Rapids: Baker Books, 2000).

Os Guinness, *Unspeakable: Facing up to Evil in an Age of Genocide and Terror* (San Francisco: Harper San Francisco, 2005).

Gary R. Habermas and J. P. Moreland, *Beyond Death: Exploring the Evidence for Immortality* (Wheaton, IL: Crossway Books, 1998).

Gary R. Habermas and Michael R. Licona, *The Case for the Resurrection of Jesus* (Grand Rapids: Kregel, 2004).

Dean Halverson, *The Illustrated Guide to World Religions* (Minneapolis: Bethany House Publishers, 2003).

Hank Hanegraaff and Tom Fortson, *7 Questions of a Promise Keeper* (Nashville: J. Countryman, 2006).

Hank Hanegraaff, *AfterLife: What You Need to Know About Heaven, the Hereafter, and Near-Death Experiences* (Brentwood: TN: Worthy, 2013).

Hank Hanegraaff, "Annihilating Abortion Arguments," available through the Christian Research Institute at www.equip.org.

Hank Hanegraaff, *The Apocalypse Code: Find Out What the Bible Really Says About the End Times . . . and Why It Matters Today* (Nashville: W Publishing Group, 2007).

Hank Hanegraaff, "Bringing Baptism into Biblical Balance," *Christian Research Journal*, 19, 1 (1996) available through the Christian Research Institute at www.equip.org.

Hank Hanegraaff, *Christianity in Crisis: 21st Century* (Nashville: Thomas Nelson, 2009).

Hank Hanegraaff, *Counterfeit Revival: Looking for God in All the Wrong Places*, rev. ed. (Nashville: Word Publishing, 2001).

Hank Hanegraaff, *The Covering: God's Plan to Protect You from Evil* (Nashville: W Publishing Group, 2002).

Hank Hanegraaff and Paul L. Maier, *The Da Vinci Code: Fact or Fiction?* (Wheaton, IL: Tyndale House, 2004).

Hank Hanegraaff, *The F.A.C.E. That Demonstrates the Farce of Evolution* (Nashville: Word Publishing, 1998).

Hank Hanegraaff, *Fatal Flaws: What Evolutionists Don't Want You to Know* (Nashville: W Publishing, 2003).

Hank Hanegraaff, *Has God Spoken? Memorable Proofs of the Bible's Divine Inspiration* (Nashville: Thomas Nelson, 2011).

Hank Hanegraaff, "How to Find a Healthy Church" (Rancho Santa Margarita, CA: Christian Research Institute, 2003), pamphlet.

Hank Hanegraaff, "The Indwelling of the Holy Spirit," *Christian Research Journal*, Spring (1997), available at www.equip.org/free/DS575.pdf.

Hank Hanegraaff, "Karla Faye Tucker and Capital Punishment," *CRI Perspective* CP1304, Christian Research Institute, P.O. Box 8500, Charlotte, NC 28271-8500 ; 1-888-7000-CRI.

Hank Hanegraaff, "Magic Apologetics," *Christian Research Journal* 20, 1 (1997), available through the Christian Research Institute at www.equip.org.

Hank Hanegraaff, *The Prayer of Jesus: Secrets to Real Intimacy with God* (Nashville: W Publishing Group, 2001).

Hank Hanegraaff, *Resurrection* (Nashville: Word Publishing, 2000).

Hank Hanegraaff, "Safe and Secure" (Rancho Santa Margarita, CA: Christian Research Institute, 1996).

Hank Hanegraaff, "The Search for Jesus Hoax," *Christian Research Journal* 23, 2 (2000), available through the Christian Research Institute at www.equip.org.

Hank Hanegraaff, *The Third Day* (Nashville: W Publishing Group, 2003).

Hank Hanegraaff, "The Unforgivable Sin," available from Christian Research Institute at www.equip.org/free/DU250.htm.

Hank Hanegraaff, "The Untouchables: Are 'God's Anointed' Beyond Criticism?" available through the Christian Research Institute at www.equip.org.

Hank Hanegraaff, "What about Halloween?" (Rancho Santa Margarita, CA: Christian Research Institute, 2001), pamphlet.

Carl F. H. Henry, *Basic Christian Doctrines* (Grand Rapids: Baker Book House, 1962).

Richard G. Howe, "Modern Witchcraft: It May Not Be What You Think," *Christian Research Journal* 28, 1 (2005), available through the Christian Research Institute at www.equip.org.

Phillip E. Johnson, *Darwin on Trial*, 2nd ed. (Downers Grove, IL: InterVarsity Press, 1993).

Walter C. Kaiser Jr., Peter H. Davids, F. F. Bruce, and Manfred T. Brauch eds., *Hard Sayings of the Bible* (Downers Grove, IL: InterVarsity Press, 1996).

Peter J. Kreeft, *Everything You Ever Wanted to Know About Heaven, but Never Dreamed of Asking* (San Francisco: Ignatius Press, 1990).

Robert Letham, *The Holy Trinity: In Scripture, History, Theology, and Worship* (Phillipsburg, NJ: P&R Publishing, 2004).

C. S. Lewis, *Mere Christianity* (New York: Macmillan, 1952).

C. S. Lewis, *The Screwtape Letters* (New York: Macmillan, 1982).

Gordon R. Lewis, "Attributes of God," in Walter A. Elwell, ed., *Evangelical Dictionary of Theology*, 2nd ed. (Grand Rapids: Baker Academic, 2001), 492–99.

John MacArthur, *Hard to Believe: The High Cost and Infinite Value of Following Jesus* (Nashville: Thomas Nelson, 2003).

John MacArthur, *Why One Way? Defending an Exclusive Claim in an Inclusive World* (Nashville: W Publishing Group, 2002).

Paul Maier, *The First Christmas* (Grand Rapids: Kregel Publications, 2001).

Paul Marston and Roger Forster, *God's Strategy in Human History*, 2nd ed. (Wipf and Stock Publishers, 2000).

Josh McDowell and Bob Hostetler, *The New Tolerance* (Wheaton, IL: Tyndale House Publishers, 1998).

Elliot Miller, *A Crash Course on The New Age Movement* (Grand Rapids: Baker Book House, 1989).

Bruce Milne, *Know the Truth: A Handbook of Christian Belief* (Downers Grove, IL: InterVarsity Press, 1999).

Marcia Montenegro, "Kabbalah: Getting Back to the Garden," *Christian Research Journal* 28, 2 (2005), available through the Christian Research Institute at www.equip.org.

James Moore, *The Darwin Legend* (Grand Rapids: Baker Books, 1994).

J. P. Moreland's two-part *Christian Research Journal* series on "The Euthanasia Debate," available through the Christian Research Institute at www.equip.org.

J. P. Moreland, *Love Your God with All Your Mind: The Role of Reason in the Life of the Soul* (Colorado Springs: NavPress, 2007).

J. P. Moreland and William Lane Craig, *Philosophical Foundations for a Christian Worldview* (Downers Grove, IL: InterVarsity Press, 2003).

J. P. Moreland, *Scaling the Secular City: A Defense of Christianity* (Grand Rapids: Baker Book House, 1987).

J. P. Moreland and John Mark Reynolds, eds., *Three Views on Creation and Evolution* (Grand Rapids: Zondervan, 1999).

Thomas V. Morris, *The Logic of God Incarnate* (Ithaca, NY: Cornell University Press, 1986).

Ronald H. Nash, *The Gospel and the Greeks* (Richardson, TX: Probe Books, 1992).

Ronald Nash, *Is Jesus the Only Savior?* (Grand Rapids: Zondervan, 1994).

J. I. Packer, *Knowing God* (Downers Grove, IL: InterVarsity Press, 1993).

Bob and Gretchen Passantino, "Christians Criticizing Christians: Can It Be Biblical?" available through the Christian Research Institute at www.equip.org.

Adam Pelser, "Genuine Temptation and the Character of Christ," available through the Christian Research Institute at www.equip.org.

Robert A. Peterson, *Hell on Trial: The Case for Eternal Punishment* (Phillipsburg, NJ: Presbyterian and Reformed Press, 1995).

John Piper, *Desiring God: Meditations of a Christian Hedonist* (Sisters, OR: Multnomah Publishers, 1986), chapter 7.

"Questions and Answers: Genesis 6:4," available from Christian Research Institute, P.O. Box 8500, Charlotte, NC 28271-8500, or call 1–888–7000–CRI.

Scott B. Rae, *Moral Choices*, 2nd ed. (Grand Rapids: Zondervan, 2000).

David A. Reed, *Answering Jehovah's Witnesses: Subject by Subject* (Grand Rapids: Baker Book House, 1996).

Robert L. Reymond, *Jesus, Divine Messiah* (Tain, Ross–shire, Scotland: Christian Focus Publications, 2003).

Richard Robinson, "Understanding Judaism: How to Share the Gospel with Your Jewish Friends," *Christian Research Journal* 19, 4 (1997), available through the Christian Research Institute at www.equip.org.

James W. Sire, *The Universe Next Door: A Basic Worldview Catalog*, 3rd ed. (Downers Grove, IL: InterVarsity Press, 1997).

R. C. Sproul, *Justified by Faith Alone* (Wheaton, IL: Crossway Books, 1999).

R. C. Sproul, *Not a Chance: The Myth of Chance in Modern Science and Cosmology* (Grand Rapids: Baker Book House, 1994).

R. C. Sproul, *Reason to Believe* (Grand Rapids: Zondervan, 1982).

Lee Strobel, *The Case for a Creator* (Grand Rapids: Zondervan, 2004).

Lee Strobel, *The Case for Christ* (Grand Rapids: Zondervan, 1998).

Lee Strobel, *The Case for Faith* (Grand Rapids: Zondervan, 2000).

Charles R. Strohmer, *America's Fascination with Astrology: Is it Healthy?* (Greenville, SC: Emerald House, 1998).

Charles Strohmer, *The Gospel and the New Spirituality* (Nashville: Thomas Nelson, 1996).

Charles Strohmer, "Is There a Christian Zodiac, a Gospel in the Stars?" *Christian Research Journal* 22, 4 (2000), available through the Christian Research Institute at www.equip.org.

Eric D. Svendsen, *Who Is My Mother?* (Amityville, NY: Calvary Press, 2001).

Joni Eareckson Tada and Nigel M. de S. Cameron, *How to Be a Christian in a Brave New World* (Grand Rapids: Zondervan, 2006).

Joni Eareckson Tada and Steven Estes, *When God Weeps* (Grand Rapids: Zondervan, 1997).

Jerald and Sandra Tanner, *The Changing World of Mormonism* (Chicago: Moody, 1980).

Peter Toon, *The Ascension of Our Lord* (Nashville: Thomas Nelson, 1984).

Jonathan Wells, *Icons of Evolution: Science or Myth?* (Washington, DC: Regnery, 2000).

James R. White, *The Forgotten Trinity* (Minneapolis: Bethany House, 2001).

Dallas Willard, *The Divine Conspiracy* (San Francisco: Harper San Francisco, 1998).

N. T. Wright, "Women's Service in the Church: The Biblical Basis," available at www.ntwrightpage.com.

J. Isamu Yamamoto's four-part *Christian Research Journal* series on Buddhism in North America, available through the Christian Research Institute at www.equip.org.

J. Isamu Yamamoto, "Zest for Zen: North Americans Embrace a Contemplative School of Buddhism," *Christian Research Journal* 17, 3 (1995), available through the Christian Research Institute at www.equip.org.

Contact Christian Research Institute

By Mail:
CRI United States
P.O. Box 8500, Charlotte, NC 28271-8500

In Canada:
CRI Canada
56051 Airways P.O., Calgary, Alberta T2E 8K5

By Phone:
US 24-hour Toll-Free Customer Service (888) 7000-CRI
US Customer Service (704) 887-8200
Fax (704) 887-8299
Canada Toll-Free (800) 665-5851

On the Internet: www.equip.org

On the Broadcast:
To contact the *Bible Answer Man* broadcast with your questions, call toll-free in the US and Canada, 1 (888) ASK HANK (275-4265),
Monday–Friday, 5:50 p.m. to 7:00 p.m. Eastern Time.

For a list of stations airing the *Bible Answer Man* or to listen to the broadcast via the Internet, log on to our Web site at www.equip.org.

ALSO FROM HANK HANEGRAAFF

The Apocalypse Code: Find Out What the Bible REALLY Says About the End Times . . . And Why It Matters Today

Most of what you've heard, read, or been told about the end times is simply wrong. Hank provides you with the code for reading apocalyptic passages for all they are worth. "This may well be the most important book I'll ever write."—HHH

Has God Spoken? Memorable Proofs of the Bible's Divine Inspiration

Are Christians guilty of blind faith, or is the bible really God's inspired word? Can you ever know for sure? Join bestselling author Hank Hanegraaff for a stirring defense of the Bible as the Word of God and your only reliable foundation for life. In answering the riveting question, "Has God spoken?", Hanegraaff uses manuscript evidence, archeology, predictive prophecy, and much more to memorably demonstrate that the Bible is divine rather than merely human in origin.

HANK HANEGRAAFF

About the Author

Hendrik (Hank) Hanegraaff serves as president and chairman of the board of the North Carolina–based Christian Research Institute. He is also host of the nationally syndicated *Bible Answer Man* radio broadcast, which is heard daily across the United States and Canada—and around the world via the Internet at www.equip.org.

Widely regarded as one of the world's leading Christian authors and apologists, Hank is deeply committed to equipping Christians to be so familiar with truth that when counterfeits loom on the horizon, they recognize them instantaneously. Through his live call-in radio broadcast, Hank equips Christians to mine the Bible for all its wealth, answers questions on the basis of careful research and sound reasoning, and interviews today's most significant leaders, apologists, and thinkers.

Hank is the author of more than twenty books, which have sold millions of copies. *Christianity in Crisis* and *Resurrection* each won the Gold Medallion for Excellence in Christian Literature awarded by the Evangelical Christian Publisher's Association (ECPA); and *Counterfeit Revival* and *The FACE That Demonstrates the Farce of Evolution* each won ECPA's Silver Medallion—the latter published in the condensed *Fatal Flaws: What Evolutionists Don't Want You to Know.*

Other noteworthy volumes include *The Prayer of Jesus*, which rose to number one on the Christian Marketplace Bestseller list October 2002. Hank exposes the dangers of both Christian and secular Zionism through his groundbreaking *The Apocalypse Code: What the Bible Really Teaches about the End Times and Why It Matters Today*, and his historical fiction series The Last Disciple Trilogy, as well as *Fuse of Armageddon*.

In *Has God Spoken?* Hank provides memorable proofs for the Bible's divine inspiration. Additional works include *The Legacy Study Bible*, *The Covering: God's Plan to Protect You from Evil*, and *The Creation Answer Book*.

He is a regular contributor to the award-winning *Christian Research Journal* and an articulate communicator on the pressing issues of our day, having spoken in leading churches, conferences, and on college campuses throughout the world (including such faraway institutions as the University of Tehran, Iran).

Hank and his wife, Kathy, live in Charlotte, North Carolina, and are parents to twelve children.